Asia Bible Commentary Series

EZRA AND NEHEMIAH

Asia Bible Commentary Series

EZRA AND NEHEMIAH

Joseph Too Shao
and
Rosa Ching Shao

General Editor
Federico G. Villanueva

Old Testament Consulting Editors
Yohanna Katanacho, Tim Meadowcroft, Joseph Shao

New Testament Consulting Editors
Steve Chang, Andrew Spurgeon, Brian Wintle

© 2019 by Joseph Too Shao and Rosa Ching Shao

Published 2019 by Langham Global Library
An imprint of Langham Publishing
www.langhampublishing.org

Langham Publishing and its imprints are a ministry of Langham Partnership

Langham Partnership
PO Box 296, Carlisle, Cumbria, CA3 9WZ, UK
www.langham.org

Published in partnership with Asia Theological Association

ATA
QCC PO Box 1454–1154, Manila, Philippines
www.ataasia.com

ISBNs:
978-1-78368-155-6 Print
978-1-78368-678-0 ePub
978-1-78368-680-3 PDF

Joseph Too Shao and Rosa Ching Shao have asserted their right under the Copyright, Designs, and Patents Act, 1988 to be identified as the Author of this work.

All rights reserved. No part of this publication may be reproduced, stored in a retrieval system, or transmitted in any form or by any means, electronic, mechanical, photocopying, recording, or otherwise, without the prior written permission of the publisher or the Copyright Licensing Agency.

Requests to reuse content from Langham Publishing are processed through PLSclear. Please visit www.plsclear.com to complete your request.

Unless otherwise stated, Scripture quotations are from the New International Version, copyright © 2011. Used by permission. All rights reserved.

British Library Cataloguing in Publication Data
A catalogue record for this book is available from the British Library.

ISBN: 978-1-78368-155-6

Cover & Book Design: projectluz.com

Langham Partnership actively supports theological dialogue and an author's right to publish but does not necessarily endorse the views and opinions set forth and works referenced within this publication or guarantee its technical and grammatical correctness. Langham Partnership does not accept any responsibility or liability to persons or property as a consequence of the reading, use, or interpretation of its published content.

To:
Esther and Robert Martin
Dorcas and Dennis Law
Joyce and Philip Co
Grace and Robert Wang
– Joseph's siblings and their spouses –
whose lives and services have touched the global community in their respective places of serving our Lord as God's servants

Ernesto and Mollie Tan-Chi, Jr.
– friends and partners in ministry at the
Biblical Seminary of the Philippines and other ministries –
for their model in serving our great and awesome God and
for their unceasing love and encouragement in our lives

CONTENTS

Commentary

Foreword xi
Series Preface xiii
Authors' Preface xv
Acknowledgments xvii
List of Abbreviations xix
Introduction 1
Commentary on Ezra 25
Commentary on Nehemiah 103
Selected Bibliography 209

Topics

Numbers and Asian Counting: Resolving Inconsistencies in the Text 32
Oral and Written History 40
Physical or Spiritual Church? 44
Facing Opposition 51
God's Word and Life 73
God or Human Protection 83
Shame and Guilt 90
Cognitive Dissonance and Compassion 99
Anxiety and Prayer 111
True Self 123
Asian Family Leadership 129
Handling Hostile Situations 139
Caring for the Poor 146
Honor and Shame 160
Leaders and Partners 168
Retelling and Memory 177
Commitments and Challenges 185
Gathering In and Reaching Out 190
Portions for Pastors 198
Mentoring 208

FOREWORD

It is a joy to survey the chapters of Dr. Joseph Shao's new commentary on Ezra-Nehemiah in the Asia Bible Commentary Series. My joy is especially full because Dr. Shao was a student of mine at Trinity Evangelical Divinity School some four decades ago. I have also had the privilege of teaching where Dr. Shao has served with distinction as president for thirty years. His work as an administrator is equally matched by his giftedness as a teacher and writer. I have also met his wife, Rosa, whose warm hospitality has been an added gift to the seminary, since she, too, has earned her PhD (in Clinical Psychology) and has taught Bible in the seminary for more than thirty years.

It is most appropriate, therefore, for Dr. Shao to be the commentator on these two books of the Old Testament, which focus on the greatness of God and effective leadership. Leadership skills are needed, as these Old Testament books stress, when the demands of administration test the foundations of our faith, both in times of great advances as well as times of testing.

Ezra and Nehemiah were two men who were willing "to stand in the gap" where few others had ventured or were willing to go. Moses previously stood in the gap (Ps 106:23), and Ezekiel tells of another time when God searched for a man to stand in the gap (Ezek 22:30). Problems for the two leaders mentioned in these two Old Testament books were not moments of despair, but rather opportunities to serve others and to call upon God to demonstrate his Lordship over all situations. Thus when Ezra and Nehemiah prayed for divine success, they honored God's name as more significant and important than the problems they faced. Moreover, their prayers were based on the word of God.

My prayer is that our Lord will use this commentary to raise up other men and women to stand in the gap regardless of how grave and problematic our times or situations may be. May the words of Scripture once more prove a blessing to all of God's people, showing all over again that men and women "do not live on bread alone, but by every word that comes from the mouth of God" (Deut 8:3).

In a day when there is a neglect not only of the Old Testament in our teaching, preaching and study of the Scriptures, but also of genuine expositions of the Bible in all its power and authority, it is a delight to recommend

Dr. Shao's special commentary on Ezra-Nehemiah. This commentary will go a long way to fulfilling both of these vacuums among the Body of Christ.

Walter C. Kaiser, Jr.
President Emeritus,
Colman M. Mockler Distinguished Professor of Old Testament,
Gordon-Conwell Theological Seminary

SERIES PREFACE

In recent years, we have witnessed one of the greatest shifts in the history of world Christianity. It used to be that the majority of Christians lived in the West, but Christians are now evenly distributed around the globe. This shift has implications for the task of interpreting the Bible from within our respective contexts, which is in line with the growing realization that every theology is contextual. Thus, the questions that we bring into our reading of the Bible will be shaped by our present realities as well as our historical and social locations. There is a need therefore to interpret the Bible for our own contexts.

The Asia Bible Commentary Series addresses this need. In line with the mission of the Asia Theological Association Publications, we have gathered evangelical Bible scholars working among Asians to write commentaries on each book of the Bible. The mission is to "produce resources that are biblical, pastoral, contextual, missional, and prophetic for pastors, Christian leaders, cross-cultural workers, and students in Asia." Although the Bible can be studied for different reasons, we believe that it is given primarily for the edification of the Body of Christ (2 Tim 3:16–17). The ABCS is designed to help pastors in their sermon preparation, cell group or lay leaders in their Bible study groups, and those training in seminaries or Bible schools.

Each commentary begins with an introduction that provides general information about the book's author and original context, summarizes the main message or theme of the book, and outlines its potential relevance to a particular Asian context. The introduction is followed by an exposition that combines exegesis and application. Here, we seek to speak to and empower Christians in Asia by using our own stories, parables, poems, and other cultural resources as we expound the Bible.

The Bible is actually Asian in that it comes from ancient West Asia, and there are many similarities between the world of the Bible and traditional Asian cultures. But there are also many differences that we need to explore in some depth. That is why the commentaries also include articles or topics in which we bring specific issues in Asian church, social, and religious contexts into dialogue with relevant issues in the Bible. We do not seek to resolve every tension that emerges but rather to allow the text to illumine the context and vice versa, acknowledging that we do not have all the answers to every mystery.

Ezra and Nehemiah

May the Holy Spirit, who inspired the writers of the Bible, bring light to the hearts and minds of all who use these materials, to the glory of God and to the building up of the churches!

Federico G. Villanueva
General Editor

AUTHORS' PREFACE

As we see the finished commentary on Ezra-Nehemiah for the Asia Bible Commentary Series, our hearts are filled with a resounding echo from the original writers themselves: "the gracious hand of the LORD our God was upon us" (Ezra 7:6, 9, 28; 8:18, 22, 31; Neh 2:8, 18). Indeed, God's powerful hand has guided us both as we squeezed out "stolen" time from our busy schedules and various commitments to bring out the rebuilding message in these two post-exilic books. Joseph, who was already burdened with the theological training of godly servants amid overwhelming demands from pastors and Christian workers in local churches and international settings, found himself in the shoes of Ezra, the teacher, and Nehemiah, the governor! Inspired by the Bible and by his Ancient Near Eastern studies training from Trinity Evangelical Divinity School and Hebrew Union College, Joseph loves to read and teach eager students the Hebrew Bible that Jesus read, which is also the foundation of Jesus's ministry. Rosa, on the other hand, stands alongside Joseph as his caring, consulting and confident helpmate. In this book, she provides her psychological and contextual input about dealing with contemporary life circumstances.

With the building projects of our seminary, the Biblical Seminary of the Philippines, the Lord gives us greater responsibility and opportunity *to equip God's workers with God's Word for God's work in God's world to God's glory.* The rebuilding of the spiritual lives of the seminarians is much more subtle and sober, a lifetime journey for both the students and the faculty. As the commentary on Ezra-Nehemiah comes to completion, we find doubled joy as we will retire from our administrative duties after serving for more than three decades.

Joseph and Rosa Shao
Biblical Seminary of the Philippines

ACKNOWLEDGMENTS

We would like to thank the board, faculty, and staff of the Biblical Seminary of the Philippines for their encouragement in our writing project. We would like to thank Dr. Walter C. Kaiser, Jr. for his foreword to the commentary. Dr. Kaiser, Joseph's mentor and teacher, inspires him toward proper methodology in preaching and teaching the Old Testament. We would like to thank Dr. Stephen Lee and Dr. Bill Arnold for the endorsements. Rosa would like to thank Dr. William Kirwan for his model on integrating Bible with clinical counseling teaching.

LIST OF ABBREVIATIONS

BOOKS OF THE BIBLE

Old Testament

Gen, Exod, Lev, Num, Deut, Josh, Judg, Ruth, 1–2 Sam, 1–2 Kgs, 1–2 Chr, Ezra, Neh, Esth, Job, Ps/Pss, Prov, Eccl, Song, Isa, Jer, Lam, Ezek, Dan, Hos, Joel, Amos, Obad, Jonah, Mic, Nah, Hab, Zeph, Hag, Zech, Mal

New Testament

Matt, Mark, Luke, John, Acts, Rom, 1–2 Cor, Gal, Eph, Phil, Col, 1–2 Thess, 1–2 Tim, Titus, Phlm, Heb, Jas, 1–2 Pet, 1–2–3 John, Jude, Rev

BIBLE TEXTS AND VERSIONS

Divisions of the canon

NT	New Testament
OT	Old Testament

Ancient texts and versions

LXX	Septuagint
MT	Masoretic Text

Modern versions

ESV	English Standard Version
NAB	New American Bible
NASB	New American Standard Bible
NIV	New International Version
NRSV	New Revised Standard Version

Journals, reference works, and series

ABCS	Asia Bible Commentary Series
ABD	Anchor Bible Dictionary
BR	Bible Review
BZ	*Biblische Zeitschrift*

JBL	*Journal of Biblical Literature*
JNSL	*Journal of Northwest Semitic Languages*
JSOT	*Journal for the Study of the Old Testament*
JTS	*Journal of Theological Studies*
KAT	*Kommentar zum Alten Testament*
NCB	New Century Bible Commentary
OTL	Old Testament Library
PEQ	Palestine Exploration Quarterly
SBLDS	Society of Biblical Literature Dissertation Series
TOTC	Tyndale Old Testament Commentaries
VT	*Vetus Testamentum*
WBC	Word Biblical Commentary
WTJ	*Westminster Theological Journal*
ZAW	*Zeitschrift fur die alttestamentliche Wissenschaft*

INTRODUCTION

Zerubbabel, Ezra, and Nehemiah exemplify three godly leaders who call three different groups of people to set out to do the impossible! Zerubbabel pilots the first and largest group of returning exiles to rebuild the temple after its destruction by Nebuchadnezzar (Ezra 2:2). Ezra, some eighty years later, directs a second smaller group of returnees to make an offering at God's temple of worship and to guide the people in learning and practicing the law of the Lord (Ezra 7:6–7). Finally, Nehemiah leads an even smaller group to build God's wall of protection (Neh 2:1, 11). There is no stopping a motivated throng that is directed by purpose-driven leaders who put themselves under God's blessed guidance. These three biblical leaders inspire the people of God to do their tasks faithfully, thereby redeeming the painful history of their exile (2 Kgs 25:20–21).

HISTORICAL SETTING

The exile of the Israelite people began with their rebellion against God as they followed the evil practices of their surrounding neighbors. For seventy years they had to live as exiles in Babylon, just as God had warned them through the prophet Jeremiah: "Therefore the Lord Almighty says this: 'Because you have not listened to my words, I will summon all the peoples of the north and my servant Nebuchadnezzar king of Babylon . . . I will bring them against this land and its inhabitants and against all the surrounding nations . . . This whole country will become a desolate wasteland, and these nations will serve the king of Babylon seventy years'" (Jer 25:8–11). The initial Babylonian invasion of Jerusalem occurred around 605 BC when Nebuchadnezzar raided Judah during the reign of King Jehoiakim and took Daniel and his three friends among his captives (2 Kgs 24:1–6; Dan 1:1–7). Then in 598 BC, Nebuchadnezzar attacked the city of Judah. The final Babylonian siege took place in 587 BC, wherein many Jews were killed, and others were taken into exile, including King Jehoiachin of Judah (2 Kgs 24:8–17; 2 Chr 36:8–10). The fall of Jerusalem immediately followed with the capture of King Zedekiah of Judah, whose eyes the Babylonians plucked out. This was the final deportation of the Jewish populace to Babylon. The prophet Jeremiah ministered among the poorest of the people, who were left behind by the Babylonian army to work the barren fields in Jerusalem (Jer 39:11–40:6). The prophet Ezekiel, on the other hand, served the exiles in Babylon (Ezek 1:1–3). Both prophets proclaimed God's judgment against the Israelite people. Nevertheless, the future rested with the cleansing of the exiles rather than those who had been left behind in Jerusalem.

The theme of God's redemption is clearly portrayed throughout the biblical narrative. When God brought about justice by sending his people into exile, he also demonstrated mercy by overseeing the people's return to Jerusalem. Even before this promise was realized, God spoke through Jeremiah, saying: "'But when the seventy years are fulfilled, I will punish the king of Babylon and his nation, the land of the Babylonians, for the guilt,' declares the LORD, 'and will make it desolate forever'" (Jer 25:12; 29:10). The last two chapters of 2 Chronicles record the early stage of the Jewish return with the decree of Cyrus, the king of Persia, permitting and prompting them to return to their ancestral land. Ezra's first three opening verses (1:1–3) repeat the last two verses in 2 Chronicles (36:22–23) almost verbatim.

God orchestrated the plan behind the return of his people after seventy years of captivity by moving the heart of Cyrus (Ezra 1:1), who issued an edict to the Jews to return (Ezra 1:1–4; 6:3–5). From many non-biblical accounts, the succession of powers dominated the ancient Near East during the first millennium BC. The Persian Empire replaced Babylon as the greatest power, following a period of wary alliance between the erratic last Babylonian king, Nabonidus, and the sagacious Persian leader, Cyrus. It was only a matter of time before Cyrus took over Babylon in 539 BC.[1] Herodotus recounted a legend that the Persians were able to enter Babylon by turning the Euphrates River into an artificial lake, thus lowering the water level enough for the soldiers to enter the city and take the Babylonians by surprise. According to Xenophon, the Persians attacked the city during a festival when "all Babylon was accustomed to drink and revel all night long."[2] All the events of Ezra-Nehemiah took place during the time of the Persian Empire.

The Persian Empire was founded by Achaemenes (ca. 700 BC). The commonly known Persian kings are as follows:

Cyrus the Great (550–530 BC), Cambyses II (530–522 BC), Darius I (522–486 BC), Xerxes I (486–465 BC), Artaxerxes I (465–424 BC), Darius II (423–404 BC), Artaxerxes II (404–359 BC), Artaxerxes III (359–338 BC).

The policy of Cyrus in allowing the exiled people to return to their homeland attests to God's fulfillment of his prophecy. God stood true to his promise and led his people back to Judah. Historians normally identify three dates for

---

1. See the translation of Cyrus Cylinder, *Documents from Old Testament Times*, ed. D. W. Thomas (New York: Harper and Brothers, 1968), 94.
2. Edwin M. Yamauchi, *Persia and the Bible* (Grand Rapids: Baker, 1990), 86.

Introduction

the Jewish return from Babylon to Jerusalem. The first Jewish exiles returned in 538 BC under the leadership of Sheshbazzar, Zerubbabel, and Joshua (Ezra 1–2). The number of those returnees was more than 49,000 (Ezra 2:64–65; compare Neh 7:66–67). Sometime later, in 458 BC, Ezra led about five thousand people from Babylon to their homeland (Ezra 7: 7–8; 8:1–14). The third and smallest group of Jewish exiles returned under Nehemiah in 445 BC (Neh 2:6, 9).

CHRONOLOGY IN EZRA-NEHEMIAH

Passages	Year (BC)	Description
Dan 5:30	539	Capture of Babylon
Ezra 1:1–4	538	First year of Cyrus
Ezra 1:11	537 (?)	First return under Sheshbazzar/Zerubbabel
Ezra 3:1	537	Building of the altar
Ezra 3:8	536	Commence the work of the temple
Ezra 4:1–5	536–530	Opposition during the reign of Cyrus
Ezra 4:24	530–520	Cease the work on the temple
Ezra 5:2; Hag 1:14	520	Resume the work on the temple under Darius
Ezra 6:15	516	Completion of the temple
Ezra 7:7–8	458	Second return under Ezra
Neh 1:1; 2:1; 5:14	445	Third return under Nehemiah; 20th year of Artaxerxes
Neh 6:15	445	Completion of the wall
Neh 8:1	445	Ezra reads the law at a public assembly
Neh 8:14	445	Feast of Tabernacles
Neh 5:14; 13:6	433	32nd year of Artaxerxes

AN ASIAN THEOLOGICAL READING OF EZRA AND NEHEMIAH[3]

Traditionally, hermeneutics implies the interpretation of God's word by focusing on the text rather than the interpreter. Thus the message of a text should not change if proper hermeneutical methods are applied. Two recent methodologies in Old Testament interpretation begin with the text. First, a narrative

---

3. See also Joseph Shao, "An Asian Reading of the Theological Themes of Nehemiah," in *Light for Our Path: The Authority, Inspiration, Meaning and Mission of Scripture,* eds. Bruce Nicholls, Julie Belding, Joseph Shao (Manila: Asia Theological Association, 2013), 119–129.

reading highlights the literary genre and how a text portrays the incidents in the story. Second, canonical criticism accepts the text as it is and accentuates the final form of the text.

In the postmodern era, however, the interpretative task takes note of the various views of the interpreter. The existential interpretation poses a provocative challenge, since there seems to be no valid empirical criteria except the aspirations and viewpoints of the interpreters. A cultural interpretation infers that a biblical text may hold interpretive appeal to various cultural people groups. Following are some key questions for this interpretive lens. Would the cultural perspectives of the interpreter influence the interpretation of the text?[4] Is there such a thing as a Western or Eastern interpretation of the text? Is it possible to remain true to the text while also considering the cultural interpretation of the interpreter?

In considering these questions, we might also observe that the heart of Western interpretation is the pursuit of truth, where knowledge is valued for the sake of knowledge. Thus the Western thinker is influenced by the desire and willingness to dig for truth. The underlying ideology is that it is possible to obtain objective knowledge in every aspect of reality. On the other hand, we might also observe that Eastern interpretation stresses personal integrity as the higher truth. Thus the cultivation of personal virtue comes before understanding intellectual truth. For Eastern thinkers who have especially been influenced by Confucius teachings, truth is associated with personal integrity. Truthful people are trustworthy, honest holders of truth. The being (person) and the doing (action) are related to one another. Thus a spokesperson of truth can also shoulder the moral consequences of truth. The Western and Eastern interpretations complement each other.

In his introduction to the "theological perspectives of Ezra and Nehemiah," Hess highlights God's ongoing plan in reversing the divine judgment with the actions of the returnees.[5] Smith presents the major themes in Ezra-Nehemiah as "the sovereign rule of God over all," "separation from impurity and dedication to worshiping God," and "faithfulness to the law in the covenant

---

4. Few books focus on specific regions. For a creative Asian interpretation of post-colonialism, see Rasiah S. Sugirtharajah, *Asian Biblical Hermeneutics and Postcolonialism: Contesting the Interpretation* (Maryknoll: Orbis, 1998). For a Majority World interpretation with a focus on African voices, see Rasiah S. Sugirtharajah, ed., *Voices from the Margin: Interpreting the Bible in the Third World* (Maryknoll: Orbis, 2006).
5. Richard S. Hess, *The Old Testament: A Historical, Theological and Critical Introduction* (Grand Rapids: Baker, 2016), 366–369.

community."[6] Goswell discusses the ethics, leadership, and lay-involvement in Ezra-Nehemiah.[7]

In the previous section, we trace the truth-seeking theological themes.[8] In this section, we present three theological motifs from an Asian perspective: honorable character, shame and disciplinary measures, and community and ancestors. By looking carefully at the texts in Ezra and Nehemiah, we can draw out these themes – not to negate the theological truths, but rather to enrich readers with cultural readings from an Asian interpreter.

Honorable Character

In Old Testament character studies, most spiritual giants start with an inner distinctive character that yields outer spiritual behavior. In Asia, honorable leaders gain respect that begins with their internal character. The four prominent characters in the book of Ezra-Nehemiah – Zerubbabel and Joshua, Ezra and Nehemiah – are introduced with the purpose of amplifying their trustworthiness. Each mini-story has its own distinct narrative introduction, which we will examine carefully in our interpretation.

Zerubbabel and Joshua, two of the twelve leaders, are the prominent leaders of the first returnees, and their names are listed before the other leaders (Ezra 2:2; Neh 7:7). They each have their respective roles in the rebuilding project. For the rebuilding of the altar, the name of Joshua as the priest appears before Zerubbabel, since this task is related to the cultic[9] aspect of worship (Ezra 3:2). For the rebuilding of the temple, however, Zerubbabel appears before Joshua, since Zerubbabel is the civil leader who is leading the people in this project (Ezra 3:8). Nevertheless, Joshua supervises the work of rebuilding the house of God (Ezra 3:9). Both Zerubbabel and Joshua are responsible for those who are involved in the rebuilding project, and so they do not compromise the integrity of the project by employing more people (i.e., "the people of the land") simply to expedite the work (Ezra 4:3–4). In Asia, leaders make important community decisions and are responsible for leading the whole group to the proper goal.

In Eastern society, the background and character of a potential leader are carefully scrutinized before any leadership tasks are assigned. Ezra is introduced

---

6. Gary V. Smith, *Ezra-Nehemiah Esther*, Cornerstone Biblical Commentary (Carol Streams: Tyndale, 2010), 15–21.
7. Gregory Goswell, *Ezra-Nehemiah*, EP Study Commentary (Darlington, UK: EP Books, 2013), 28–32, 36–40.
8. See the section titled "Theological Themes."
9. In this book, "cult" and "cultic" are used in reference to a particular system of religious worship, especially with reference to its rites and ceremonies.

by his priestly genealogy and then identified as the priest (Ezra 7:11–12, 21; 10:10, 16).[10] His ancestral roots can be traced back to Zadok, Phinehas, Eleazar, and Aaron (Ezra 7:1–5). Zadok is the priestly line that remains faithful during the time of David while the line of Eli goes astray (1 Kgs 2:27, 35; Ezek 44:15–16). Phinehas is the decisive priest who asserts his zealous devotion to the Lord's honor at a crucial stage in the wilderness to avert a plague (Num 25:6–18; Ps 106:30–31). Eleazar is the faithful priest who supports Joshua (Josh 24:33). Aaron, of course, is the chief priest during the time of Moses. This impressive priestly line certifies that Ezra is qualified to serve as the priest.

Ezra is a scribe ("teacher," NIV) who is well-versed in the law of Moses (Ezra 7:6). He is introduced as a model learner who teaches by his exemplary character (Ezra 7:10). Ezra internalizes God's instruction and teaching by devoting himself to careful study, probing and seeking for the truth, and then living out the truth himself before teaching the law to others. Moreover, Ezra is known to King Artaxerxes as "the priest, a teacher of the law of the God of heaven" (Ezra 7:11–12, 21), and so he is entrusted to teach the law and to bring back the articles of worship to God's house. At the square before the Water Gate, all the people of God invite Ezra to read God's law (Neh 8:1, 4). Thus his integrity is widely known and he is accepted as trustworthy, both to the king and to ordinary people. Hence Ezra's inner quality makes him a leader in the community. Having earned respect and honor because of his exemplar character, we later learn that the reputable titles of "priest" and "scribe" are given to him (Neh 10:1; 12:36).

Likewise, Nehemiah, is introduced as a man of prayer (Neh 1:4–11; 2:5). His written prayer conveys his trust in God (Neh 1:8–9). His inner preparation over four months confers his upright character (Neh 1:1, 2:1). As a trusted cupbearer, he can speak freely to the king even while his queen is present (Neh 2:6). As a man of prudence, he carefully examines the broken wall before he persuades the crowd to join the cause of rebuilding (Neh 2:12–15), and he displays a discipline of silence before acting outwardly (Neh 2:12, 16). Having established Nehemiah's character, he is later identified as the governor and the leader of the third returnees (Neh 8:2, 9, 13).

Similarly, in the Asian context, though titles and expertise are important, they must be reinforced with a trustworthy personality.

---

10. H. G. M Williamson, *Ezra, Nehemiah*, Word Biblical Commentary (Waco: Word, 1985), 91, compares the genealogical record with 1 Chronicles 6:1–15. Likewise, Mark A. Thronveit, *Ezra-Nehemiah*, Interpretation (Louisville: John Knox Press, 1992), 40, acknowledges the person and mission of Ezra and compares the record with that of 1 Chronicles 6.

Introduction

Shame and Disciplinary Measures

Honor and shame are not only biblical concepts, but they are also embedded in Asian culture.[11] Western interpreters tend to look at sin and guilt as guiding concepts in the interpretation of the text. Though sin and guilt are noticeable in Ezra-Nehemiah (Ezra 9:6–7, 13; 10:13; Neh 1:6; 9:2, 37; 13:27), the concepts of honor and shame are more prominent. Both Ezra and Nehemiah use shame and disciplinary action to bring about change. Shame can be defined as a feeling of humiliation for oneself and others. Shame pertains to the inner core of a person's being and longing – how we feel about ourselves, our sense of being shameful or loathsome as people. Guilt pertains to a person's actions and can be atoned for and even removed by compensation. Shame, however, lies much deeper and can be very difficult to erase.

Ezra and Nehemiah demonstrate appropriate Asian ways for leading people. In the Western world today, leaders are often encouraged to be non-offensive, whereas in Asia, leaders tend to confront people because the feeling of shame can be redemptive and instructive, deterring reprehensible actions that may lead to sinful acts against brothers and sisters.[12]

In confronting the issue of intermarriage, Ezra feels shameful and offers a private prayer to the Lord highlighting his shame (Ezra 9:5–6). Note that his personal shame comes before his statement about the community's guilt and sins (Ezra 9:6–7). To deal with intermarriage, Ezra issues a public proclamation, listing the names of everyone involved in order to shame the guilty families. From personal shame to public shame, the communal list serves as a warning for the future generation (Ezra 10:18–44) and a teaching tool to guide the community.

Shame and anger are interrelated emotions. Anger can be a coverup for shame. Nehemiah shows his anger, but he diverts his own hidden and painful feelings of shame with disciplinary measures that shame the offending party. In dealing with poverty, Nehemiah is so angry with the community for failing to

---

11. Biblical scholars and practitioners have started to look at honor and shame as topics worthy of study. See Bin Kang, "The Rhetoric of Honor and Shame as a Significant Role in Understanding the Judgement Oracle against Tyre in Ezekiel 28:1–19," Master of Theology Thesis, Asia Graduate School of Theology, 2019; Daniel Wu, *Honor, Shame, and Guilt: Social-Scientific Approaches to the Book of Ezekiel* (Winona Lake, IN: Eisenbrauns, 2016); Jerry Hwang, "How Long Will my Glory Be Reproach?," "Honour and Shame in Old Testament Lament Traditions," Old Testament Essays 30/3 (2017): 684–706; Jayson Georges, "Get Face! Give Face! A Missional Paradigm for Honor-Shame Contexts," *Evangelical Missions Quarterly* 53, no. 3 (July 2017): 1–6.
12. Jesus's cleansing of the temple in the New Testament may be viewed from this angle, as a way to shame the culprits who are doing business instead of praying.

love their lesser brothers and sisters (Neh 5:6–8) that he summons the priests, nobles, and officials to change. In a public confrontation, he shakes the folds of his robe to shame those who did not keep their promise (Neh 5:9–13).

Nehemiah, knowing that Tobiah has occupied a chamber in the house of the Lord, shows his anger by throwing all of Tobiah's household furniture out of the chamber in order to cleanse the house of God (Neh 13:7–8). This disciplinary action brings honor to God but shame to Eliashib, who made this arrangement for Tobiah. Of course, Tobiah is also shamed when his goods are thrown out of the room in the courts of God.

Within this culture of shame, Nehemiah confronts Jews who have mixed marriages and whose children cannot speak Hebrew. He curses them, beats them, pulls their hair (Neh 13:23–25), and reprimands them (Neh 13:26–27) – actions that both publicly shame the offenders and also motivate others to give up the idea of a mixed marriage. Honor and shame are complementary concepts, where the shaming of an offending party honors a non-offender for doing what is right and just for the community.

Lastly, Nehemiah says that he drove an offending priest away because he defiled the priesthood by marrying a foreigner (Neh 13:28). Though a minor incident, Nehemiah publicly shames the priest for his unpleasant marriage association.

These four incidents in Nehemiah illustrate the culture of shame, where culprits are confronted and publicly humiliated and disgraced. The shame culture is also used as a teaching opportunity for the younger generation. In the case of Tobiah, the new generation learns a lesson about sacredness and how to distinguish right from wrong. The shamed offenders of mixed marriages learn the biblical principle of marriage purity. By purifying the priesthood, Nehemiah upholds the Torah teaching as applicable to all men and women, thereby proclaiming that no one is above the law.

Community and Ancestors

In Asian culture, the common interests and values of the community are held above the rights of individual people. Ancestors are remembered for their positive contributions in their descendants' lives.[13] In post-exilic writings, there are many listings of names. The genealogical accounts reflect strong statements about the community and their value. For Asians, time is continuous

---

13. For traditional African thinking on how ancestors who have died may play an active role in the lives of their descendants and the proper biblical view, see Yusufu Turaki, "The Role of the Ancestors," in *Africa Bible Commentary* (Nairobi: WordAlive Publishers, 2006), 480.

Introduction

in nature. Thus who the people of God are in the present era emanates from previous generations.

In Ezra-Nehemiah, there are many lists of people that reveal the community's unity in supporting God's ministry. Some passages identify groups without names, but other texts provide names. The different lists of people give a clear statement about the commitment of the post-exilic community.[14] For some lists, the author enumerates names without additional descriptions. Other lists provide the names of the younger generation along with their ancestors for two or even three generations. The inclusion of the ancestors traces the roots as a sign of respect and remembrance that encourages the new generation to uphold the spiritual heritage of their families.

The whole community supports the rebuilding of the altar and the temple. Joshua has a supportive group of priests, whereas Zerubbabel has his building associates (Ezra 3:2, 8). Following the advice of the prophet Jeremiah to pray for their sojourned community, many remnants happily dwell there (Jer 29:4–9). Not every family is willing to go up to Jerusalem. To commend them for their willingness to heed God's opportunity for them to return to Judah and Jerusalem, the lists consist of the names of the first and second returnees (Ezra 2:2–70; 8:1–14). The genealogical record of the first returnees in the book of Nehemiah functions as an inspiration for those who are willing to "go up" and live in Jerusalem (Neh 7:4–23). Following their ancestors, they should be joyful that they are now in Judah. Although the names of the third returnees are not listed explicitly in the book of Nehemiah, the names of the previous returnees could encourage the younger generation to recall their spiritual heritage and to faithfullycontinue their own spiritual journey.

Ezra selects a group of capable leaders to find and enlist the Levites to join the caravan to Jerusalem (Ezra 8:16). A group of thirteen leaders stands with him while he is reading the Torah (Neh 8:4), and thirteen Levites instruct the people in the law (Neh 8:7). The heads of all the families, along with the priests and Levites, gather around Ezra to learn more about the words of the law (Neh 8:13). When the Israelites confess their sins, the sixteen named Levites lead their prayer of confession before the Lord (Ezra 9:4–5). Thus Ezra is accompanied by a group of supportive leaders and Levites.

---

14. Community is more important than the individual in Asia. Individual rights are subordinated to the rights of community. In Asia, especially in the Chinese society, lists of names and pictures of groups are published in the newspaper to inform the public about their contribution. Special donations are also given in the memory of ancestors to show forth the descendants' filial piety and so that the ancestors may be remembered by younger generations.

Nehemiah has a group of active builders who play different roles within the society as they rebuild the wall (Neh 3:1–32). The leaders, priests, and Levites, who understand the teaching of the law, affix their seals to express their commitment (Neh 9:38–10:27). Those who are willing to live in Jerusalem – the descendants of Judah, Benjamin, the priests and the Levites – list their names along with their ancestors (Neh 11:1–19). Hence, the obedient community makes possible both the rebuilding of the wall and the re-education of the people.

In Ezra-Nehemiah, the post-exilic community functions as a wholesome entity. Though these books may not bring out the unity of "all Israel" (as in the Chronicles), we can see the unity of the people as they face different challenges, held together by their common spiritual legacy.

THEOLOGICAL THEMES

Four of the theological concerns expressed in Ezra-Nehemiah are worthy of further study: prayer, lists, obedience, and leadership.[15] First, because Ezra-Nehemiah was written in the post-exilic era, *prayers* are emphasized. The people have learned that they need to wait upon the Lord for their commitment, commendation, confession, and confidence. Second, the *lists* of items or names in Ezra-Nehemiah conveys the people's ideology about God's faithfulness and the legacy of the faithful returnees in the community. Third, having lived through the painful experience of exile, the people express their desire for *obedience* to God by following the teaching of the Torah. Fourth, the theme of *leadership* is revealed through the actions of Zerubabbel, Ezra, and Nehemiah, whose leadership styles are worthy to examine and emulate.

Theology of Prayer

Ezra-Nehemiah contains various and significant types of prayers that reveal the post-exilic development of prayer. With the challenges faced by people after the exile, fasting and praying become linked (Ezra 8:21; Neh 1:4; 9:1). Along with prayers, the book records emotional actions, such as weeping, throwing oneself down, and wearing sackcloth as expressions of lament (Ezra 9:3; 10:1; Neh 9:1). Some prayers are brief while others are long. Some prayers ask God for intervention while others express faith before God. The wording

---

15. To understand the theology of Ezra-Nehemiah with a link to the New Testament, see Paul J. Kissling, "The So-Called 'Post-Exilic Return': Already-But-Not-Yet in Ezra-Nehemiah," *Stone-Campbell Journal* 17 (2014): 207–220.

Introduction

and vocabulary used in the prayers reflect the piety of the Old Testament believers along with a consistent faith that the Almighty God listens to human prayers.[16] The prayers also reveal the liturgical traditions that were handed down from one generation to the next. The prayers in Ezra-Nehemiah can be broken into the following genres: *commitment, commendation, confession, confidence,* and *celebration.*

Prayer of commitment

The prayer of commitment affirms the Lord's mightiness and acknowledges humankind's frailty. The motive of this prayer is to commit oneself to the Lord for service and to prepare one's heart for ministry. It is a humble request to serve God by following his will and seeking his goodness and timely intervention.

Before Ezra departs on a journey to Jerusalem, he declares a fast to ask for a safe journey (Ezra 8:21–23). He testifies that the gracious hand of the Lord is upon him as he looks to God for guidance. Ezra commits himself and his journey to the Lord, trusting God's gracious hands to protect him.

When Nehemiah learns about the destructive conditions of the wall of Jerusalem, he prays to the God of heaven for guidance (Neh 1:1–11). The motive for his prayer is to wait upon the Lord as he commits himself to the Lord's work, asking the Lord to grant him success so that he may get involved immediately (Neh 1:11). When given a chance to speak before King Artaxerxes, who earlier issues a decree to prohibit the people from rebuilding the city (Ezra 4:7–21), Nehemiah prays to the Lord before opening his mouth. His silent personal prayer depicts his commitment to the Lord and his willingness to entrust the matter to the Lord (Neh 2:4). Though it is a challenge to present his plans before the king, nothing will hinder him from his access to the Lord – not even a royal decree – and nothing will prevent him from his desire to rebuild the wall for the Lord!

This genre of prayer includes the following four elements: first, addressing God's name (Neh 1:5); second, acknowledging God's justice (Neh 1:6–7); third, affirming God's power (Neh 1:8–9); fourth, anticipating God's action (Neh 1:10–11).

Though Nehemiah hopes for instantaneous action, he has to wait for four months before his prayer is finally granted. In Nehemiah's prayer, King Artaxerxes, who is the monarch of the Persian empire, is addressed as "this man," reducing him to a puny man before the Almighty God. At the proper

---

16. See Philip Yancey, *Prayer: Does It Make Any Difference?* (London: Hodder & Stoughton, 2006).

historic moment, Nehemiah knows that God can intervene and that prayer is the avenue to bring the matter before him.

Prayer of commendation

The prayer of commendation, or the prayer of praise, is an important genre in post-exilic prayers that depicts God's goodness, steadfast love, and faithfulness and focuses on God's loving actions toward his people. This prayer encourages all the people to participate in singing and shouting praises to the Lord, either through voice or musical instruments. Praise is a way to thank God for his blessings, mercies, and goodness.

When the builders finish laying the foundation of the temple of the Lord, they utter a simple prayer of praise to express their thankfulness to the Lord for his love and mercies (Ezra 3:10). Filled with gratitude, the people sing out, "He is good; his love endures forever" (Ezra 3:11). God's goodness and steadfast love are standard phraseologies in the post-exilic era (compare Pss 100:5; 106:1; 107:1; 118:1–4; 136).

In Nehemiah, two choirs sing and rejoice as they walk on top of the completed walls, praising God along with the gathered officials, priests, women, and children (Neh 12:31, 40–43). The choirs express their praise in song and are accompanied by many musical instruments, such as cymbals, harps, and lyres, following the great musician David's command (1 Chr 25:1; compare Neh 12:24, 45).

Prayer of confession

Confession focuses on human sinfulness, disobedience, and stiff-necked arrogance. In confession, people do not complain about human suffering and divine punishment but ask the Lord to intervene and forgive. This genre of prayer describes the ultimate problem of human weakness, particularly disobedience to God, and affirms God's goodness and faithfulness, often comparing human failures with God's graciousness.

Realizing the seriousness of intermarriage, Ezra tears his tunic and cloak, pulls hair from his head and beard, and offers a prayer of confession to the Lord (Ezra 9:6–15). Similarly, the Israelites gather to confess and worship the Lord a few days after the reading of the Book of Moses (Neh 9:5–37). Their communal prayer of confession uses historical imagery and traces the obstinacy of the people from past to present. A prayer of confession may involve weeping or throwing oneself to the ground as a sign of repentance (Ezra 10:1).

One characteristic of the post-exilic prayer of confession is the identification of people as sinners. Ezra includes himself as the guilty party whose sins are higher than their heads (Ezra 9:6–7, 10, 13). On the communal day of confession, the Israelites pray and confess before God, tracing the cyclical history of their failures in sinning against God and acknowledging their arrogance. This intentional acknowledgment, remembering the sins of the past generations, would move them forward. Rather than separating themselves from what has happened in history, the post-exilic Israelites constantly include themselves as members of the guilty party (Neh 9:32, 36–37). Both individual prayers of confession and corporate prayers of confession are included in the repertoire of these prayers.

The prayer of confession includes the following four elements: first, acknowledging humankind's sinfulness (Ezra 9:6–7; Neh 9:16–17); second, appreciating God's deeds (Ezra 9: 8–9; Neh 9:5–15, 19–25); third, admitting humankind's disobedience (Ezra 9:10–12; Neh 9:26–31); fourth, accepting God's punishment (Ezra 9:13–15; Neh 9:32–37).

The prayer of confession appeals to God's compassion and love. God is "a forgiving God, gracious and compassionate, slow to anger and abounding in love" (Neh 9:17, 19, 27, 28, 31). This prayer recalls God's deeds for his sinful people and also accepts God's punishment for their wickedness and rebellion.

Prayer of confidence
While leading the rebuilding of the wall, Nehemiah turns to God and prays about the challenges he is facing (Neh 4:4–5). In his prayer of confidence, he confides in the Lord about his troubles. Other scholars may want to classify this genre as an imprecatory prayer, or the cursing of one's enemies before God (as in the Psalms). Yet Nehemiah's prayer expresses an unflagging trust that God will deal with his enemies justly and absolutely. Knowing that the rebuilding of the wall is God's project and that this God-given task is being ridiculed and despised, Nehemiah firmly believes that God will intervene on his behalf, judging and punishing his enemies for their sinfulness. Hurling insults at Nehemiah, who is God's servant, is tantamount to hurling insults at the Lord, and so Nehemiah trusts that God will be a righteous judge.

The prayer of confidence includes the following three elements: first, stating one's trust in God ("Hear us, our God," Neh 4:3a); second, describing one's trouble (". . . we are despised," Neh 4:3a); third, making a request ("Do not cover. . . ," Neh 4:4; "Remember . . . what they have done," Neh 6:14).

Similarly, Nehemiah utters a short prayer when his life is threatened, asking God to strengthen his hands (Neh 6:9). Upon discovering the plot of his enemies, he pours out his feelings to God instead of using tactics to fight back

(Neh 6:14). He believes that because the building project is God's work, and the Lord commissioned him to mobilize forces for this task, any hindrances are indirect attacks against the Lord.

The prayer of confidence and trust in the Lord's intervention includes two elements. First, there is an element of urgency ("Hear us, O our God," Neh 4:4). Second, there is an element of conviction. Knowing that God will intervene on their behalf, Nehemiah exclaims, "we are despised" (Neh 4:4), because of the insults that have been hurled at the builders who are working on God's project (Neh 4:1–3, 5). Facing these challenges, he prays, "Now strengthen my hands" (Neh 6:9). Nehemiah's prayer of confidence states the evil deeds of his enemies (Neh 6:14) while both asking and asserting that God will fight for him (Ps 94:1).

Prayer of celebration

The nature of a prayer of celebration is testimonial and consists of three elements: (1) invoking God ("Remember me . . . my God," Neh 5:19a; 13:14); (2) requesting mercy (". . . show mercy to me," Neh 13:22; "Remember me with favor," Neh 5:19a); (3) presenting a finished task (". . . for all I have done for the people," Neh 5:19b; 13:14, 22, 29, 31). The first element, "Remember me," is a simple and humble request to the Lord, who oversees all the actions of human beings. The second element, the request for mercy, acknowledges that humankind is a vessel for God's blessings. Anticipating God's favors allows men and women to share his blessings with others (Neh 5:14–18). The more blessings that God bestows, the more those blessings can flow to others. The third element, presenting a finished task, is not meant to be boastful, but is a celebration of accomplishment, a reverential report from a servant to his master that all the assigned tasks have been accomplished (Neh 13:14, 22, 31). Though the task at hand may prove to be difficult, the servant can tackle the job and overcome the evil deeds of his enemies to accomplish the mission of his master (Neh 6:14; 13:29).

Nehemiah utters several short prayers of celebration (Neh 5:19; 13:14, 22, 29, 31). Even as these prayers could be mistakenly identified as Nehemiah's boastfulness of his actions, they actually reveal his honesty and positive request before God. The content of these "remembrance" prayers are reports to the Lord about what he has done[17] and are interspersed among his accomplishments for the Lord. The short prayers ask the Lord about "his remunerative

---

17. We consider the "remembrance" prayer of Nehemiah 6:14 as a prayer of confidence, asking God to intervene on his behalf.

righteousness rather than his retributive righteousness."[18] The remunerative righteousness focuses on God's gracious gift, whereas retributive righteousness concentrates on human righteousness and the expectation of God's reward. God's generous righteousness gives Nehemiah the courage to offer these votive prayers. Nehemiah is not asking for reward, but he expresses his sincerity that he has done things according to God's desire. His godly actions are only possible because of God's generous and gracious gifts. His desire is to bring glory to God. Moreover, the prayers are private and are part of Nehemiah's memoir.

Theology of Lists

There are many lists in the Ezra-Nehemiah memoirs, which indicate the religious interests and ideology of the books as well as the composition of the post-exilic community. The list of sacred vessels indicates the importance of religious items to the people. The lists of people depict the various family groups and also establish relevant groups in their religious historical account.

List of sacred vessels

The list of sacred vessels serves as a historical link between the first and second Temple (Ezra 1:7–11; see also 5:13–15; 6:3–5). Whereas Nebuchadnezzar removed the vessels of the first Temple (2 Kgs 24:13), Cyrus restored them to their original purpose in Jerusalem, giving theological validity to the second Temple. In returning, Ezra follows the mission of carrying the sacred vessels for the temple (Ezra 7:19; 8:25–34).

The list of sacred vessels reveals the overall concern of the post-exilic era, tracing its legitimacy to the first Temple of Solomon. The vessels are the same vessels used at the Solomonic Temple, which Nebuchadnezzar carried away from Jerusalem and which will be returned to their proper place (Ezra 1:7, 11; compare 2 Kgs 24:13; 25:13–15; 2 Chr 36:7, 10, 18). With the return of the sacred vessels, the Temple worship can be restored. The careful listing also demonstrates the importance of counting the vessels in order to transfer them to the rightful place of worship.

Lists of people

The lists of people consist of returnees, genealogical records, and the faithful and unfaithful members of the returned community.

---

18. Derek W. H. Thomas, *Ezra & Nehemiah: Reformed Expository Commentary* (Phillipsburg, NJ: P & R Publishing, 2016), 286.

Returnees

The list of the first returnees chronicles the heads of families who are willing to return from exile after having settled down in Babylonia (Ezra 2:1–70; Neh 7:4–65). The list of the second returnees consists of priests (Ezra 8:2), the royal line (Ezra 8:2b–3a), and the twelve lay families (Ezra 8:3b–14). The twelve heads of families call to mind the twelve leaders of the first return (Ezra 2:2; Neh 7:7) in connection with the twelve tribes of the Exodus event. The second return can be seen as a second exodus. Compare with the first exodus, the first and second returnees are limited in numbers (Num 1:44–46). The returnees are the rightful heirs of Israel and provide a theological answer to the judgment of the prophets: though God led them to the wilderness, God is now bringing them back as the remnant.

Genealogical record

The genealogical record of Ezra is carefully traced to Aaron (Ezra 7:1–6), testifying that the Aaronite genealogy, or the priestly genealogy, connects with the last pre-exilic high priest, Seraiah, whom the Babylonians executed after the fall of Jerusalem (2 Kgs 25:18–21). The purpose of the genealogical record is to establish Ezra's legitimacy as the priest. He is not only a scribe who carefully transmits the law of Moses but is also a teacher of the Lord's instructions for the post-exilic community.

The list of priests and Levites accomplishes the following: (1) it lists those who return from the exile (Neh 12:1–9); (2) it gives the chronological listing of high priests (Neh 12:10–11); and (3) it furnishes the names of priests and Levites from the time of Joiakim, the immediate generation after the return (Neh 12:12–26). This list shows that the priestly line is never interrupted, even when there is divine judgment for human sins. God shows his mercies through the list of priests and Levites.

The genealogical record of Ezra and the list of priests and Levites in Nehemiah confirm the legitimacy of their work by tracing their genealogy to the previous generations.

Faithful and unfaithful members

The faithful and unfaithful returnees are carefully recorded for posterity. The unfaithful are guilty of intermarriage (Ezra 10:18–44), whereas the faithful participate in the rebuilding of the wall (Neh 3:1–32), join Ezra in the reading of the law of Moses (Neh 8:4–7), and seal their names in order to acknowledge their commitment publicly (Neh 10:1–27). Of course, the faithful members also want to live in Jerusalem (Neh 11:1–19).

The faithful members may be the descendants of pious families, but there are also others who have joined the faithful community and are starting out fresh in their walk with the Lord.

Theology of Obedience

Both Ezra and Nehemiah emphasize the importance of the law of Moses. The law is to be revered, read, studied, interpreted, and obeyed. Of course, the ultimate goal of the law of Moses is obedience. In Ezra-Nehemiah, the law of Moses is at the forefront of many activities.

The written law of Moses is followed in building the altar, offering sacrifices, and celebrating the sacred feasts (Ezra 3:2–6). Ezra, a teacher who is well-versed in the law of Moses, devotes himself to studying and observing the law of the Lord and teaching its decrees and laws to Israel (Ezra 7:1–10). Moreover, Artaxerxes, the Persian King, commissions Ezra to come to Jerusalem to teach the law of his God (Ezra 7:14, 25–26), whose commands and counsels are to be obeyed and followed (Ezra 9:14; 10:3). Torah obedience is the purpose for the reading of the law of Moses.

While Ezra reads the law, the Levites instruct the people, making it clear so that they can understand it. In response to the words of the law, the people weep (Neh 8:9). The heads of all the families, along with the priests and the Levites, gather to listen to the law and then follow it carefully as they celebrate the Feast of Tabernacles (Neh 8:14–17). Moreover, the people seal the document with their names and publicly agree to obey the Lord (Neh 10:1–39). As they understand the law of God, they become more willing to obey the word. On the second return of Nehemiah to Jerusalem, the Book of Moses is read aloud, and the people understand the meaning, but it takes the presence of Nehemiah to implement the law (Neh 13:4–11, 15–22).

Theology of Leadership

Both Ezra and Nehemiah trace the importance of building a team, working collaboratively with people in leading a ministry, and encouraging weaker or marginalized team members.

Team building

As the first returnees arrive in Jerusalem, they are led by a group of twelve leaders (Neh 7:7; Ezra 2:2), including Zerubbabel and Joshua, who partner together to lead their associates to rebuild the altar and the temple (Ezra 3:2, 8–9). Likewise, Ezra leads a second group of returnees to Jerusalem (Ezra 8:1–14), and along with his team brings about the reformation of the people's faith (Ezra 10:5–6).

Nehemiah's team-building strategy includes three important features. First, Nehemiah *chooses* a team of trustworthy persons whom he can count on to face strenuous challenges and to labor closely with him. This team is comprised of his brothers (Neh 1:2), his men (Neh 2:12), and his guards (Neh 2:9). The guards escort him to return to Jerusalem without any trouble (Neh 2:9–10). His men help him to survey the site in the middle of the night in order to observe what he needs to do with the wall (Neh 2:11–16). His men are comprised of a trusted group of confidants who work together to look at the damaged portion of the wall. The group he gathers is loyal, reliable, and dependable. His team stands behind him to support him and to help implement the rebuilding efforts.

Second, Nehemiah *commands* his team, giving them clear instructions and earning their respect. When he faces opposition at the wall, ". . . half of my men did the work, while the other half were equipped with spears, shields, bows and armor" (Neh 4:16). As he commands the people to work longer in order to repair the wall quickly (Neh 4:21) and to stay in Jerusalem to avoid propaganda schemes (Neh 4:22), he orders his team members ("my brothers," "my men," and "the guards") to watch diligently and to act responsibly by preparing for a possible attack by their enemies (Neh 4:23). By staying close, each with a weapon, they are not only protecting the wall, but are also prepared to fight a possible skirmish. Hananiah (Hanani), Nehemiah's brother, is a trustworthy person whom he puts in charge of Jerusalem (Neh 7:2).[19] When Nehemiah wants to implement Sabbath keeping among the people, he orders his men to stand at the gate at sundown to make sure that it remains shut until after the Sabbath so that no one can work or conduct business (Neh 13:19).

Third, Nehemiah *compliments* his team. In his memoirs, which summarize his accomplishments, he includes his brothers as part of his faithful team. Unlike previous governors, who put heavy tax burdens upon the growing community by demanding food, wine and silver from them, no one on his team demanded the governor's food allowance (Neh 5:14); rather, they forfeited that right without complaint. Nehemiah also compliments his men for working diligently at the wall rather than getting sidetracked by business affairs in the community. With their privileged position close to him as the governor, they could have used their power to acquire land and appoint more landlords, leaving more landless people in the community. Instead, they worked closely

---

19. We see Hanani and Hananiah as the same person.

at the wall and concentrated on the rebuilding task (Neh 5:15–16). Their faithful, diligent, and focused service amplifies Nehemiah's leadership.

Collaborative leadership
Zerubabbel and Joshua collaborate with one another in the rebuilding of the temple and in their common task of leading the people, with Zerubbabel working as a civil leader and Joshua as a religious leader. As the two prophets Haggai and Zechariah challenge them to finish the rebuilding, they set their hearts to the work of restoring the temple (Ezra 5:1–2).

Zerubabbel and Joshua also work closely with the heads of the families of Israel. These family heads support the rebuilding of the temple through their actions and through praise (Ezra 3:12–13). The family heads also help the leaders facing the opposition to rebuild the temple (Ezra 4:2–3).

Likewise, Ezra sets apart twelve of the leading priests to deal with the offerings that he brings to Jerusalem (Ezra 8:24–27). The leading priests help Ezra in handling the articles consecrated to the Lord.

Before Nehemiah arrives on the scene as governor, there are already key political leaders in the community (Neh 2:10, 19). Although Nehemiah has a team consisting of his brothers, men, and guards who may be able to assist him in the rebuilding of the wall (Neh 4:23), he also recruits new leaders from their Jewish community such as the priests, nobles, and officials to join him in the rebuilding project. First, Nehemiah challenges the leaders to support his work (Neh 2:16–17). Second, Nehemiah calls the leaders to make strategic plans in facing difficulties (Neh 4:14, 19). Third, Nehemiah commits the key leaders to push for positive changes (Neh 5:7, 12). Nehemiah is a great leader who understands the dynamics of the post-exilic community.

Moreover, as a political leader and building manager, Nehemiah works closely with Ezra, the priest, teacher, and scribe. After Nehemiah and his leadership team complete the wall, Ezra can fulfill his duty as the teacher of the law.[20] Nehemiah and Ezra serve together at the Water Gate as Ezra reads the law of Moses to the people. Then both Nehemiah and Ezra call the people to a celebratory feast (Neh 8:9). Though they have different viewpoints (Ezra 8:22; Neh 2:8–9) and different ways of handling their anger regarding intermarriages

---

20. The quiet thirteen years of Ezra should not be a problem, as not all actions of Ezra and Nehemiah are part of the recorded events in Ezra-Nehemiah. The fact that Ezra is invited to read the law of Moses shows the respect of the people in acknowledging his role as the teacher of the law.

(Ezra 9:3; Neh 13:25), they collaborate with one another, and both take part in the festive group as they dedicate the wall to the Lord (Neh 12:33).

Encouraging weaker team members

In the post-exilic community, there are more priests than Levites (Ezra 2:36–40; Neh 7:39–43). In fact, during the second return with Ezra, there are initially no Levites in the caravan (Ezra 8:15). The Levites have lower status in the temple service and perform the more menial tasks, but without them, the worship of the post-exilic community cannot be handled properly. Thus Ezra recruits some Levites to join him (Ezra 8:16–18). Some of the returning Levites settle in Jerusalem, while others settle in their ancestral properties outside Jerusalem. But in the dedication of the wall, the decision is made to seek out all the Levites from their scattered dwellings to come to Jerusalem for the celebration (Neh 12:27–30). Inviting the "weaker" Levites to participate restores their role as part of the team. After the wall dedication, another decision is made to provide them with respectable provisions (Neh 12:44–47; 13:13). Together, Ezra and Nehemiah make sure that all the Levites, musicians, and gatekeepers join together to serve God and the people. The healthy financial system of tithes and offerings strengthens the longevity and service of the entire community.

COMPOSITION

Many biblical scholars see the composition of Ezra-Nehemiah, together with the Chronicles, as completed in the late-Persian period (about 400–333 BC) by one editor. The similarity between these books in style, choice of words, theme, and theology seems to suggest a common authorship. Later extensive research, however, points toward great differences in the Hebraic language usage and theological emphases, suggesting that the authorship of Ezra-Nehemiah differs from Chronicles.[21] With the final form as the accepted methodology, most scholars recognize Ezra-Nehemiah as a unified material.

Ezra was one of the descendants of Hilkiah, the priest under King Josiah (2 Chr 34:14). Ezra probably edited this book around the fifth century as he

---

21. Though M. A. Throntveit accepts Ezra-Nehemiah as an independent work that does not have common authorship with Chronicles, his earlier study shows that it may not be easy to prove its separation on linguistic ground. See "Linguistic Analysis and the Question of Authorship in Chronicles, Ezra, and Nehemiah," *VT* 32 (1982): 201–216. Likewise, David Talshir, "A Reinvestigation of the Linguistic Relationship between Chronicles and Ezra-Nehemiah," *VT* 38 (1988): 165–193, concludes his studies with an argument for its common authorship. Talshir, however, does not include Nehemiah's Memoir in his study, which in itself is already a wrong methodology.

Introduction

recorded the first two returns. Sheshbazzar and Zerubbabel led the first group of returnees, which is described in the first six chapters. Ezra, whose name does not appear until chapter 7, led the second group of returnees. This second portion of the book is Ezra's memoir.

Nehemiah, who served as cupbearer to Artaxerxes king of Persia, wrote his personal memoirs that account for the condition and the accomplishment of the royal grant for the Jewish people to return to their homeland. A large portion of Nehemiah's memoir is found in Nehemiah 1–7 and parts of chapters 11–13.

RELATIONSHIP WITH CHRONICLES

As early as L. Zunz (1832) and F. C. Movers (1834), Ezra-Nehemiah is considered to be part of the work of the Chronicler. Many more recent scholars also argue that the theme of Ezra-Nehemiah is the same as the Chronicles.[22] The two works share similarities in essentially two areas. First, both works have common verses (Ezra 1:1–3; 2 Chr 36:23–23). Second, both works have similar ideology: (a) the legitimacy of the returned community (Ezra 10:1–17; Neh 13:1–3; 1 Chr 17:1–14); (b) the importance of the temple (Ezra 3:6; 1 Chr 22:2, 4, 15; 2 Chr 2:9, 15–16); (c) an emphasis on the cult (Ezra 3:2–6; 6:16–22; Neh 12:27–30, 44–47; 1 Chr 23–26; 2 Chr 2–7; 2 Chr 2:3; 8:13); (d) an emphasis on musical instruments (Ezra 3:10; Neh 12:35; 1 Chr 15:19; 16:5–6; 2 Chr 5:12–13); and (e) the listing of names (Neh 11:3–19; 1 Chr 9:2–17).

By investigating the treatment of significant OT theological themes in Ezra-Nehemiah and Chronicles, Japhet (1968) and Williamson (1977) were instrumental in presenting the differences between the two works.[23] Their basic finding – that Ezra-Nehemiah and Chronicles are two different works – has become the accepted norm. Following is a comparison of the different treatment given to some of the theological themes within each work. David's name is merely cited for his contribution (Ezra 8:20; Neh 12:24, 45).

First, Ezra-Nehemiah accentuates the exodus event (Neh 9:9–12), presenting all three of the returns as a second exodus in fulfillment of Isaiah's

---

22. David J. Clines, *Ezra, Nehemiah, Esther*, NCB (Grand Rapids: Eerdmans, 1984), 25–31, argues for the same ideology between Ezra-Nehemiah and Chronicles. Though Joseph Blenkinsopp, *Ezra-Nehemiah*, OTL (Philadelphia: Westminster Press, 1988), 53–54, accepts the differences between both works, he lists few similarities.
23. Sara Japhet, "The Supposed Common Authorship of Chronicles and Ezra-Nehemiah Investigated Anew," *VT* 18 (1968): 330–371; H. G. M. Williamson, *Israel in the Books of Chronicles* (Cambridge: University Press, 1977).

prophecies (42:13–16; 43:14–21; 52:1–12).[24] Chronicles, however, is quite silent on this matter, preferring to emphasize the theme of David and his Davidic covenant (in nineteen of its sixty-five chapters) and to trace back to Adam to provide a link to David (1 Chr 1:1). Ezra-Nehemiah, by contrast, merely cites David's name for his contribution (Ezra 8:20; Neh 12:24, 45)[25] and connects the post-exilic community with the pre-exilic community (Ezra 1:7; 3:1–7; Neh 13:1). Thus the most important history for Chronicles is David's kingship (1 Chr 10:1–9) and his involvement in the cult (1 Chr 22:1–26:32), and it purposefully omits his adultery.

Second, Chronicles highlights the immediate retributive effect of the people's sins, whereas Ezra-Nehemiah is silent about this.[26] Though Ezra-Nehemiah is very sensitive about the subject of sin, it does not present any immediate retribution.

Third, Ezra-Nehemiah stresses the importance of marriage in the covenantal family and is against mixed marriages (Ezra 9:1–10:17; Neh 13:23–24). The evil consequence of Solomon's mixed marriage to Pharoah's daughter is condemned explicitly by Nehemiah (Neh 13:26), whereas Chronicles fails to mention the many altars that he had sacrificed to gods because of his pagan wives, perhaps in an effort to avoid tarnishing the image of Solomon (see 1 Kgs 11:1–13). Moreover, Chronicles offers a theological explanation about how Pharoah's daughter did not stay in the temple complex because of the ark (2 Chr 8:11; compare 1 Kgs 9:24; 7:8).

Fourth, Ezra-Nehemiah emphasizes the political reality, which is that only two tribes, "Judah and Benjamin," returned from exile, whereas Chronicles prefers to use the more inclusive terminology, "all Israel," to express the unity of Israel (Ezra 4:1; Neh 11:4; 1 Chr 9:1; 11:1; 13:6) and to depict an idealized post-exilic history. Thus Ezra-Nehemiah is more exclusive and separatist, presenting the two tribes as "the holy seed" who are willing to be obedient to the Lord and to make a stand (Ezra 9:2; 10:1–17; Neh 9:2; 13:23–27), whereas Chronicles is inclusive and open to the northern tribes of Israel and to internationalism (Ezra 4:1–4; Neh 10:28–31; 1 Chr 1:1–9:44; 2 Chr 30:1).

Finally, Ezra-Nehemiah follows the teaching of the exilic prophet Ezekiel by highlighting the importance of Sabbath keeping as a gift from the Lord to the Israelites (Ezek 20:12, 20). Chronicles, on the other hand, is noticeably silent about the importance of the Sabbath (Neh 10:31; 13:15–22).

---

24. Mark A. Throntveit, *Ezra-Nehemiah*, Interpretation (Louisville: John Knox Press, 1992), 44.
25. Blenkinsopp, *Ezra-Nehemiah*, 51.
26. Sara Japhet, *I & II Chronicles*, OTL (Louisville: Westminster/John Knox Press, 1993), 44–45, presents the view that God's rule in Chronicles is direct, immediate, and individualistic.

THE BOOK OF EZRA

EZRA 1–6

PERIOD UNDER ZERUBBABEL: TEMPLE REBUILT

The book of Ezra narrates the return of the people of God to Jerusalem and Judah under the leadership of three key leaders. The first section, Ezra 1–6, traces the return under the leadership of Zerubbabel and Joshua in rebuilding the temple of God in Jerusalem. The second section, Ezra 7–10, traces Ezra's guidance in rebuilding the people of God. All three godly leaders are concerned with the worship of the people of God.

The narrative begins in 539 BC with the conquest of Cyrus of Babylon. With this victory, Cyrus proclaims a decree during in 538 BC to allow and urge the people of God to return to Jerusalem and Judah to rebuild the temple. This decree fulfills the word of the Lord through the prophet Jeremiah. As the people return to Jerusalem, they build an altar (537 BC), worship the Lord, and then begin to rebuild the foundation of the temple on its original site (around 536 BC). When faced with opposition from the local people, as recorded in Ezra 4:1–24, the construction halts between 530–520 BC, during the reigns of Persian Kings Xerxes (Ahasuerus) and Artaxerxes I. With the encouragement of the prophets Haggai and Zechariah, the people resume the rebuilding under Darius in 520 BC and finally complete the temple in 516.

EZRA 1:1–11

THE VERDICT OF FREEDOM: GO, GO, GO!

On September 28, 1901, a group of Filipino in Balangiga, Eastern Samar, launched a sneak attack on US troops, killing forty-eight of the seventy-five soldiers as the village church bells rang. In retaliation, one US commander ordered the killing and burning of more than 2,500 Filipino males above the age of ten. As a memorial to the slain American soldiers, the Balangiga bells were taken from a church in Balangiga as American military "war booty." Two of the bells were placed in F. E. Warren Airforce Base in Wyoming, and one was placed in a US war museum in South Korea. On December 11, 2018, the Balangiga bells were reunited when the US returned them to the Philippines. The return of these historical bells symbolizes the re-bonding of friendship between the US and the Philippines after the Balangiga massacre.

Ezra 1 is about the miraculous return of the precious "lost" gold and silver articles of the temple of Solomon to Jerusalem after the proclamation of King Cyrus of Persia. As pointed out in the introduction, the beginning portion of Ezra is a verbatim account of the end of 2 Chronicles 36. Ezra records the rise of the Persian Empire with the enthronement of Cyrus, who exercised authority over the Jewish exiles. Yet God did not forget his promise to his people in exile. After seventy years of captivity, he allowed them to return home by the decree of this foreign king. Ezra describes two groups of returnees from Babylon. The first group comes back to rebuild the temple (Ezra 1–6) under the leadership of Zerubbabel.

The verdict of freedom, "Go, Go, Go," can be traced back to the prophecy of Jeremiah (Jer 25:11–12; 29:10). With the edict of Cyrus, the Jews are free to "go" up to Jerusalem (v. 3).

1:1–4 THE KING MOVED BY GOD

Cyrus, the king of Persia, rose to power in the Near East and unified the Medes and Persians into a strong empire, treating the inhabitants of the conquered cities with mercy. Although Cyrus was not a Jew, God worked through him to return the exiled Jews to their homeland and to return all the temple articles that had been taken by Nebuchadnezzar. Thus the prophecy of Isaiah (44:28–45:6) and Daniel (5:29; 6:28) was fulfilled.

The opening verse not only describes the change of foreign rule in the lives of the exiles, but also declares the Lord's sovereign claim over his people as he stirs the heart of Cyrus, king of Persia (1:1).[1] The Lord himself moves the heart of a foreign leader, King Cyrus of Persia, to free God's captive people. The main emphasis of Ezra-Nehemiah is God's sovereignty and providence over the history of humankind in order to carry out his will.

With the eyes of faith, Ezra sees the realization of God's prophecy "to fulfill the word of the Lord spoken by Jeremiah" (1:1a; compare Jer 25:11–12; 29:10). God raises up a ruler of another nation to fulfill his purposes. The first year of Cyrus is reckoned from October of 539 BC, the time when he entered the Babylonian city in triumph, as chronicled by historians. Cyrus, who only twenty years previously had been a vassal king to the Mede, Astyages, astonishingly rose to power over the Near East after a series of victorious conquests.

Jeremiah's words also call to mind the prophecy in Jeremiah 51, which says, "See, I will stir up the spirit of a destroyer against Babylon . . . the LORD has stirred up the kings of the Medes, because his purpose is to destroy Babylon" (1, 11). In moving the heart of Cyrus, the Lord guides Cyrus toward his plan. The Hebrew, "stir up," connotes active arousal, a lifting up for action (Isa 41:2, 25). The most striking parallel for this phrase appears in Isaiah 45:13: "I will raise up Cyrus in my righteousness: I will make all his ways straight. He will rebuild my city and set my exiles free, but not for a price or reward, says the LORD Almighty."

God's stirring within Cyrus results in the edict of Cyrus, which is circulated widely in his powerful realm and preserved for posterity with a written decree. In the ancient Near East, important matters were registered in writing, as evidenced by the thousands of clay tablets and other inscriptions regarding laws, receipts, and contracts that have been found. A written proclamation was not only intended to preserve a record but was also used to announce or display public information.

The edict of Cyrus follows the lenient policy of his reign and the Persian kings after him. The motivation behind the decree is political, although it sounds religious. Tolerance of the religious customs of the people under Persian

---

1. The heading for Cyrus's decree also serves as a superscription to Ezra 1–6. See Raeyong Kim, "A Study on the Connecting Links in the Book of Ezra-Nehemiah," *Korean Journal of Christian Studies* 84 (2012): 5–19, which presents several links in Ezra-Nehemiah and argues for their function and importance.

rule could keep stability in the empire. The famous Cyrus Cylinder, a clay barrel with a long inscription, states, ". . . to the cities of Ashur and Susa, Agade, Eshnunna, the cities of Amban, Meturnu, Der, as far as the region of the land Gutium, the holy cities beyond the Tigris whose sanctuaries had been in ruins over a long period, the gods whose abode is in the midst of them, I returned to their places and housed them in lasting abodes." Cyrus helped his subjects restore their places of worship and even asked them to pray for his long life.

Although there is no mention of Jerusalem in the list of sanctuaries outlined in the above inscription, the decree recorded in Ezra 1:2–4 (along with the one written under the Aramaic version in Ezra 6:3–5) are very much in keeping with the intent of the Cyrus Cylinder. This affirms that God controls all the happenings in the world and even makes the leaders of empires carry out his designated tasks. The gracious blessing of Cyrus frees his people to go up to Jerusalem in Judah and rebuild the temple of the Lord (1:3). Note that the object of worship is not Cyrus, but the Lord. God is alive, and he is concerned about the welfare of his people. He gives power and appoints people to accomplish his will.

After seventy years of captivity, there were two new generations of Jewish descendants who had already established roots in the diaspora. This left few who might consider returning, and so those who remained were encouraged to assist those who set out. Looking into details of the provisions, Cyrus ordered the Jewish colony in Babylon to help the returning group offset the huge cost of transporting their goods all the way to Jerusalem by giving them silver and gold, goods, livestock, and freewill offerings. The provisions are quite similar to the exodus event, wherein the Israelites were instructed to bring along silver and gold, goods and livestock when they set out to leave Egypt (Exod 3:22; 12:38–39).

The "freewill offering" in Cyrus's provision refers to one of the three subtypes of a peace offering that was to be used in sacrifices (Lev 7:11–18) for festival meals at Passover (2 Chr 35:8), Pentecost (Deut 16:10), and Tabernacles (Ezra 3:5). More broadly, freewill offering refers to voluntary gifts brought to the Lord. The people of God used freewill offerings to erect and furnish the tabernacle (Exod 35:29; 36:3). They were given during the time of Hezekiah for the first temple (2 Chr 31:14) and also for the second temple (Ezra 1:6; 8:28). A freewill offering is a spontaneous act of individual piety rather than a prescribed ritual of the community written in the Mosaic law.

For a good gesture, Cyrus would pay for the cost of the temple from the royal treasury (Ezra 6:4). This symbolizes the official support of Cyrus. But the versatile Jews, noted for their ability to survive in the most difficult situation, were not too impoverished to extend financial assistance.

1:5–11 THE PEOPLE MOVED BY GOD

The response to the edict of Cyrus came from two sectors: the family heads of Judah and Benjamin and the priests and Levites (1:5). The family unit is the basic system in the Israelite society, and each "family head" leads his respective family. The post-exilic community is comprised of the tribes of Judah and Benjamin (1:5; 4:1; 10:9; Neh 11:4),[2] and priests and Levites, who are in charge of the worship. Because building the temple is the focus of their return, the priests and Levites will be needed, but God works in the hearts of both groups to return to Jerusalem. Returning to a land impoverished by wars and famine would not be easy and would include leaving behind possessions, ties, and business enterprises.

As the people prepare to return, all their neighbors assist them by giving them many goods. These neighbors were not necessarily from the Jewish clan. The incident echoes the exodus scene, where the Israelites asked for goods, such as articles of silver and gold, from their Egyptian neighbors before they fled (compare Exod 3:21–22). In their return to Jerusalem from Babylonia, a similar situation occurs, which fulfills the decree of Cyrus (1:4).

In verse 7, Cyrus returns the articles that Nebuchadnezzar plundered from the temple of the Lord in his conquest of Jerusalem in 586 BC to symbolize his victory. By returning the stolen articles, Cyrus shows his desire to honor the beliefs and customs of his subjects. These articles will be returned to the temple of the Lord, where they belong.

To ensure an accurate account of the transferred goods, Cyrus assigned Methredath as the treasurer, with further accounting assigned to Sheshbazzar, the prince of Judah. The naming of the people and titles of those who are responsible for properly transferring the articles expresses a meticulous and conscientious accountability procedure.

In managing the details of the inventory, each item is given a specific number denoting its value. The exiles bring 5,400 articles of gold and of silver from Babylon to Jerusalem (1:11). The articles are probably those used in the

---

2. Chronicles prefers to use "all Israel" to describe the returned community in order to project an ideal community, though it does record that only Judah and Benjamin returned from exile (see 1 Chr 9:1–3).

Jewish temple, and the gold dishes might be the vessels used to collect the blood of the slaughtered sacrificial lambs.

This assembly of Israel, those that come back from the exiles, claims the legitimacy of religious traditions (6:19–20; 8:35; 9:4; 10:7, 16),[3] even over the ethnic population that did not go into exile.[4] In comparing the partial list in the two previous verses, however, the sum does not add up to 5,400. The partial list may refer only to the most important items. These articles are delivered from Babylon to Jerusalem, where a thrilling atmosphere of reception awaits the returning company as they carry their valued possessions, anticipating the rebuilding of the temple of God. For their return proves that God honors his covenant of saving grace to the nation he called his own.

The Jews in the diaspora are blessed to have King Cyrus, a Persian ruler, issue a royal decree for them to return home, with God stirring before and behind them. Similarly, many overseas Chinese have started visiting their hometowns and renewing their ties with relatives and friends in China. The once "iron door" of China has swung wide open for trade, tourism, education, and even mission. For example, in the Philippines, as early as the 1980s, many Chinese-Filipinos began to travel back home and to send support to their kin. To date, many overseas Chinese ethnic groups have returned home to rebuild and repair their ancestral houses and lands. Some contribute money to repair roads and infrastructures, while others build schools and factories and set up businesses. Many Christians participate in the rebuilding of God's sanctuaries in China. Being able to return to their hometowns is a joy for ethnic Chinese who have resided in other countries.

The hope of regaining ownership of one's home fuels the decision to return. In one instance, a Chinese lady from the Philippines was thwarted in her efforts to regain ownership of her grandfather's property in Xiamen, China, and yet she was comforted by the prospect of arranging for the property to be used by the family clan there.

---

3. Ezra 6:16 (Aramaic) refers to the same group.
4. Joseph Blenkinsopp, *Opening the Sealed Book: Interpretations of the Book of Isaiah in Late Antiquity* (Grand Rapids: Eerdmans, 2006), 64–71, argues that the sectarian phenomena in the early Persian period can be traced back to Isaiah.

NUMBERS AND ASIAN COUNTING: RESOLVING INCONSISTENCIES IN THE TEXT

Ezra 1 gives an inventory of articles belonging to the house of God (Ezra 1:9–11) and a summary statement that there were 5,400 articles of gold and silver (Ezra 1:11). The precise number of the enumerated vessels does not add up to the summarized figure. How should we resolve this discrepancy?

The Western way of counting tends to be very precise. If we follow this way of counting, we would definitely want to find a valid reason for the discrepancy. Was the original list lost? Was there a miscalculation? Does the Ezra 1:9–10 only present the important vessels?

First, the Eastern way of counting tends to round up numbers. Second, the number normally reflects approximation. Larger numbers tend to reflect the significance of matters being mentioned. This does not mean that Asians do not want to be precise, but the discrepancy in counting can point us toward the bigger picture in the narrative. The purpose of this passage is to reveal the cultic continuity of the returnees with the temple vessels along with the covenantal faithfulness of God to his people. While the Babylonians took the vessels as plunder, God's promise to bring the people back includes the return of the temple vessels because life under God includes worship. This might be the case here. In Ezra 1:9–10, the total number of temple articles is 2,499. But in Ezra 1:11, the total number is 5,400. Hence, a round number and a larger number which signifies the importance of the temple vessels.

In many East Asian cultures, we encounter a different way of counting one's age. In traditional Chinese reckoning, newborns are one year old at birth. On New Year's Day, another year is added to the person's age.

As more Chinese live in westernized societies, many follow the Gregorian calendar, but among other Chinese, they still identify themselves according to the lunar calendar, differentiating their "virtual age" *xūsuì* (虛歲) from their "solid age" *zhousùi* (周歲). The former reflects the Chinese reckoning, while the latter reflects the Gregorian reckoning.

One's "virtual age" begins in the uterus. A newborn is one year old, because the baby has been living in his or her mother's womb for almost a year. This Asian reckoning is very biblical, as reflected in Psalm 139:15–16: ". . . when I was woven together in the depths of the earth, your eyes saw my unformed body; all the days ordained for me were written in your book before one of them came to be."

Female family members celebrate birthdays that end in even, round numbers as they reach fifty, sixty, seventy, or eighty, using the Gregorian, or "solid age," calendar. In contrast, male family members celebrate birthdays that end with nine, such as fifty-nine, sixty-nine, seventy-nine, and eighty-nine, using the Lunar, or "virtual age," calendar. The reason for this difference is related to the homonym for the number nine, *jiu* (九), which sounds like "long." Thus celebrating one's age that ends in nine expresses the wish of the family members for their patriarchs to live long, *zhang zhang jiu jiu* (長長久久). Similarly, the saying, "nine is not far from ten" *jiu bu li shi* (九不離十), has the same homonym as, "in nine you do not die" *jiu bu li shi* (九不離世), which means that by celebrating a birthday ending in nine, you do not die.[1]

Rosa Ching Shao

---

1. See http://i-explorechina.com/chinese-customs-culture-traditions/chinese-jubilees-celebrating-big-birthdays-in-china, accessed July 14, 2017.

EZRA 2:1–70

THE FIRST RETURNEES: WHO'S WHO?

A Christian school has just rebuilt their administration building. At the front of the new building, the administration prominently displayed a photo gallery with pictures of the founders and the board members. These pictures honor the founders for their significant contributions and also encourage the young generation to follow in their footsteps. Ezra 2 records a list of many names, which honors the first returnees to Jerusalem after the exile.

The faithful remnants, listed according to family, return to their ancestral town. Though the number of people is not enormous, their presence is a substantial illustration of God's grace. Many in the post-exilic community are accustomed to a comfortable life in the foreign land, and so they do not plan to return to their desolate homeland. Zerubbabel, the governor, and Joshua, the priest, lead the first batch of returnees.

2:1–70 LIST OF RETURNEES

The list of returnees also appears in Nehemiah 7:6–73, with minor variations. These two lists are almost the same, with a few textual variants. In Ezra 2:2, eleven leaders are named, whereas twelve leaders are named in Nehemiah 7:7. Ezra 2:69 provides a round number for the offering figures, whereas Nehemiah 7:70 breaks the account into more precise and varied offerings.[1] Both lists legitimatize their respective functions, with Ezra 2 recording the first returnees who come to build the temple and Nehemiah 7 providing demographic data for the relocation to Jerusalem recorded in Nehemiah 11. Moreover, both lists provide continuity within the Israelite community, with Ezra's list connecting the returnees with Israel's pre-exilic past by using geographical names, and the list in Nehemiah 7 linking the first returnees with the dwellers in Jerusalem and Judah (Neh 11:1–36).[2]

The first returnees have been living in exile in Babylon since the captivity, but they are now returning to Jerusalem and Judah. In the list, they are counted

---

[1]. It is generally accepted that Nehemiah 7 reflects the original list. See Williamson, *Israel in the Books*, 29.
[2]. Thronveit, *Ezra-Nehemiah*, 19, 93.

as the people of Israel, whereas those who are choosing to remain in exile are excluded. The list identifies the heads of families, priests, and Levites, along with the names of the musicians, gatekeepers, temple servants, and servants of Solomon. The total number of returnees is less than 50,000 but would be more than those who were taken to exile in Babylon. The list serves as a testament to God's providence in looking after the people of God.

2:1–2 Leaders

Ezra 2:2 names eleven leaders, whereas Nehemiah 7:7 names twelve leaders, with the addition of Nahamani. The number twelve connects with the twelve tribes of Israel and Judah, showing some relationship with the first exodus. The return of the community is the second exodus. The twelve leaders are leading the people of Israel back to their land, as proclaimed and prophesied by the prophets (Isa 44:24–45:7; compare Jer 25:12–14).

The two important leaders are Zerubbabel and Joshua. Zerubbabel is a descendant of the Davidic family and the grandson of Jehoiachin. He is usually referred to as the son of Shealtiel (see Ezra 3:2, 8; Hag 1:1). In the genealogy listed in Chronicles, he is the son of Pedaiah (1 Chr 3:19) and the brother of Shimei. He is the biological son of Pedaiah and, perhaps through marriage or adoption, he is also linked with Shealtiel (Deut 25:5–10). Joshua, known as the son of Jozadak (Ezra 3:2; Hag 1:1), is generally listed after Zerubbabel. He is the grandson of Seraiah, the last officiating high priest before the exile (2 Kgs 25:18; 1 Chr 5:40). Joshua is the high priest of the post-exilic community (Zech 3:1). Hence, the returnees have a leader from the David lineage and a high priest from the priestly line of Aaron.

2:3–35 Laymen Listed by Family and Town

The subsequent names are listed according to family heads (2:3–19), and then by ancestral towns (2:20–35). The ancestral towns are within the borders of the pre-exilic kingdom of Judah, excepting Lod, Hadid, and Ono (2:33), which are further west. Listing the ancestral towns fulfills the promise of the prophets, which is that the exiled people shall return to their hometowns. As members of the post-exilic community, the returnees are identified by their family heads and ancestral homes.

Having followed the advice of Jeremiah to build houses, settle down, and plant gardens during their sojourn years in Babylon, it is not easy for the people to return to Jerusalem (Jer 29:4–6). The returnees are the faithful ones who are willing to risk their lives yet again in order to resettle the land of their forefathers.

We see a modern equivalent for identifying through family heads and ancestral towns in the Philippines. Filipinos normally identify themselves either through ancestral clans or their places of origin. Historically, the political leaders in the Philippines all descend from ten elite family clans, who marry among their own kinsmen. President Rodrigo Duerte is the only president with an unknown family background. The three former presidents, Joseph Ejercito Estrada, Gloria Macapagal-Arroyo, and Benigno Aquino, are from significant political clans. Other Filipinos whose clans may not include famous people usually prefer to identify themselves by the locality of their birth or the place where they have spent most of their lifetime. With so many Filipinos traveling abroad now, people often identify themselves with geographical regions or even specific towns and barrios.

Likewise, the Chinese community uses clan names as well as geographical names to identify people. In Southeast Asia, the Chinese community is organized through clan associations, which consist of clan leaders who are active in helping their families, clans, and communities. The majority of people in the greater Chinese community recognize the names of clan leaders, which are listed in the newspaper. Ordinary members of the community only need to utter the name of their clan leaders to identify themselves with a particular clan. It is the responsibility of clan leaders to call a clan into unity and to serve as examples by generously giving and gently caring for people in their clan as needs arise. Some clan associations are very exclusive in their socio-civic activities and care only for the needs of their own members, whereas others are quite inclusive and extend help to the greater community. Many clan associations build classrooms in remote areas to promote education and a brighter future for children.

The Chinese community also organizes around place names. In the early 1960s and 1970s, student application forms in Chinese schools in the Philippines included information about the place name of one's ancestry (*ji guan*, which literally means, "place of origin").[3] Likewise, in the Chinese diaspora throughout the world, the younger generation still identifies the ancestral home (*lao jia*, or literally, "old home") of their parents. This identification helps identify the origin of the ancestral clan. The elder people in the family tell the younger generation about their hometown in Mainland China, sharing interesting anecdotes about their native land. Fathers often bring the younger generation to tour ancestral places and to meet relatives who may still be living there.

---

3. The modern *pinyin* is used to transliterate Chinese words.

This system of identifying oneself through place names can also be observed in Chinese cemeteries in the Philippines. There are beautiful Chinese cemeteries in the mega-cities of Manila, Cebu, and Davao. The existence of these grand and well-built mausoleums for the dead seems paradoxical, given the hundreds of homeless who squat around them. Manila Chinese cemetery has even become a tourist spot for foreigners. When the first-generation immigrants from southern China came to the Philippines, most of them were poor, hardworking, and thrifty. Because they had no money, they could not own any land. When the second and third generations were born, they inherited large fortunes from their hardworking parents, and so they were able to buy land so they could honor their parents by building a mausoleum where they could "live" decently after death. As Chinese immigrants without Filipino citizenship, they could not own any property except the land where they were burying their ancestors. In such a "city" for the dead, the younger generation had to indicate the places where their ancestors had come from so that they could be properly identified. Thus the place names for the deceased are inscribed on top of the front wall when one enters the mausoleum and also on the tombstone. The place name not only denotes the family root of an ancestor but is also meaningful for the younger generation, so that they know where their *lao jia* (literally, "old home") is.

2:36–67 Priests and Temple Personnel

The listing of priests and temple personnel follows the traditional listing, beginning with the priests (2:36–39), then the Levites (2:40), musicians (2:41), gatekeepers (2:42), temple servants (2:43–54), and servants of Solomon (2:55–57). Only four priestly family groups are listed – Jeshua, Immer, Pashhur, and Harim – whose families are listed again in Ezra 10:18–22. The numbers of the priests and temple personnel add up to 4,289 or approximately 10 percent of the total number of the returnees. In the post-exilic period, a priestly hierarchy eventually developed, which culminates in the emergence of the twenty-two (Neh 12:1–7) and twenty-four priestly courses (1 Chr 24:7–19). The development of the list from four priestly families to twenty-two, and eventually to twenty-four priestly families, could possibly relate to their identity in the family records (Ezra 2:61–62). As their priestly identity is proven, more families are acceptable to render service. The priestly courses not only identify the priests with their priestly clan, but also involve more priests in the service.

There are only seventy-four Levites among the first returnees, a small number that may be attributed to the following. First, the primary responsibility of the Levites is to help the priests in the temple, but this duty could not be exercised during the exile. Hence, their role has become insignificant (compare Ezek 44:10–14). With their limited role and insecure position, they are less motivated to return to Jerusalem. Second, given their lowly status, few would have gone into exile in Babylon (2 Kgs 24:14; 25:12). In the law of Moses, the Levites are classified together with the aliens, orphans, and poor in need of provisions (Deut 12:19; 14:27, 29).

Six family groups cannot prove their lineage (2:59–62), which is significant for the returnees. As in the first exodus, many non-Israelites go up to Jerusalem with the returnees (Exod 12:38), along with a few sympathizers. Of these six undocumented families, three are among the priestly line. Because there are strict restrictions around eating sacred food, these three families cannot receive the priestly privilege without clear lineage. However, these "unclean" families can be restored if a priest ministering with the Urim and Thummim decides to restore them (2:63). Among these three undocumented priestly families, the Hakkoz family appears to be reinstated during the return of Ezra and Nehemiah (2:61). Meremoth, a descendant of Hakkoz, is very active in the post-exilic society (compare 8:33; Neh 3:4, 21).

Following this first genealogical record, a summary is given. The numbers coincide with the list in Nehemiah 7, except for the account of the men and women musicians. Significantly, animals are listed after the servants, for they belong to the caravan. As with the exodus account, livestock are part of the caravan (Exod 12:38; compare Jonah 3:7). The animals are brought along not only for offerings, but they also constitute property for the people's resettled life in Jerusalem.

Ezra 2:69 provides a round number for the offering figures, whereas Nehemiah 7:70 breaks the account into more precise and varied offerings.[4]

2:68–70 Giving and Settling

When the first returnees arrive in Jerusalem, the heads of the families give freewill offerings generously to restore the temple on its foundations. Their generosity demonstrates their specific purpose in coming back: to rebuild the house of God (2:68). The theology of giving in accordance with their ability follows the antecedent theology of giving during the wilderness period (2:69; compare Lev 1:3, 10, 14). Giving is a response to God's love.

---

[4]. It is generally accepted that Nehemiah 7 reflects the original list. See Williamson, *Israel in the Books*, 29.

Settling in their ancestral towns is a fulfillment of the promise proclaimed by the prophets (2:70; 3:3) and realized with their return from Babylon to Jerusalem (compare 1:11). Thus the priests, Levites, musicians, gatekeepers, temple servants, and the rest of the Israelites all return to their hometowns.

> ### ORAL AND WRITTEN HISTORY
>
> Asians tend to emphasize the oral transmission of a story rather than a written record. In many traditional Asian churches, people seldom communicate through writing. Instead, important historical events and names are quoted from memory, and we rely on stories to be transmitted from one generation to the next. While oral stories can transmit historical facts for two or three generations, it may become quite difficult to "prove" the reliability of the history later on. Even with a written record, disputes often occur about who is telling the history accurately.
>
> Oral history tends to be relational, following concurrent events rather than straight facts. Asian communities also tend to understand history as cyclical rather than linear and weave together both good and bad contents. The names of the first returnees are listed and numbered carefully in the post-exilic community (2:3–60). Names are important because they testify about the involvement of people in a ministry. Pastors need to update their members' personal data in order to have a working pool of people to enlist as co-workers, prayer partners, and even financial supporters. The lists in Ezra-Nehemiah remind us that people are essential in the restoration of a worshipful community.
>
> The narration also records the free will offerings made by this first batch of returnees toward the rebuilding project for God's house. While the names of the returnees are listed individually and regionally, the offering amounts are summarized. To ensure the wholesome management of church funds, it is important to keep track of the church's financial accounting. There are different ways of approaching this, and some churches print code names or numbers for donors in weekly church bulletins, while others openly divulge the names and amounts given by donors. The latter method may serve to keep the accounts accurate and might encourage reluctant givers to follow others' good examples. The former method, however, proves one's sincerity in giving anonymously. Both accounting methods are biblical, and so each church should adopt whichever method suits and serves its overall function as well as its members.
>
> Rosa Ching Shao

EZRA 3:1–13

WORSHIPING TOGETHER: FIRST THINGS FIRST

After a 7.8 earthquake struck a church in Dagupan City on the coast of the Philippines the church suddenly sank one floor below the ground. The city appeared to be doomed to extinction because the soil behaved like liquid during the earthquake. After the tragic event, some concerned friends suggested relocating the church to a suburb, but members were determined to continue worshiping in the same place because the locality had so many historical memories attached to it. Initially, members met at a corner lot where it would be safe to worship. After much prayer, the church was eventually renovated.

Ezra 3 is about the Israelite people rebuilding the worship place in Jerusalem after seventy long years of exile in Babylon. As the first batch of returnees sets foot on their desolated temple ground, their main priority is to restore the altar and the temple. Under the direction and leadership of Zerubbabel and Joshua, they begin to rebuild the altar, facing intense opposition from their enemies in the land around them (3:1–6). They overcome their fear and manage to rebuild the altar on its original foundation (3:3) and then lay the foundation of the temple (3:7–13).

3:1–6 REBUILDING THE ALTAR

The seventh month is the sacred month for the Jews (see Lev 23:23–36). As soon as the people are settled in their towns, they gather together in one accord in Jerusalem. Settling in their own towns is part of God's promise spoken through the prophets (Isa 40:1–2; Jer 33:12–13) and fulfills the promise given through Moses and later implemented by Joshua in distributing the land. This promise-fulfillment theme reminds the people of God's faithfulness.

The returned community is connected with the community before the exile, and so restoring temple worship is the first priority. During the exilic period in Babylon, the sacrificial system may have been functioning, but it may not have been done properly, or it may have been discontinued over time (see Jer 41:5). In Abram's journey with God, he always built an altar to the Lord whenever he arrived in a new place (Gen 12:7–8). Worshiping through offering at the altar is part of the religious practice of the people in the Old Testament.

Thus building the altar for burnt offerings on its original foundations is the first aspect of restoring worship (3:3). The altar has to follow the law of Moses (3:2; compare Exod 20:24–26; 27:1–8) and must be built on its original place (1 Chr 22:1). Moses is depicted as "the man of God" for his role as a prophet (3:2; Deut 33:1; Josh 14:6), and the post-exilic writing defines his role in the cultic worship (1 Chr 23:14; 2 Chr 30:16) along with David, the man of God (Neh 12:24, 36). Just as Moses receives revelation about the blueprints for the tabernacle, David receives detailed plans for temple worship (Exod 25:8–9; 1 Chr 28:19).[1] Moreover, the biblical narrative makes it clear that unlawful altars should never be constructed (Amos 3:14; Hos 8:11; 1 Kgs 12:28–33).

Zerubbabel and Joshua lead the rebuilding project of the altar of the God of Israel. Because of Joshua's role as the high priest, his name is listed before Zerubbabel's (3:2). Under their leadership, and despite opposition from the people around them, the Israelites assemble "as one man" and build the altar on its old foundations (3:1). In spite of their fear of their enemies, they sacrifice burnt offerings on the restored altar (3:3), which is a symbol of God's presence and protection. Building an altar of worship draws the people before God and also announces to the enemies of the land that surrounds them their united purpose and commitment as a nation to serve God.

The altar enables the people to begin sacrificing morning and evening offerings (Exod 29:38–42; Num 28:3–8), which consist of a year-old lamb along with flour, oil, and wine. Other feasts, such as the Feast of Tabernacles and other sacred feasts will soon follow (3:4–5). The law of Moses prescribes daily burnt offerings, New Moon, or monthly offerings, other appointed feasts, as well as freewill offerings (Num 28–29; Lev 22:17–25). With the altar in place, the returned community can restore and regularize the religious practices of the previous sacrificial rituals, which demonstrate the people's sincere repentance for their sins and earnest seeking of God's guidance. By performing all these religious rites in accordance with the law of Moses, the people rededicate themselves to obey God's commands, having learned this lesson the hard way.

---

1. Dean Ulrich, "David in Ezra-Nehemiah," *WTJ* 78 (2016): 55.

3:7–13 REBUILDING THE TEMPLE

The returned community prepares to lay the foundations to rebuild the temple. Again, we see continuity in the striking resemblance between the rebuilding and the building of the first temple. For the rebuilding, the masons and carpenters are provided with money as well as daily provisions of food, drink, and olive oil (3:7); this mirrors the provisions of wheat, barley, wine, and olive oil for the first temple workers (compare 1 Kgs 5:11; 2 Chr 2:10, 15). The material used to build the first temple and also to rebuild the temple are cedar logs from Lebanon (2 Chr 2:3, 8), and in both cases the logs are transported by sea to the port of Joppa (2 Chr 2:16).

The chronology of beginning the rebuilding during the second month (3:8) is similar to the chronology given to the first temple (1 Kgs 6:1, 37; 2 Chr 3:2). As in the building of the first temple, the Levites are appointed to supervise the rebuilding (3:8), since they are not responsible for carrying the tabernacle and its articles (1 Chr 23:4). In the wilderness period, the minimum age to begin listing the Levites is thirty years (Num 4:3, 23, 30), but they can start serving at twenty-five (Num 8:24). When David organizes the Levites, he also starts counting them at thirty (1 Chr 23:3), but they can enter into service at twenty (1 Chr 23:24, 27). For the returned community, the paucity of the Levites (2:40) requires their participation as overseers at the age of twenty (3:8).

All members of the returned community join together in the rebuilding (3:8), with specific names identifying the priests and Levites who supervise the work (3:9). The solemnity of the occasion is evidenced by the presence of the priests, who are dressed in proper vestments with trumpets to praise the Lord as the builders lay the foundation of the temple. Trumpets and cymbals are often used in summoning the congregation and are included in religious ritual celebrations (Num 10:1–10; 1 Chr 16:5–6; 2 Chr 25:11–13). Because the sons of Asaph have returned as singers (2:41), the task of singing and praising the Lord with cymbals according to the direction of King David is given to them (3:10–11). Their religious participation is possible through the prescription of David, who introduced innovative changes in the guidelines for temple organization and proper worship (2 Chr 8:14; Neh 12:24, 36).[2]

The content of the praise: "He is good, his love . . . endures forever" has become the accepted phraseology in the psalms of praise (Neh 3:11; Pss 100:5;

---

[2]. Gregory Goswell, "The Absence of a Davidic Hope in Ezra-Nehemiah," *Trinity Journal* 33 (2012): 19–31.

106:1; 107:1; 118:1–4; 136:1). The goodness of God is very much related to his steadfast love, especially as the returnees experience his grace. It is but natural for most of them to show forth their joy by great shouts of praise. Completion of the foundation for the temple needs the great effort and support of the whole community. As they start to praise the Lord, no one seeks personal praise; instead, everyone praises God for what has been accomplished at this point of their congregational worship.

Fifty years after the destruction of the temple, the rebuilding process began (536 BC). Some older priests and Levites who had seen the first temple weep in sorrow, perhaps relinquishing their pride, and surrender all their shortcomings to God. They can remember Solomon's more glorious, elaborate, and ornate temple, which was decorated with vast amounts of gold and precious stones and took over seven years to build. As they lay the foundations of the temple, surrounded by ruins and debris, they are struck by the great contrast between grandeur and gravity. Yet the returned community rejoices over God's grace and grieves their sins, and their joyful praise and sorrowful penance travels afar, ringing loud and clear.

PHYSICAL OR SPIRITUAL CHURCH?

The post-exilic community functions as a team. The leaders set good examples for their followers through their integrity and authentic living. They lead their core members to build up the community and to restore worship by building the physical sanctuary. It really is a joy to see stricken and barren houses of worship become promising and lively again. It is equally joyful to see God's people serve God in new communities.

Do we need to build a physical structure for God's ministry? Or should we focus on building up the body of Christ spiritually? These questions seem to be oft-repeated by leaders in Asia today. Many church buildings are being built upon the foundations of historic churches, which is a testament of God's grace and faithfulness from the old generation to a new generation of believers. Other pastors and mission directors have a more futuristic outlook, building churches on prime locations in major cities to target newly relocated people. In mega-cities today, the location of a church building and easy accessibility are important for church growth. Thus through urban planning, some churches plan their meeting places around different modes of transportation, such as ample parking for cars, or being situated near a bus or train line. Such considerations are made before the church building has even been constructed.

The leaders of the Methodist Church in Singapore and Malaysia strategically planned to build churches in settled communities where people in the neighborhood could easily come to worship. They have blossomed and become the largest denomination in both countries.

Other churches seek to draw various people groups to the Lord by focusing on people rather than buildings. In some creative access nations (CAN), the only way to worship the Lord is to meet in various houses. Some Filipinos worship through "mobile" churches, renting vehicles to worship for a few hours.

Obviously, people are more important than church buildings. The issue of "church with walls" (physical property) versus "church without walls" (people as worshipers) is an age-old concern. Ideally, God's work calls for his people and a place of meeting (like a building) to expand his ministry. God is building a people of power when tasks are assigned to them.

We need vision and goals for any work that we do for the Lord, for if we fail to plan, we plan to fail. We also need more spiritual leaders who can work with people at their level, shoulder to shoulder. The Chinese have a saying that a mountain cannot hold two tigers, for when two tigers fight, one will get injured. Indeed, it is difficult for two gifted and outstanding leaders to oversee a task together. In mission work, however, we need many able, available, and amiable leaders to keep growing and gaining new heights for both the spiritual and physical church of God. Leaders who partner with others will definitely produce greater accomplishments for the kingdom of God.

Just like what we see from Erza 3, people like Joshua and Zerubbalel are called to lead in the rebuilding of the altar and temple; the people around them gave a shout of praise seeing the foundation of God's house laid (Ezra 3:11). With this temple, the people could worship more intently and keenly, leading to their spiritual growth in God; this is likened to the rebuilding of the inner walk with God.

Rosa Ching Shao

EZRA 4:1–24

MOUNTING OPPOSITION FOR THE TEMPLE: NO, NO, NO!

It may be easier to rally the people of God to build a visible sanctuary to worship the Lord than to raise funds for some other invisible cause. In the Christian world, worshipers often prioritize visible structures, such as God's sanctuary. Migrants from Wunzhou, China, who moved to Europe from the early 1980s through to the present, gave to the Lord for building projects before establishing their own businesses. In Italy alone, they helped build around ninety churches, and in Spain, they helped build more than fifty. God has also blessed their businesses and families. Building a sanctuary is a great idea, but it can be difficult to mediate the different opinions among church members. Opposition voices can cause disunity, which can form divisive groups inside churches.

Ezra 4 describes the various oppositions faced by the returnees as they rebuilt the temple and the city. The hostility from the opposition takes the subtle form of cooperation (4:2), an accusation (4:6), and finally the brutal stoppage of the work (4:23). All three forms of opposition become obstacles to the work of rebuilding. The first portion of the chapter focuses on the rebuilding of the temple and explains why the work is stopped until the reign of Darius king of Persia (4:1–5). The second portion covers a latter historical period during the reigns of Xerxes (4:6) and then Artaxerxes (4:7–23) and emphasizes the rebuilding of the city walls and foundations. The narration concludes with a remark about the standstill of the temple rebuilding project (4:24).

This chapter consists of two salient themes: opposition against the people of God and the efforts to counterattack that opposition. In the first round of resistance against the work of God's people, the opposition is identified as the enemies of Judah and Benjamin (4:1), who settle in the city of Samaria (4:10). The second round of resistance is identified by a list of those who are responsible for drafting the letter of complaint to King Artaxerxes (4:7–8), followed by the list of regions who support the opposition, including Erech, Babylon, Susa, Samaria, and the region beyond the Euphrates River (4:9–10). Two literary markers, which serve as a "summary notation" of the opposition, offer a coherent purpose for the chapter (4:4–5, 24). Thematically, the events in this chapter focus on the temple rebuilding by God's people and the related opposition to that project.

4:1–5 NOT ALLOWING ENEMIES TO PARTICIPATE IN REBUILDING

The Israelites who have returned to Jerusalem are from the tribes of Judah and Benjamin (4:1; compare 3:1). They are quite clear in their goal to rebuild the temple for the Lord. Because the first temple was in Jerusalem and was part of David's aspiration to honor God, the descendants of these tribes have a natural inclination to worship and to build a temple for the Lord (4:3). The temple of the Lord differs from other secular structures and buildings, because it is to be used only by those who have faith in the Lord. The rebuilding project gives those who have gone through exile a chance to demonstrate their faith and fidelity to God. Because of their experience as exiles, they are predisposed to exclude their enemies.

The first round of opposition to the rebuilding can be divided into three scenes: (1) the enemies express their desire to participate in the rebuilding of the temple (4:1–2); (2) the people of God express their desire to build a house to their God as commanded by King Cyrus (4:3); and (3) the enemies attack (4:4–5).

Although the enemies claim that they have been worshiping the same God since the time of Esarhaddon, they have been singled out as the enemies of Judah and Benjamin (4:1–2). In the Exodus account, a "mixed multitude" of god-fearers joins the Israelites (Exod 12:38), so why are they being excluded now? Through their exilic ordeal, the people of God have become very careful, and they are afraid that having the enemies of Judah and Benjamin participate in the rebuilding might bring problems in the long run. Moreover, the syncretistic theology of their enemies might be motivating their desire to participate.

Indeed, under the expansionist program of Assyria, the enemies of Judah and Benjamin were brought by the Assyrian King Esarhaddon (681–669 BC) from other parts of his empire. Esarhaddon settled them in the land when most of the northern tribes were deported after the fall of Samaria (721 BC). Sargon II also brought in people at the time of his conquest (2 Kgs 17:24). During this time, some people living in the north continued to participate in the custom of offering sacrifices and visiting Jerusalem during exile (Jer 41:5).

The people of God express their desire to build the temple by themselves. Zerubbabel, Joshua, and the other family heads of Israel claim that they are the only ones authorized by King Cyrus to participate in rebuilding the temple. The temple is meant to honor the Lord, the God of Israel, and they are his chosen people. This exclusivity is meant to ensure the uniqueness of their belief, so that the effort and motive of rebuilding of the temple will be pure. The chapter ends with a repetitive resumption summary (4:4–5) that establishes a clear time frame for the ongoing opposition, from the time of Cyrus to the reign of Darius.

In the history of churches in Asia, a look into the church growth process discloses a few negative factors, such as church splits. Sadly, church splits often happen because of personality clashes between the leaders or some petty matters. When initially establishing a church, most people rally together around a common goal, subsuming their own desires and motives under the big umbrella of that shared vision. Once the church is established, or once a building project is finished, a battle around different goals may create dissension. Those who have not been supporting the project financially may express critical comments that are motivated by underlying selfish interests. As fractions occur, an outgoing group of dissenters may form an independent entity, thus creating a church split. Sooner or later, another church split may occur within that newly formed church. Such splits might be avoided if these "enemies" were identified so that their appalling intentions could be made.

As the world becomes a borderless village, many migrations have occurred both globally and locally. In our postmodern time, people are not only moving around to different countries and seeking greener pastures, but they are also finding it difficult to make single-minded decisions. We are living in the information age, so nothing is final or absolute. Relationships nowadays come and go.

4:6–24 NOT ALLOWING REBUILDING BY ACCUSATION

This second round of opposition occurs during the time of Xerxes and Artaxerxes I. Even though Xerxes (486–465 BC) and Artaxerxes I (465–424 BC) ruled after Darius I (522–486 BC), this seeming digression shows that similar problems existed during the time that Ezra was being written. The opposition during the time of Artaxerxes deals with the rebuilding of the city walls rather than the temple (4:12–13, 16).

The passage between 4:8 and 6:18 is written in Aramaic. Because Aramaic was the official language during that time, the correspondence in verse 8 begins in Aramaic, demonstrating the editor's careful use of the sources that were at his disposal.

The identification of Judah and Jerusalem explain why the opposition is included here. Xerxes (MT Ahasuerus) is the Greek name of the Persian king (4:6), who passed through Palestine during 485 BC to stop the rebellion of Egypt against Persia.

The opposition theme during the time of Artaxerxes, along with the record of an exchange of letters (4:7–23), is a key to understanding the roles of Ezra and Nehemiah in their historical context. Artaxerxes I sends Ezra to make reforms in Jerusalem (7:12–26). Thus Ezra should be in Jerusalem when the complaint from Israel's enemies is filed (see 4:12) and the king's decree is given (4:21). Nehemiah, who is in Susa, serving as cupbearer under Artaxerxes I (1:1, 11), understands the enormous challenge, for it will not be easy to reverse the king's decree.

The opposition to the city walls begins in the days of Artaxerxes (4:7). The name Bishlam could well be Belshunu, the governor of Beyond the River during that time. The letter, along with its effect, is written in Aramaic. Bishlam and his associates are merely handling a complaint letter filed by Rehum and Shimshai. The gist of the letter is to call to the attention of the king that a project to rebuild the city and its wall is now in progress. The authorized returnees are the ones who are rebuilding the wall and its foundations (4:12). The king is the one who has commissioned them to come to Jerusalem. This group could very well be the party of Ezra who came up in 458 BC. The letter argues that harm could be inflicted on the king if the rebuilders do not pay taxes and tribute. They even politely encourage the king to verify why the rebellious city was destroyed. The ultimate purpose, of course, is to insinuate doubts and hatred against the Jews.

After being fed such spiteful and provocative words, the king sends a decree to Rehum, Shimshai, and those living in Samaria and elsewhere in Trans-Euphrates. The function of the letter is to stop the work in order to protect the royal interests. Research finds that the city has a long history of revolt against kings, and so with the blessings of the king, Rehum and Shimshai immediately implement his decree.

The timing of the rebuilding of the city wall, the restoring of the foundations, and the stoppage of the work, point toward 445 BC, when Nehemiah hears about the wall of Jerusalem being broken down and its gates burnt with fire (Neh 1:1–3).

The literary marker "thus," which is used as a participle in 4:24, is used by the editor to pick up where he left off in 4:5. The resumptive summary states that the work of the temple is halted till the reign of Darius king of Persia. "The second year of Darius king of Persia" marks an important time frame for the stoppage of the rebuilding, an impasse that will soon be challenged by the prophets.

FACING OPPOSITION

How do we turn any conflictual crisis into a win-win situation? Some pressures may force people who are serving the Lord to run away into depression, but they can enable others to fly high and face the opposition squarely. The Chinese word for crisis (*wei ji* 危機) is actually a combination of two words: danger (*wei xian* 危險) and opportunity (*shi ji* 時機). With God's help, one can pass through the Valley of Baca (literally, weeping) and make it a place of springs (Ps 84:5). A problem can enable a mature leader to make key decisions for the glory of God. A frustrating situation can force a mature Christian to wait on the Lord (Isa 40:27–31) and become more resilient in the process.

In Chinese society and East Asian cultures, there are three commonly recognized religio-philosophical traditions: Confucianism, Taoism, and Buddhism. In a peaceful situation, Confucianism is normally accepted as a way of life. When there is a hierarchical structure in place, and each person knows his or her role in society, the Confucius teaching about harmony, serenity, and prosperity is the guiding principle. But when there are problems, traditional Chinese may appeal to Lao Tzu for his organizing system of belief. Taoism teaches that life needs balance between two opposite poles, Yin and Yang. Whatever comes down will go up, and whatever goes up will come down. This philosophy results in minimal action. When there is opposition or suffering, some traditional Chinese may appeal to Buddhism. Buddhism teaches that life is full of suffering, and so we need to accept an unfulfilled life and put everything aside, especially material enjoyment and family life.

When Christians face disappointments or frustrations, especially with our Christian friends, we need to trust the Lord and prayer. In responding, we can either: (1) retreat and leave the place of frustration or disappointment; (2) react with hurt feelings; and (3) recognize the situation and rise above the occasion.

We see the first option played out in Ezra 4. On two separate occasions, God's people stop the work of rebuilding after they meet mounting opposition (4:23–24). When we retreat because of opposition, nothing can be accomplished. In fact, retreating may encourage the opposition to assert themselves even more forcibly. Withdrawal will never solve any problems and may even yield more frustrations.

In the second option, we feel the heat of the opposition and react. Humanly speaking, we may want to recount our pains and hurts to others and nurse ill feelings. But the more we revisit our frustrations and hurts, the more we experience hurt. We can allow them to become huge issues that become obstacles for our healing. It would be far better for us to release our hatred and learn how to forgive and forget. As we lay our burdens at the cross, at Jesus's feet, we can rest and trust God to help us find a solution, even when there seems to be no way out (see 1 Cor 10:13).

In the third option, we try to accept the situation, including any criticisms or mistakes we have made. By going back to the drawing board, we can gain fresh perspective, knowing that God is always good and in control. As Peter reminds us, ". . . those who suffer according to God's will should commit themselves to their faithful Creator and continue to do good" (1 Pet 4:19).

I can recall a time when our youth put on a puppet show at our church entitled "Antshillvania," and everyone who watched the show was clamoring for its repeat performance. Our puppeteers were excited and encouraged, but they wanted to bring the message of "our loving heavenly Father, longing for the return of his prodigal son," to other schools who had not been founded by Christians.

The writer and a few members of the puppet group went to a nearby Buddhist secondary school to talk with the school director, a gentle and soft-spoken Buddhist nun. After hearing the gist of the story, she told us that we could perform the play as long as we took out the name of Jesus Christ at the end of the show.

The writer sensed a kind of the "foot-in-the-door" technique, which describes "a means of social influence wherein the target of social influence is first asked to agree to a small request, but later is asked to comply with a larger one."[1] All throughout the conversation, she was curious about how we could make those different kinds of ant puppets and props from scratch! The writer could see that the school was eager to learn how to make puppets and arrange presentations from us. Without consulting the rest of our puppeteers, the firm reply was, "Sorry, but that is the only uncompromising truth in the whole story of the prodigal son." Though we did not get to stage our puppet show, we did get to proclaim the unchanging and incomparable name of our Lord Jesus Christ, the Name wherein every knee shall bow, and every tongue confess that "Jesus Christ is the Lord of lords."

Rosa Ching Shao

---

1. Feldman, *Social Psychology*, 407.

EZRA 5:1–6:22

THE DECREE TO BUILD: YES, YES, YES!

The Philippine government likes to construct monuments and statues to commemorate important events in the life of the country. In 2017, some people protested the placement of a statue of a woman along a prominent street in Metro Manila to commemorate war crimes against Filipino women. But as soon as the responsible organization showed the authorities a permit, the statue was built without further hindrance. Ezra 5–6 is about obtaining certified royal permission to continue rebuilding the temple.

The prophets Haggai and Zechariah encourage the returned community to continue the rebuilding, since work has been stopped for a long period of time – possibly as much as ten years – due to fierce opposition from enemies of the Israelites. Tattenai, the governor of Trans-Euphrates, questions whether or not the Jews have the authority to rebuild, and his inquiry triggers research into the original edict of Cyrus in the royal archives (5:6; 6:6). This turns out to be a blessing to the Jewish people, as the existence of an authentic decree from Cyrus charges Darius to proclaim a new decree, which authorizes the Jews to finish rebuilding the temple (6:6–12).

The resumption of the temple rebuilding project begins around 520 BC during the second year of King Darius's reign (4:5, 24). The second temple is completed during the sixth year of Darius's reign (6:15). The theme of "the house of God in Jerusalem" links these two chapters together (5:2, 14, 16; 6:5, 7, 12). The God of Israel cares for the people of God through the prophecy of the prophets (5:1). Their unswerving command convinces the people to work together in finishing the temple (6:14). As they celebrate the Passover, they seek the Lord, the God of Israel (6:21–22).

These two chapters can be divided into the following scenes: (1) resuming God's work (5:1–5); (2) retrieving Cyrus's decree (5:6–17); (3) rediscovering Cyrus's decree (6:1–5); (4) rebuilding God's temple (6:6–12); (5) rejoicing at God's temple (6:13–18); and (6) remembering God's grace (6:19–22).

5:1–5 RESUMING GOD'S WORK

The prophets Haggai ("The Feasts") and Zechariah ("Yahweh remembers") are among the first batch of the returned exiles, and they actively promote the rebuilding of the temple in Jerusalem. Through their exhortation and preaching, the Israelites resume the rebuilding. Haggai's first prophecy is dated 29 August 520 (Hag 1:1), and the rebuilding work begins on 21 September 520 (Hag 1:15). Zechariah is identified as a descendant of Iddo, a prominent member of the priestly family (Neh 12:4, 16). Both prophets successfully inspire the other Jewish leaders to continue rebuilding the temple of God after many years of delay due to setbacks from their enemies (5:2; see also Hag 1:14). By preaching the messages of God, the two prophets help the Israelites remember their primary task in returning to Jerusalem (6:14).

The prophet Haggai proclaims that the temple must be restored so that God may dwell in the midst of his people once again. He encourages the returned families to get involved with the rebuilding project, asking them to "give careful thought" (Hag 1:5, 7; 2:15, 18). Haggai's prophecy seeks to assure the people of the presence of the Lord and strengthen both Zerubbabel and Joshua (Hag 2:1–5). The returned community is not rebuilding the temple in order to earn the favor of the Lord, but to give an outward sign of their inner devotion to God. The rebuilding flows out of their desire to offer honor, respect, praise, thanksgiving, and glory to God.

If Haggai preaches to the people from the human plane, then Zechariah prophesies from the heavenly perspective. Zechariah's main message is to show how God cares for his people. God has roused himself from his holy dwelling to complete his task of bringing the kingdom on earth (Zech 2:13). In a series of eight visions, the prophets describe God's actions on behalf of his people and for their land. God bestows a clean garment for Joshua (Zech 3:1–5) and promises the hands of Zerubbabel that those who laid the foundation of the temple will complete it (4:9). With the completion of the temple, all the nations will gather to worship the Lord in Jerusalem (Zech 8:20–23).

Governor Tattenai, Shethar-Bozenai, and their associates, ask who authorized the Jews to restore the temple. They also ask for the names of the builders. But God watches over the Jewish elders (5:5), who are the leaders of the community (5:9; 6:7), and so the work does not stop. The imagery of God's watchful eye denotes God's protection over his people (see Ps 11:4; Zech 9:8) and symbolizes his presence (Ezek 1:18; 10:12).

Behind Tattenai's inquiry is God's sovereignty. On the human plane, the query of the Persian officials prompts the royal court to search for the original decree of Cyrus. Upon finding that decree, Darius is prompted to endorse and support the rebuilding project. In the official Persian inquiry, Tattenai records the names of many builders, along with their leaders (5:4, 10). The rebuilding project requires the participation of many people, the devout leadership of Zerubbabel and Joshua, and the faithful support of the Jewish elders. Moreover, through the timely encouragement of God's prophets, along with divine protection through God's overseeing eyes, the work cannot be stopped!

5:6–17 RETRIEVING THE EDICT OF CYRUS

As the Jewish people proceed with the reconstruction of the temple, the non-Jews who live nearby attempt to hinder their progress. Tattenai, Shethar-Bozenai, and their associates retaliate against the Jews by writing an official report to King Darius, stating the reason for their inquiry on the rebuilding project (5:8–10), relating the response from the Jewish elders regarding the inquiry (5:11–16), and asking for permission to search the royal archives for any such decree from King Cyrus (5:17).

According to the report, the Jews are working diligently on the temple of the "great God," a phrase that reveals their reverence for the God of the Jews, and their work is progressing rapidly (5:8). The significant materials, such as large stones and timbers, depict the seriousness of the returned community. As part of the inquiry, Tattenai and his associates record the names of the leaders of the project (5:10).

In response to the inquiry, the Jews state their identity as "servants of the God of heaven and earth" (5:11). They also explain that they are rebuilding the temple because the Lord handed them over to Nebuchanezzar due to the sins of their forefathers, and Nebuchanezzar destroyed it (5:12). They further explain that Cyrus issued a decree in his first year as king, ordering the Jewish people to rebuild the temple of God, and allowing them to return to Jerusalem with the gold and silver temple articles that had been taken away during their captivity (5:13–14). The Jewish people also note that Cyrus appointed Sheshbazzar as their governor, who laid the foundations of God's house in Jerusalem (5:15–16).

Traditionally, Sheshbazzar ("Shamash protects the son") is identified as the Babylonian name of Zerubbabel ("Seed of Babylon"), following the identity in Josephus.[1] Both Sheshbazzar and Zerubbabel are designated as "governor of Judah" (Ezra 5:14; Hag 1:1). Both Sheshbazzar and Zerubbabel receive credit for laying the foundation of the temple (5:16; 3:8–10).

---

1. Josephus Ant 11.1.3 §13–14.

Modern scholarship prefers to treat Sheshbazzar and Zerubbabel as two distinct persons,[2] since it is unlikely that a Jew would have double Babylonian names. Sheshbazzar is identified as "the prince of Judah" and later as an "appointed governor" (1:8; 5:14–15). Unlike Zerubbabel, the Davidic ancestry of Sheshbazzar is not clear, though not totally absent. It is probable that he is the first Judean governor after the Babylonian exile, while Zerubbabel is the second governor. Both are involved in the work of the temple.

6:1–5 REDISCOVERING CYRUS DECREE

Darius issues an order to search the archives for the original decree of Cyrus. A written scroll is found in Ectabana, the summer palace of the Persian king. The winter palace is in Susa (Neh 1:1). A written scroll, rather than written tablets, reflects the usage during that time.

The original decree of Cyrus confirms the rebuilding work that the Jews are doing during the time of Darius. The scroll may be a summary of the original decree, since it is included in Darius's own decree (6:3–5).

There are two salient points of comparison between the summary and the original decree. First, the timing of the decree is marked as the first year of Cyrus in both (6:3; 5:13; see also 1:1). It is also the very first important element in that decree for the rebuilding of the temple. Second, the decree stipulates that the gold and silver articles from the house of God should be returned to their original place (6:5; 5:14; compare 1:9–11). Cyrus's decree asserts that the costs for rebuilding the house of God are to be paid by the royal treasury (6:4). It also includes a description of the temple, stipulating that it should be built with large stones and timber (6:4; compare 5:8).

6:6–12 REBUILDING GOD'S TEMPLE

Darius fully supports the rebuilding of God's temple, and so he instructs Tattenai and Shethar-Bozenai to implement a new decree. Paradoxically, their original inquiry about the rebuilding cast a veil of suspicion over the project (5:6; 6:6). After summarizing the original decree of Cyrus, Darius issues his decree, which fully endorses and affirms the rebuilding of the temple. The decree not only prohibits Tattenai and Shethar-Bozenai from interfering by commanding them to stay away from the project (6:7), but it also demands that the expenses are to be paid by the royal treasury – specifically, from the

---

2. ABD 5:1207–1209.

revenues of Trans-Euphrates (6:8). Thus these two meddling skeptics have to support the project out of their treasury. Remarkably, King Darius, who is a foreign ruler himself, orders the non-Jews not to interfere, giving the Jews and Jewish elders a free hand to finish rebuilding God's temple (6:7). Moreover, whatever is needed for their offerings to the God of heaven, such as young bulls, rams, and male lambs, together with wheat, salt, wine, and oil, will be provided for them daily (6:9). Through God's astonishing and miraculous intervention, the enemies' scheme ends up benefiting God's people. Of course, underlying the decree, the king may have a selfish motive of asking the Jews to pray for the well-being of the king and his sons (6:10).

In the ancient Near East, most kings helped provide for the needs of the rebuilding of temples. Oftentimes, written prayers were placed on the foundation to benefit the kings. These prayers normally included a wish for a long life for the king and a desire for him to win over his enemies.[3] On one hand, Darius's hope that the Jewish elders will pray for his well-being is predictable. On the other hand, his decree is an amazing miracle for God's temple. The temple of the God of heaven will be rebuilt, and the people can offer prayers for the king while also offering pleasing sacrifices to God.

Moreover, Darius decrees that no one shall change this edict. Anyone who dares to alter the decree will be punished harshly; for his house will become a pile of rubble, and he will suffer a shameful and painful death (6:11). He also utters a strong curse against any king or people who try to destroy the dwelling of God in Jerusalem, the city of God's people (6:12).

In researching the history of missionary work in Asia, the earliest records about the establishment of churches may uncover rare and exciting findings that could bring much gratified joy to present-day believers. Jean Uayan, a faculty member from the Biblical Seminary of the Philippines, has recently completed her archival research on the earliest Protestant Chinese churches in the Philippines to determine if they were founded by Western missionaries or by the local Chinese people themselves.

Her work took her on a long journey into the mission records, church documents, and even oral interviews with surviving founders and members of six Chinese churches in the Philippines. Using meticulous qualitative and descriptive approaches, the result of her almost two-year study yielded exciting updates about the emergence of the Protestant Chinese churches in the

---

3. See Joseph Too Shao, *A Study of Royal Hymns and Prayers*, Dissertation Series 10, Bible and Literature 7 (Hong Kong: Alliance Biblical Press, 2002).

Philippines. With voluminous documentation, her findings reveal that the earliest Protestant Chinese church to be established in the Philippines was the "Chinese Presbyterian Church in Iloilo," which was founded in 1911 by local Chinese, rather than St. Stephen's Parish, which has generally been acknowledged as the first parish established by the Chinese-Filipino Christian community.[4] In her final analysis, only one church, the Chinese United Evangelical Church, was truly native, as it was founded by a group of local Protestant Chinese believers. This church later changed its name to the United Evangelical Church of the Philippines.[5]

6:13–18 REJOICING AT GOD'S COMPLETED TEMPLE

This summary notation explains how Governor Tattenai, Shethar-Bozenai, and their associates carry out the instructions in the decrees of Cyrus, Darius and Artaxerxes with diligence (6:13). Tattenai has been neutral in making inquiry and making sure that the decree is fully implemented. Inspired by the prophecies of Haggai and Zechariah, the Jewish elders oversee the rebuilding of the temple and finish the whole project according to God's command and as decreed by the foreign rulers of the land (6:14). The temple of God is completed on the third day of the month of Adar, during the sixth year of the reign of King Darius, around 516 BC (6:15). Thus the temple is completed in about four years.

As soon as the temple is finished, the post-exilic community celebrates with joy. As with their celebration during the inauguration of the first temple, they sing for joy and honor the second temple (1 Kg 8:63), making a burnt offering with many bulls, rams, and lambs, along with a sin offering of twelve goats, corresponding to the twelve tribes of Israel (6:16–17). Although Solomon offered far more cattle and sheep, the essence of their feasting and temple dedication is just as meaningful and truthful. The arrangement of twenty-four divisions of priests and twenty-two groupings of Levites is credited to David in Chronicles. He made this revision possible for the post-exilic community, according to the written law (6:18).

---

4. Jean Uy Uayan, *A Study of the Emergence and Early Development of Selected Protestant Chinese Churches in the Philippines* (Carlisle, UK: Langham Monographs, 2017), 90–109.
5. Uayan, *Study of the Emergence*, 179–207, 285–286.

6:19–22 REMEMBERING GOD'S CARE

On the fourteenth day of the first month, the exiles celebrate the Passover (6:19), which is the first Passover since the exile. The priests and the Levites, following the laws of Moses, observe the purification rites so that they can be considered ceremonially clean (6:20).

The narrative emphasizes the religious purity in the celebration. Following the antecedent practices of Passover observances, the foreigners can be integrated into the community as long as they follow the "entrance" requirement of following the Lord (Exod 12:43–49; Num 9:1–14; Deut 16:1–8; Josh 5:10–12; 2 Kgs 23:21–23).[6] Hence, along with the Israelites who returned from the exile, those who have separated themselves from the unclean practices of the land in order to seek the Lord join in the Passover celebration (6:21).[7] The purpose of the separation is to ensure that there will be a consecrated community joyfully worshiping the Lord. They celebrate the Feast of the Unleavened Bread for seven days, a practice that is written in the law of Moses.

The closing summary notes that "the LORD has filled them with joy by changing the attitude of the king of Assyria" from hindering them to assisting them in their work on the house of God by providing full financial support. Indeed, the fact that the work on the temple for the God of Israel is endorsed and encouraged by a non-Jewish ruler is a cause for a joyful celebration (6:22).

---

6. Peter H. W. Lau, "Gentile Incorporation into Israel in Ezra-Nehemiah?" *Biblica* 90 (2009): 356–379.

7. The issue in Ezra-Nehemiah is whether the separation means emphasizing genetic purity or religious purity. Nehemiah 10:28 could also be an inclusive statement about those who desire to make a decision to seek the Lord.

EZRA 7–10

PERIOD UNDER EZRA: PEOPLE REBUILT

The second section of the book of Ezra starts during the reign of Artaxerxes I. In 458 BC, the seventh year of Artaxerxes, Ezra leads the second group of returnees to Jerusalem. With the authority given to him as a priest from the line of Aaron, Ezra brings with him the law of Moses to teach the people, along with other financial resources for the temple of God. Anticipating the proper worship of the Lord, Ezra makes sure that the Levites and temple servants are in his entourage. After handing over the gifts they are bearing to a leadership team, they offer burnt offerings to the God of Israel. Ezra's most important tasks are the bearing of the law and the renewal of the people of God.

EZRA 7:1–28

THE MAN FOR THE HOUR: HEAR YE! HEAR YE!

The spiritual legacy of a person who serves the Lord is very important. My father, who is a second-generation servant of the Lord, traces our roots to a small village in TongAn. Every New Year's Eve, our small family clan in Manila would gather to have a year-end thanksgiving service. My father would recount how the gospel was brought to our village with Grandpa Shao, who professed to become Christian and eventually a servant of the Lord in Xiamen. Today, many Christian families in the Xiamen are writing the family clan history, tracing their spiritual heritage.

The narration in Ezra begins with the genealogy of Ezra, who is the most important person in the book and who is instrumental in leading the second group of returnees back to Jerusalem. Whereas Zerubbabel and Joshua lead the people to rebuild God's temple (Ezra 1:1–6:22), Ezra helps to rebuild God's people (Ezra 7:1–10:44). The timeline moves from the completion of the second temple under the sixth-year of Darius (515 BC) to the seventh year of Artaxerxes I (458 BC).

With the completion of the temple, which is a prerequisite for the observance of rituals and sacrifices, Ezra can focus on establishing God's law as the norm for godly living in the post-exilic community. Because of the people's disobedience of God's law, Israel was removed from her land and sent into exile. The Persian king, Artaxerxes I, sends Ezra to Judah to help rectify this problem by carrying out a program of religious education to the post-exilic community. Other biblical writers call Ezra the "scholar priest" because of his expertise in expounding on and teaching God's law.[1]

The return of Ezra to Jerusalem is recorded in chapters 7 and 8. Chapter 7 focuses on Ezra's genealogy and the edict of Artaxerxes I and can be divided into two main sections. The first section briefly describes Ezra's coming to Jerusalem (Ezra 7:1–10), and the second records his commission from Artaxerxes I (Ezra 7:11–28), whose decree sends Ezra to Jerusalem with a clear

---

1. Derek Kidner, *Erza & Nehemiah: An Introduction & Commentary*, TOTC (Downers Grove: InterVarsity Press, 1979), 61.

purpose as a personal envoy of the king. Chapter 8 lists the family heads and the key descendants of the second returnees and gives details about how Ezra starts his journey back to Jerusalem.

Thematically, Ezra is both the main character of chapter 7 as well as the author. Ezra starts with his genealogical record and introduces his role as a teacher who is well-versed in the law of Moses (7:1–6). The chapter ends with his doxology to the Lord and a description of how God strengthened him to gather leading men to go up to Jerusalem with him (7:28).[2] The expression "the hand of the LORD is on me"[3] describes God's bountiful blessing on Ezra by working through his life for the people of God. The Lord is his personal God (note the possessive pronoun, 7:6, 28). The title "the God of Israel" links these two sections together. The Lord, the God of Israel, gives the law of Moses to his people (7:6). Ezra sets his heart to the serious study of God's law, and now he commits to teach God's word and its life application to God's people in Jerusalem. Jerusalem is identified as the dwelling place of the God of Israel, as mentioned in the decree of Artaxerxes (7:15).

7:1–10 THE COMING OF EZRA

Ezra's genealogy begins with Seraiah, who was the last chief priest before the exile (2 Kgs 25:18), and traces back to Aaron, the brother of Moses, who is considered to be the very first chief priest of Israel. Though it is a shortened genealogical record that includes seventeen names, the list includes many important priests in the history of Israel. Hilkiah, the high priest during the time of Josiah, was known for his discovery of the book of the law (7:1; 2 Kgs 22–23; 2 Chr 34; 35:8). Zadok, the chief priest during the time of David, was in charge of the ark and took part in anointing Solomon (7:2; 2 Sam 15:24–29; 1 Kgs 1:8; 2:35; Ezek 44:15–16). Eleazar, the chief priest after death of Aaron, served during the time of Moses and Joshua (7:5; Num 20:25–28; Josh 24:33). This is Ezra's rich spiritual heritage.

The purpose of the genealogy is to convey Ezra's significant role in teaching the law, following his priestly ancestors. Ezra's legitimate Aaronide genealogy prefigures the historical fact that the cult will be perpetuated once again. The

---

2. Since Jerusalem is high in its elevation, "going up" usually refers to the pilgrims who go to Jerusalem to worship (see Pss 120–134). The modern Israelites who return to their homeland use *aliyah* ("going up") in referring to their return to Jerusalem.
3. The exilic prophet Ezekiel first uses the expression, "the hand of the LORD," to indicate his special prophetic relationship with God (Ezek 1:3; 3:14, 22; 8:1; 33:22; 37:1; 40:1).

genealogy legitimizes the existence and authority of Ezra as the priest during the post-exilic period.

The genealogical record of Ezra is a linear genealogical list that ascends in order from the descendant to the ancestor. The list can be compared to another more expanded list that descends in order from the ancestor to the descendant (1 Chr 6:3–15). Whereas the Chronicle's list starts with a horizontal record, recording twenty-three generations from Aaron to the time of exile, the list in Ezra is a vertical list that omits six generations between Azariah and Meraioth. The names that appear in Chronicles but not Ezra are: Amariah, Ahitub, Zadok, Ahimaaz, Azariah, and Johanan (1 Chr 6:7–11; compare 7:3). Moreover, the list in Ezra identifies Ezra, rather than Jehozadak, as the son of Seraiah. The word "son" in the Hebrew language also refers to ancestry, and so the purpose for this replacement is to establish Ezra's continuity with the exilic history. As the key descendant of Seraiah, Ezra shows his involvement in the post-exilic period (1 Chr 6:14–15; compare 7:1).

During a memorial service for Lim Ng SiokOan, who died at the age of ninety-three, her pastor honored her trustworthiness and said that she had served the Lord faithfully without changing her membership to another church. Indeed, this lady was a third-generation Christian who had survived four Episcopalian rectors of the St. Stephen's Parish Church in the Philippines. A committed leader of her church, she worked closely with the Filipino churches under the Episcopal diocese, and her predecessors served in various capacities in the church in China. Though her church went through different crises, difficulties, and leadership changes, she continued to worship the Lord and devoted herself to ministering with others. Two additional generations from her lineage continue to serve God as leaders within the church.

After listing Ezra's priestly genealogy, Ezra is introduced as "a teacher well-versed in the Law of Moses" (7:6; see also 7:12, 21). The role of a teacher (literally, "scribe") in this context is directly related to the written Torah. In pre-exilic time, a scribe was a secretary (2 Sam 8:17; 20:25), a royal messenger (2 Kgs 18:18), an official in charge of legal documents (Jer 32:12–15), or a minister of finance (2 Kgs 22:3). During the exile, the scribes became a professional class in handling the Torah. During this time, the law of Moses became the center of all Jewish life, and the exiled Israelites were determined to study it. The scribes occupied themselves in gathering all the sacred literature of Israel, interpreting it diligently, and guarding its purity.

Ezra functions as an interpreter and a teacher of the law as well as a student and an expositor of the law (7:10). He exercises the office of teacher and priest by reading the law to the people (Neh 8:13–18). Similar to Moses during the wilderness period, Ezra is assigned a unique teaching role as a priest. This special role is amplified during the post-exilic period, and many priests bear this role in Chronicles' parallel account of the book of the Kings (compare Mal 2:7). People come to the priests for inquiries regarding the clarification of the law (compare Hag 2:10–13).

Ezra also enjoys another special privilege, for "the hand of the LORD his God was on him" (7:6; see also 7:9, 28; 8:22, 31; Neh 2:8, 18). The expression "hand" comes from an anthropomorphic notion that conveys royal bounty (1 Kgs 10:13; Esth 1:7; 2:18). Hence, the hand of the Lord signifies that bountiful blessings are being bestowed upon the recipient, Ezra. This overflowing favor and special blessing strengthen Ezra with a desire to accomplish great tasks for God.

The second group of returnees consists of "some of the Israelites, including priests, Levites, musicians, gatekeepers, and temple servants" (7:7). This resumptive summary[4] of the returnees lists those who return to Jerusalem.[5] Indeed, there are some Israelites who would prefer to stay in Babylonia, but others decide to return home to Judah. The caravan follows the same order as the first returnees, naming the laity before priests, Levites, and other temple personnel (2:3–59; Neh 7:8–61). As with the first returnees, the musicians and gatekeepers are considered as Levites. Their family heads are listed with proper names in Ezra's memoirs, except for some unknown temple personnel who may be ranked under these family leaders (8:1–14).

The caravan comes up to Jerusalem in the fifth month of the seventh year of King Artaxerxes I (7:8). The journey begins on the first day of the first month (8 April 458) and ends on the first day of the fifth month (4 August 458; compare 8:32–33). The first month coincides with the exodus from Egypt that occurs in the first month (Exod 12:2; Num 33:3), whereas the fifth month commemorates the destruction of the Solomonic temple (2 Kgs 25:8). These textual details establish a link with the first exodus from Egypt, where Ezra is bringing the second group of returnees out of their shameful and painful history up to Jerusalem.

Ezra starts out by counting the people (8:15), then prepares the caravan through a fast by the Ahava Canal (8:21), and then they set out together on the

---

4. It is a commonly accepted view in literary study that in biblical narratives, a "resumptive summary" gives the reader an overview of what happens in the introduction even before the events really happen.
5. Ezra 8:15–20 describes how the Levites are able to join the caravan.

twelfth day of the first month (8:31). A delay is caused by the absence of Levites in the original caravan (8:15–16). Ezra, along with his caravan, starts journeying from Babylon in the month of Nissan and arrives at Jerusalem in the month of Ab. The whole journey traverses some thirteen hundred kilometers.

Ezra has a very special role in leading the caravan to Jerusalem. Because he is a disciplined man, the caravan reaches Jerusalem. As a teacher of the law, he "set his heart to study the Law of the Lord, and to do it and to teach . . ." (7:10, ESV). Ezra's devotion begins with his heart, his passion "to study," "to do" and "to teach" God's law. In the Old Testament, the heart is the primary seat for decision-making. Moses reminds the people of God to "love the Lord with all your heart . . ." (Deut 6:5). The wisdom literature also teaches about the importance of guarding the heart (Prov 4:20–23). To "study" means to dig deeper into the written word, carefully understanding the teaching of God's law. Ezra needs to study earnestly and accurately in order to be able to interpret the law. To "do" (observance, NIV) means that he practices what he learns from his study of God's law. The psalmist blesses those who both study the law and live accordingly (Ps 1:2–3). To "teach" (teaching, NIV) is to transmit one's learning into the practical realm, living it out authentically. Walking one's talk is the best way to teach and influence others. Thus Ezra sets an example as a model teacher.

Bob and Esther, a missionary couple, worked diligently in two remote regions in the Philippines: Daet in the southern region and Tuguegarao in northern Luzon. They committed themselves to learning the local dialects so they could teach and preach God's word to the native people. During their four years of working and living among the people, they were able to plant an indigenous church, but they were waiting for money to be able to build a church building. They often had to wait for foreign funds, because so many members were not aware of the biblical principle that "it is more blessed to give than to receive" (Acts 20:35), and so they began to teach their local church about the biblical principle of giving tithes and offerings to God. When the missionary couple was about to fly back to the US for a new assignment, they learned that a family from their church in the north had come to visit them. This family brought with them a stack of gold bars that they had hidden underground as family treasure. They had been enlightened by the missionary couple's teaching on tithing and wanted to donate the gold toward the building project. It was thrilling not only to see those shiny gold bars, but even more the beaming hearts of this family, who gave out of joy and love as taught by God's word.

7:11–28 THE COMMISSIONING OF EZRA

Like the edict of Cyrus, which commissioned the first returnees to return to Jerusalem, Artaxerxes commissions Ezra to return to Jerusalem. This royal edict from a non-Jewish ruler gives Ezra both extensive authority as well as comprehensive support for his mission. The king's letter of authorization assigns Ezra with four specific missions in Jerusalem. First, Ezra's *administrative mission* is to lead the Israelites who want to return back to Jerusalem (7:12–13). Second, Ezra's *didactic mission* is to conduct inquiry into Judah and Jerusalem regarding obedience toward the law (7:14). Third, Ezra's *cultic mission* is to bring back gifts and sacrifices for the temple of the God of heaven (7:15–24). Fourth, Ezra's *social mission* is to appoint magistrates and judges to administer justice and to teach God's laws (7:25–26).

The first mission is a political move, extending a friendly gesture to the Israelites who want to return home. Ezra is commissioned to lead these people back to Jerusalem. The second mission refers to Ezra's spiritual role as a teacher of the law of Moses. The third mission deals with Ezra's cultic duty as the priest in leading the people in proper worship of the God of Israel. The fourth mission pertains to Ezra's social duty to oversee justice in the society.

In the royal edict, the titles of God are used interchangeably. The title "the God of heaven," as an abbreviation for the God of heavens and earth, implies that Israel reveres and worships the Creator God, the great transcendent God (7:12, 21, 23). The expression "the God of Israel" describes the God who cares for his people, Israel, and whose dwelling is in Jerusalem (7:15). The name "the God of Jerusalem" denotes the God who loves Zion, the place where he chooses to dwell and keep his name, and the place where Ezra is commissioned to go (7:19; compare 7:16, 17).

7:11 Introduction of the Edict

Since the edict is an official Persian document, it is written in Aramaic (7:12–26). The edict is introduced as a "copy of the letter" (Persian-loaned words). Ezra is both the priest and the teacher, with the dual role of leading God's people to true worship and teaching them to learn and understand the law in order to implement righteousness in the society. The Persian kings commonly used the title "king of kings" for themselves in their official documents, since they were the kings of the great empire. In the edict of Artaxerxes, Ezra is acknowledged as the priest and teacher of the law of the God of heaven. He is the instrument of dispensing the grace of God.

7:12–13 The First Mission: Administrative Duty

Artaxerxes addresses Ezra directly, calling his attention to the law of "your" God (7:14, 26), the laws of "your" God (7:25), the altar of the temple of "your" God (7:17), the will of "your" God (7:18), the temple of "your" God (7:19, 20), and the wisdom of "your" God (7:25). King Artaxerxes not only has confidence in Ezra as his royal representative, but he also acknowledges the God whom Ezra is serving. Ezra refers to the Lord God of Israel, the God of heaven, as "my" God (7:28). The possessive pronoun is very significant, as it reflects Ezra's relationship with his God.

The edict coincides with the policy of Cyrus and serves as a renewal of the permission to return to Jerusalem (7:13; compare 1:3). Any Israelite, including priests and Levites, is allowed to go with Ezra. Quite similar to the first return, there is a distinction between the laity, the priests, and Levites. Artaxerxes grants permission for the people of Israel to return as a friendly political motion. He charges Ezra with the responsibility to lead the Israelites back to Jerusalem.

7:14 The Second Mission: Didactic Duty

In the Persian tradition, a king normally has seven advisers who are responsible to give counsel to the king (7:14; compare Esth 1:14). Ezra's role is to inquire whether the law of the Lord is being observed in Judah and Jerusalem. The expression "the Law of your God, which is in your hand" refers to the Pentateuchal law (7:14). This law is already known by the general public and especially by the Jews in Judea. As the priest and the teacher of the law, Ezra is asked to examine how the people are following and obeying the law of their God. He is also instructed to teach them to understand and obey the law. Ezra's spiritual duty as the teacher of the Israelites is made possible because Artaxerxes publicly identifies Ezra as a "scholar priest" and an expert in Jewish law.

7:15–24 The Third Mission: Cultic Duty

Ezra is instructed to take with him the silver and gold that the king and his advisers have freely given to the God of Israel, which Ezra may have obtained from Babylonia (7:15; compare 1:4). The return of these gifts connotes the Persian king's full endorsement of the Jewish people's return to Jerusalem for the benefit of Judah. Ezra is instructed to take gifts to the temple from three sources: gifts donated from the Persian king and his advisers, gifts from the people of Babylonia, and freewill offerings from the Babylonian Jews and priests (7:16). As with any offerings in the Old Testament, the rule of thumb is the giver's willingness to give the gift. For Jews who prefer to stay in Babylonia, they can participate in the return through their freewill offerings for the temple. For Jews who are choosing to return, their freewill offerings are collected at the outset of the journey. All the contributions are clearly listed upon arrival in Jerusalem (8:26–27).

The temple is identified as the dwelling of the God of Israel (7:16–17) and the house of the Lord in Jerusalem (7:27). These descriptions refer to the second temple, the temple that Zerubbabel rebuilt.

The contributions are used to buy the necessary animals and accompanying offerings for the temple sacrifices. Bulls, rams, and male lambs are commonly used in the sacrificial system (7:17; see also 6:9, 17; 8:35). The grain offerings accompany animal sacrifices, and drink offerings follow burnt and peace offerings (Num 15:1–10). The altar of the temple refers to the sacred altar in Jerusalem. Because the first returnees built the altar of the Lord, the second returnees can offer their sacrifices on the altar.

Inasmuch as the funds from the royal treasury will be used to cover the needs of the temple, there will still be some money left. The leftover money is spent in accordance with the will of God. The guiding code allows Ezra and his fellow Jews to spend the money as they see fit for the temple.

The articles of the temple are to be delivered to the temple (7:19; 8:26–27), which echoes the theme during the first return under Cyrus (1:7–11; 5:14–15; 6:5). Ezra is quite careful in following through on this order upon his arrival in Jerusalem (8:26–27, 33–34). Any additional needs are supplied from the royal treasury. Again, Artaxerxes emulates Cyrus's generosity in supporting the temple (compare 6:4).

The final verses of this section stipulate the generous grants that are to be given to Ezra from the treasuries of Trans-Euphrates (7:21–22). These verses also exempt all the cultic officials from taxes (7:24). Ezra is introduced once more as a priest and a teacher of the law of the God of heaven (7:21; see also 7:12).

The grant of up to a hundred talents of silver from the treasuries of Trans-Euphrates is enormous (7:22). In the early Achaemenid period, according to Herodotus (3:91), 350 talents is the total tax contribution of the entire satrapy annually. The phrase "whatever the God of heaven has prescribed" (7:23) relates to the offerings of the sacrificial system, which means that the grants are related to God's temple. The king places his full trust in Ezra.

The other contributions are related to the temple offerings (7:22). The contribution of "wheat" is related to grain offerings (Lev 2:1), and "wine" is related to drink offerings (Exod 29:40–41; Lev 23:13, 18, 27; Hos 9:4). The "olive oil" is used for the temple lamp (Exod 27:2) and in connection with other offerings (Lev 2:4; 14:10–18). "Salt" is used for grain offerings and other types of offerings (Lev 2:13).

The king's generosity is motivated by his fear of God's wrath (7:23). Of course, the king also wants to gain favor and blessing from the God of heaven for himself and his sons. God's wrath speaks of his intervention on behalf of his people (Josh 22:20; 2 Kgs 3:27). The wars and revolts are interpreted theologically, and the king is hoping to turn away troubles and problems in his empire (compare 6:10).

7:25–26 The Fourth Mission: Social Duty

Ezra's fourth mission is to appoint magistrates and judges to administer justice to the people. The positions are synonymous and are meant to ensure that the law of Moses will be administered in the Judean community. Moreover, Ezra is instructed to teach the law to those who do not know it. According to the book of Deuteronomy, a judiciary system with judges and officers also needs to be appointed (Deut 1:16–17, 16:18).

Whoever disobeys the law will be penalized. The power to appoint magistrates and judges is serious enough to include punishment as a deterrent. The law that Ezra is to implement is both "the law of your God and the law of the king" (7:26), which reflects Ezra's social mission. The king even specifies the kinds of punishment that are to be carried out against those who disobey the law of God: death, banishment, confiscation of property, or imprisonment (7:26).

How should we interpret Ezra's commission, especially the instructions to implement the religious law and the secular law of the Persian king? Currently, there are three possible ways to interpret this matter: imperial authorization, geopolitical strategy, and priestly ideology. Regarding the first interpretation, many scholars support the theory of imperial authorization, which argues that the local rules were elevated to the status of Persian imperial law. With the vast area of Persian provinces, the imperial authority that was issued in writing was based on a norm that was proposed by subordinates to the empire. Thus "the law of your God" can also be "the law of the king." Regarding the second interpretation, some argue that Persian support for the authority of the Torah and the use of a cultic point as their administrative center was a geopolitical strategy for Persian provincial governance. Thus by supporting the temple, the Persian king could supervise the people living in Judah and Jerusalem. Timothy

Lim argues for a third interpretation, which is that the priestly ideology in the edict uses the language of volition. He argues that the edict in Ezra is initiated by the Persian court but shaped by the priestly theology of divinely inspired action. Thus because the God of Israel is behind the enthusiastic edict of Artaxerxes,[6] the Persian king supports the authority of the Torah.

7:27–28 Ezra's Doxology

This section is a doxology of praise to the Lord for intervening by moving the king's heart to honor the temple of God. These verses mark the return to the "memoirs of Ezra" and revert back to the Hebrew language.

The title "the God of our ancestors" is a particular nomenclature designated for Yahweh (7:27) that stems from the informing theology of Deuteronomy (Deut 26:7; compare 1:11, 21; 4:1; 6:3; 12:1), which is that God cares for the patriarchs by fulfilling what he has promised. This theology is based on the belief that the God of Abraham, Isaac, and Jacob is the same God who brings them up to Jerusalem with his steadfast love (*hesed*). The Lord restores his people and his temple, using the Persian king as his instrument. Just as the God of "our" fathers acted in the past, God is also acting in the present and will definitely be acting on our behalf in the future.

Ezra connects "the hand of the Lord" (7:6, 9, 28) with the idea of gathering the people to return to Jerusalem. As with the first returnees, it is not easy to convince the people to join him in returning to Jerusalem, but the Lord's hand gives him courage and strength to accept this challenging task. Just as God moved in Cyrus's heart during Cyrus's time (1:5), the hand of the Lord is now moving in Ezra as he gains the courage to lead the people to go up to Jerusalem with him.

---

6. See the various scholarly discussions of the edict of Artaxerxes in Ezra 7:12–26 since 1985, Timothy H. Lim, *The Formation of the Jewish Canon* (New Haven: Yale University Press, 2013), 54–62.

GOD'S WORD AND LIFE

Paul's charge to Timothy is a great reminder for Bible teachers to spend time studying God's word so that they might teach others to understand it and walk accordingly: "You then, my son, be strong in the grace that is in Christ Jesus. And the things you have heard me say in the presence of many witnesses entrust to reliable people who will also be qualified to teach others" (2 Tim 2:1–2).

The Old Testament uses the imagery of a "tree" to portray the lives of the people of God who follow God's teachings. The tree absorbs water and produces leaves and fruit in season (Ps 1:2–3). Likewise, the righteous person is portrayed as a "palm tree" and a "cedar" (Ps 92:12). A palm tree has a long slender trunk with foliage at the top, and its roots go very deep to seek water. It is associated with an oasis where God's people camp when they need water (Exod 15:27; Num 33:9). Palm trees produce dates, which can serve as food. The cedar of Lebanon has a straight trunk and deep roots (Judg 9:15). Because of all the water in the mountains of Lebanon, its cedars have thick foliage (Ps 104:16; Ezek 31:3–9). Both of these trees illustrate the balanced life of a righteous person.

We might know all the biblical truth and yet fail to live out its essence in our daily, practical lives. Students of the word who have been trained systematically and dogmatically should beware of how "knowledge puffs up while love builds up" (1 Cor 8:1). Jesus calls us to live as his disciples, so that our "righteousness surpasses that of the Pharisees and the teachers of the law" (Matt 5:20). The Pharisees were exacting and scrupulous in their attempts to follow after the Mosaic law, but they were content to obey God's laws outwardly without allowing God to change their hearts or inner attitudes. They looked pious on the outside, but they were far from God's kingdom. Jesus wants our righteousness to be lived out of love and obedience to his word – not out of legal compliance. Jesus speaks of a righteous living that goes beyond keeping the law to living by the principles behind the law. Likewise, James reminds the believers: "Do not merely listen to the word, and so deceive yourselves. Do what it says" (Jas 1:22).

One great insight into Ezra's teaching is the way that he stays with the people and lives in their midst. Ezra's personal study of God's word is just as devoted as his study of God's word with the people. True leaders identify with and serve their followers. Rather than trying to become the focus of attention or the locus of power, Bible teachers should focus people's hearts and minds on Christ, the main character of God's word. Ezra studies and teaches God's word in order to benefit the people and ensure their obedience to God – not to him. Richard Foster reminds us that "Those who take on the mantle of leadership do so for the sake of others, not for their own sake. Their concern is to meet the needs of the people, not to advance their own reputations."[1]

Rosa Ching Shao

---

1. Richard Foster, *The Challenge of the Disciplined Life* (San Francisco: HarperCollins, 1998), 235.

EZRA 8:1–36

THE SECOND BATCH OF RETURNEES: HERE THEY COME!

Churches often compile a complete list of pastors and key leaders for easy access. Such lists not only provide a convenient source of contact information, but they are also important historical documents. Written records for each year help younger generations remember the leaders who preceded them and served faithfully in a church's ministries.

Chapter 8 begins by listing the family heads and the key ancestors of the second group of returnees to Jerusalem. The narrative chronicles of the second returnees to Jerusalem detail how the family heads come to Jerusalem under Ezra's leadership and how he helps to bring back the precious temple articles to the priests who are responsible for them. Whereas most of the previous chapter is narrated in the third person, this chapter narrates the same events in the first person from Ezra's perspective.

In the first group of returnees, there were some 42,000 persons; the second group of returnees is much smaller, with some 1,500 men and, if counting all the family members, about 5,000 people in Ezra's caravan (8:21).

8:1–14 RETURNING FAITHFUL LEADERS

Ezra 7:28 through the end of Ezra 8 is part of the Ezra memoirs, where the speaker and writer is Ezra himself. In this section of the Ezra memoirs, Ezra records a list of the returnees, which he divides into three sections: the priests (8:2), the royal line (8:2c–3a), and the laity (8:3b–14). Most of the Israelites have grown accustomed to the Babylonian lifestyle and opt to remain there rather than return to Jerusalem with Ezra. Thus the "family heads" who return with Ezra during the reign of Artaxerxes I deserve to be recorded. The family is the basic unit in ancient Israelite society, and the father signifies the head. Within this accountability system, members of the family clan are accountable to the "head" of their father's household.

The first section of the list records leading priests (8:2). Unlike the list of the first returnees, this list places the names of the priests ahead of the royalty and laity. Given Ezra's role as both priest and scribe, this is not surprising.

Since the priestly descendants provide spiritual leadership for the group, this ideology may follow the theology of Ezekiel 40–48, which gives priority to the spiritual leadership of the priests.

Both Phinehas and Ithamar are descendants of Aaron; the former is a grandson of Aaron, and the latter is the fourth son of Aaron (Exod 6:23–25; 1 Chr 6:3–4, 50). Eleazar, the third son of Aaron, inherits his father's office and carries on an important role in history (Num 4:16; 20:25–26, 28; 26:1, 2, 63; Deut 10:6; Josh 14:1; 19:51; 21:1; 24:33). Eleazar's son, Phinehas, defends the true worship of Yahweh and thereby becomes a model of godly leadership for subsequent generations (Num 25:7; 31:6; Josh 22:13; Judg 20:28). The Lord bestows priesthood on Phinehas and his descendants, and all the priestly factions (Aaronites, Levites, and Zadokites) are related to Phinehas. Ithamar, on the other hand, is in charge of the Levites, the lesser clans of Gershon and Merari in particular (Exod 38:21; Num 4:28, 33; 7:8). Thus Phinehas and Ithamar represent two branches of priests who are descendants of Aaron (1 Chr 24:1–3). This archaic connection is important for the post-exilic community, showing its continuity with the origin of priesthood from Aaron. The descendants of Ithamar are prominent in the post-exilic community, along with their family head, Daniel (compare Neh 10:6).

The second section of the list records the family heads of royal lineage (8:2b–3a). The list of the first group of returnees does not include any descendants from the royal line, and so this is a new development. The servants of Solomon, who are listed among the first returnees, are not descendants of the royal line. Although Zerubbabel has royal blood, the first returnees concentrate mainly on the rebuilding of the cult, and so laity and other related cultic officials are listed. The second returnees have some descendants of royal blood joining them in the caravan. There must be a purpose for this listing and the inclusion of royal lineage.

David, of course, is the historic king of Israel and Judah. Though David is long dead, his idea of setting up Jerusalem as the religious capital and the center of the nation has long been a historical ideal. In the Chronicler's history, Moses and David are linked together. The liturgical calendar of Sabbaths, New Moons, and the three annual feasts (the Feast of Unleavened Bread, the Feast of Weeks, and the Feast of Tabernacles) are based on the Torah of Moses (2 Chr 8:13). David decreed "the divisions of the priests for their duties, and the Levites to lead the praise and to assist the priest according to each day's requirement" (2 Chr 8:14; see also 1 Chr 23:1–26:23). With the descendants of David as part of the caravan, the return to Jerusalem bears greater significance.

The post-exilic community hopes for the rebuilding of Jerusalem, and the royal descendants add value to their cause and involve David vicariously through his descendants. Indeed, these accompanying royal descendants could be an inspiration for the community.

The ancestry of Hattush, an important royal descendant after the exile (8:2), can be traced back four generations to Zerubbabel and before him to Jehoiachin, the last king before the exile (1 Chr 3:17–22). Though Jehoiachin went into exile, his descendants through Hattush are returning to Jerusalem. Whereas the Chronicler lists Johoiachin as a captive (1 Chr 3:17), Ezra lists Hattush as a descendant of David, which frames his history from a positive theological perspective. As descendants of the Davidic dynasty, the descendants of Hattush remain connected to a royal line. This reflects the beauty of the Davidic covenant (2 Sam 7:16), where the Lord promises David that there will be a seed to continue his kingship and sit on the throne. Thus the descendants of Hattush not only show continuity with the generation before the exile, but they also signify hope for the post-exilic community. Shekaniah is the grandfather of Hattush (1 Chr 3:22), and he links Hattush with Jehoiachin, the last surviving king.

The third section of the list records the laity, who are grouped under the twelve family heads (8:3b–14). The laity represent those who are willing to return to their hometown and who are fundamental to the rebuilding of Jerusalem. Just as there are twelve leaders who lead the first group of returnees, these twelve family heads also stand for the twelve tribes of Israel (2:2; Neh 7:7). The ideal twelve is very much part of the eschatology of the post-exilic community (compare 8:24, 35). Though small in number, the second batch of returnees is the legitimate representative and heir of Israel.

The twelve family heads and their respective leaders are identified cautiously, using the following formula: "the descendants of *[x, y]*, and with him *[number]* men." Compared with the first group of returnees, the laity in the second group is smaller in number. The registering of the number under each respective family head shows the importance of accurate accounting. There are many members under each particular family clan who are willing to return with Ezra.

The naming of people under their family heads seems to be an important item in the list, starting with the descendants of Parosh (8:3b; compare 2:3; Neh 7:8). Except for the descendants of Joab, the descendants of all eleven family heads have joined both groups of returnees.

Davao Evangelical Church in the Philippines started out with a handful of devoted Christians and grew to about thirty-three members before they invited their first full-time pastor, Rev. Wesley K. Shao (my father), who served them for ten years. Over the course of fifty years, the church was blessed by a series of good shepherds who watched and cared for the growing congregation. In time, the church founded Davao Christian High School, which has a large enrollment of students each year. The church has also nurtured many dedicated members, who have gone on to serve God in various roles as pastors, missionaries, and Christian teachers. The church member directory records several generations of faithful believers from the same households. Some family clans include three generations of full-time church workers. In fact, many of the church's present leaders and coworkers are young families who are following the footsteps of their parents and grandparents in serving God.

In reminiscing about God's faithfulness during the early struggles of this Davao church, Rev. Shao always thanks God for the wonderful way that so many of its members are serving the Lord fervently. He recalls how during the beginning stage of the church, a group of devoted believers was planning to hold a weekly Sunday service, but many of the non-believers were busy opening their shops and doing business on Sunday mornings, and so a Sunday evening service was designed to reach out to them. Initially, only three Chinese non-believers came to that service, but in time they became the patriarchs of several generations of believers in the church, many of whom are now full-time Christian workers and alumni from the local Chinese-Filipino seminary, the Biblical Seminary of the Philippines. In fact, the great majority of the graduates from this seminary come from this church in the southern part of the Philippines. God is faithful, showing his love to a thousand generations, and raising Christian families to serve him. Carefully listing and tracing family relationships are a good way to write church history and to encourage pastors to remain faithful to God's work.

8:15–20 RECRUITING SERVING LEVITES

As Ezra assembles the people at the Ahava Canal, he notices the complete absence of Levites. This mirrors the first return, where the caravan only included a few Levites (2:40). The Levites have special responsibilities on the march to Jerusalem, for without their service, worship in the post-exilic period cannot be carried out in accordance with the Mosaic law. Moreover, the group of returnees needs to be represented by both priests and Levites. As a servant of God, Ezra seeks to recruit the Levites (8:15–17), sensing that any recruits must come from God's provision (8:18–20).

Ezra takes three days to prepare and gather the people (8:15; compare 8:32; Neh 2:11). As he conscientiously surveys those who will accompany him to Jerusalem, he cannot find any Levites. The people are the basic unit of the covenanted family; the priests lead them in worship; the Levites assist the priests in the worship service.

Compiling and checking over lists are connected to the biblical notion of responsibility (compare Num 1–3). In the first exodus, the priests are in charge of the tabernacle, whereas the Levites are assigned to carry the items for the tabernacle (Num 3:24–31, 35–37; 4:24–27, 31–33). The Levites have the specific task of assisting the priests as they travel back to Jerusalem (8:24, 29). As a team with members who are all equally necessary, or the analogy of one body with significant parts, the Levites have an important role to play as those who are designated to serve the priests.

Ezra calls for other valuable leaders to help. Nine men are leaders, and two are men of learning. The "leaders" (literally, "heads") could well be the selected few who have talents surpassing others, whereas the "men of learning" (literally, "men who give understanding") could be men with insights who know how to interpret and teach the law. Among the leaders, only Shemaiah and Zechariah are family heads from the preceding list (8:16; see 8:3, 13), which means that there are more leaders than those listed in Ezra 8:2–14.

The purpose of sending the eleven men to Iddo, the leader in Casiphia, is to bring back "attendants" (literally, "servers") for the house of God. Casiphia, an unknown place, could be a cultic center of worship. During the exile, the development of cultic centers was inevitable, because Jerusalem was too far and inaccessible to the exiles.

It is not easy to convince people to join them within such a short span of time. Ezra acknowledges God's gracious hand in helping him tackle this recruiting process (8:18, compare 8:22, 31). As a man of God, Ezra looks at the pressing issue before them from the perspective of God. God's bountiful bestowal of blessings enables Ezra to accomplish his task. Thirty-eight Levites join the caravan, along with 220 temple servants with registered names.

Among the Levites, Sherebiah, a capable man (literally, "man of prudence"), is specially mentioned. Sherebiah descends from the line of Mahli, who is from the line of Merari, who is the grandson of Levi (Exod 6:16–19; 1 Chr 6:16, 19; 23:21–23). Sherebiah comes with his descendants and brothers and serves as the leader of the eighteen Levites. Sherebiah becomes one of the important Levites in the post-exilic community (8:24; Neh 8:7; 9:4, 5; 10:12; 12:24).

Likewise, Hashabiah and Jeshaiah are descendants of Merari, who are traditionally responsible for carrying the tabernacle (Num 3:33–37; 4:29–33). Hashabiah has a significant role in the post-exilic community (8:24; Neh 12:24). Though Ezra's caravan does not carry the tabernacle, as in the first exodus, the descendants of the Levites through the Merarites (Sherebiah, Hashabiah, and Jeshaiah) symbolically return with the caravan to assist in the second temple.

As with the first returnees (2:43–58), the temple servants (literally, "given as gift") respond well to the challenge to return to Jerusalem. This is the only place where the founding of temple servants is mentioned (8:20). They are incidentally mentioned in 1 Chronicles 9:2. Just as the Levites are given to assist the priests (Num 3:9; 18:6), the temple servants are attributed to David, who founded them to assist the Levites. During the wilderness period, the Levites were the only assistants, and they assisted Aaron and the priests. Now, in the post-exilic times, the Levites have temple servants to assist them in fulfilling the levitical tasks (1 Chr 23:28, 32). For the post-exilic community, David developed, amplified, and reformed some of the Levitical functions in the prescription under the law of Moses (compare 1 Chr 23:3, 25–27; 2 Chr 8:14). Whereas Moses set up the full sacrificial system, David strengthened the administrative aspects of the system (compare Neh 12:24, 36, 45–46).

8:21–30 REGROUPING FOR THE JOURNEY

The preparations for this journey can be seen as the caravan regroups for their spiritual needs (8:21–23) and administrative concerns (8:24–30). With four months (8:31b; 7:8–9) to travel as a large group, Ezra needs to give instructions that will prepare the caravan to ensure that their offerings will be brought to the temple safely and properly.

At the same place where Ezra assembles the people, the Ahava Canal, he proclaims a fast. Prior to exile, fasts were practiced by individuals or smaller groups as rites of mourning (Judg 20:26) or personal penance (Ps 35:13; 1 Kgs 21:27). In the post-exilic period, fasting becomes more prominent. Though fasts are still an expression of private piety (10:6; Neh 1:4), public fasts become more established (9:1; Esth 4:3, 16; Zech 7:2–7; 8:19), and the temporary abstention from food becomes an act of devotion to express one's faith. In the inter-testamental period, fasting becomes a popular religious exercise, with the belief that it has value in itself, and is commended alongside prayer and almsgiving (Tobit 12:8; Judith 4:9).

The fasting initiated by Ezra has a specific purpose, which is to humble themselves as a group and pray for a safe journey (8:21). "Humble" literally means "afflicting," "submitting," which is to accept one's position as the weak and disadvantaged. God takes care of the afflicted, who are more prone to depend on God. God's protection is necessary for a perilous, four-month journey away from their comfortable environment. "Safe journey" literally means "straight path," "right way," which will lead them to the right destination without obstacles or hindrances by plausible enemies.

Ezra does not want to ask for an armed escort from the king as an expression of his faith in God. This decision is totally different from Nehemiah (compare Neh 2:8–9, 18). Though both know that "the gracious hand of our God" is upon them, Ezra wants to depend solely on God, whereas Nehemiah identifies the armed escort as God's provision. Ezra is a purist, who puts trust in God and God alone, whereas Nehemiah is a pragmatist, who views the armed escort as a sign of God's providential care. Moreover, the different roles of Ezra, a priest, and Nehemiah, a governor, most likely influence their respective decisions. Inasmuch as both Ezra and Nehemiah are used by God, God's protection in their lives has different applications. There is no spiritual contest about who is more advanced or mature in their faith.

Ezra's challenge to fast and pray makes the people more focused; for the risk of enemies is real during their four-month journey to Jerusalem (compare 8:31). Ezra is bringing many treasures that have been entrusted to the Israelites, along with a huge amount of money funded by the king's order (8:36). In refusing to have a royal armed escort, he is putting his faith in God, who will watch over the caravan and protect them from enemies and bandits along the way (8: 31). This decision to wait before God through fasting and prayer and then prepare the group through further instruction from God reflects the spiritual journeys taken by other Israelites who have been instrumental in carrying out great and mighty tasks for the Lord (compare Deut 29–30; Josh 5:13–15).

A high-level Christian executive who travelled in Asia and many other countries held a diplomatic passport that enabled him to pass the immigration counter in a relatively short span of time. Government officials from various countries often escorted him and showered him with hospitality and respect. During his travels, he visited many missionaries to uplift and encourage them, and he saw his travel privileges as God's provision for this work. After he accepted early retirement, he continued to serve as a volunteer executive of a Christian organization, but he now holds an ordinary passport, where he has to wait in line for clearance whenever he travels. He no longer receives a diplomatic escort – except, perhaps, some modest provisions from the Christian groups he visits. He says that holding either passport is a provision of God. "Different roles, lifestyles, and provisions, but the same God who provides my timely needs."

In dealing with many administrative concerns, Ezra appoints twelve of the leading priests and twelve Levites (8:24) and then gives them direct and clear instructions about what is expected of them as they transport the precious articles for the temple (8:28–29). He singles out Sherebiah and Hashabiah, who might be the recent recruits (8:18–19; compare Neh 12:24) and confirms their leadership for greater accountability. Pointing out these particular leaders' names might encourage greater liability and commitment to their assigned tasks.

Ezra weighs out the contributions to ensure that nothing will be lost during the transport to Jerusalem. Because both the priests and Levites have respective roles in the second temple, he gives the responsibility for safeguarding, handling, and delivering the contributions to the twelve priests and the twelve Levites (8:30, 34). The king, his advisers, his officials, and all Israel participate in giving freewill offerings for the house of God. The gifts are notably huge, for all the participants give generously for the needs of the temple. Silver is listed first, quite consistently, before gold (8:26–27; 1:4).

Ezra clearly tells the priests and Levites that both the deliverers and the delivered things are consecrated, because the contributions are specified for the Lord, the God of their fathers (8:28–29). Though delivering things may seem like a mundane task, it is a holy duty. Thus the priests and Levites are to be faithful and careful in fulfilling their assigned task.

8:31–36 RETURNING TO JERUSALEM

Ezra begins his journey on the first day of the first month (7:9), checking his caravan for three days (8:15), searching for Levites (8:16–20), proclaiming a fast (8:21), and regrouping his team for final instructions before moving on (8:24–30). Finally, on the twelfth day, they leave and experience God's gracious protection (8:31). The delay between the original intention to leave on the first day and their final departure is caused by the need to search for the Levites (compare 7:9).

When they arrive at Jerusalem, they rest for three days, perhaps to recuperate from the stress and weariness of traveling (8:32). Practically, a rested mind can work more effectively than a tired one. On the fourth day, they proceed to the house of God, weighing out the freewill offerings to two priests and two Levites (8:33). Meremoth, son of Uriah, the priest, understands the order of Ezra and Nehemiah. From the list of the first returnees, Hakkoz is listed as one of the priests without proper family records (2:61; Neh 7:63). His position as "priest" is now restored through his descendant, Meremoth. The same Meremoth, the son of Uriah, son of Hakkoz, who built two portions of the wall of Jerusalem, may not have had the title "priest" directly attributed to him; however, his work on the second segment of the wall is approximate to the priestly section (Neh 3:4, 21). His name might be so common that no identification is needed. Jozabad, son of Jeshua, might be the same Levite who moved and resided in Jerusalem (Neh 11:16).

Ezra is entrusted to bring the freewill offerings to Jerusalem. At the beginning of the journey, after properly weighing out the precious articles, he entrusts them to the twelve leading priests and twelve Levites and gives them clear instructions. Two groups of people are called to participate in transporting these articles to the proper authority at the other end. As the caravan arrives in Jerusalem on the fourth day, the very first day after they have rested, Ezra weighs out the entrusted treasures to the two priests and two Levites again. Both the exact numbers and precise weights are recorded and counted (8:34).

After the long journey, the people offer burnt offerings for thanksgiving and sin offerings for cleansing. Finally, the edict of Artaxerxes is fulfilled (7:17). The Persian officials, including the royal satraps and governors of Trans-Euphrates, show their support to the people and the temple.

GOD OR HUMAN PROTECTION

Ezra must have undergone an internal psychological struggle with respect to accepting or refusing support from the pagan king. Is this provision a gracious blessing from God, or a reflection of his dependence on the pagan king? For the long journey back to Jerusalem, Ezra refuses to accept any military escort. Yet Ezra agrees to receive substantial financial support from the pagan king, his advisers, and officials (Ezra 8:25, 36). How can these seemingly inconsistent responses from Ezra be reconciled?

As in Roman mythology, traditional Chinese mythology has over two hundred protective gods and goddesses and over one thousand spirits. Each town and district has its own nature spirits (*kuei-shen*, 鬼神),

which one can worship and seek for protection. In many Chinese graveyards, a statue of the earth spirit (*Tudi Gong*, 土地公) guards and protects the dead. Each of the gods and goddesses has their own part to play in the lives of the people.[1]

As a priest, Ezra prioritizes his situation. For protection from enemies on the road, he leads the people of God to wait upon the Lord through fasting and praying. Inasmuch as the Persian King may want to help, Ezra prefers to receive protection from his great God. This is a teachable moment for all the returnees. Just as the Lord led Joshua to Canaan, Ezra wants the returnees to humble themselves and ask God for help. The experience of waiting upon the Lord is a lasting lesson for them about trusting the Lord. Ezra says that he was ashamed to ask the king for an escort to protect the caravan, because he told the king that "the gracious hand of our God is on everyone who looks to him, but his great anger is against all who forsake him" (Ezra 8: 22). By refusing a royal escort, Ezra validates the people's great confidence in God as all-seeing, all-knowing, and all-abiding, and the Lord answers their prayers (Ezra 8:23). As the Psalmist proclaims, "My help comes from the Lord, the Maker of heaven and earth" (Ps 121:2).

Regarding the donations from the pagan king, Ezra accepts the royal offer because the Israelites are giving as well (Ezra 8:25). Because he is commissioned by the pagan king to tackle the task of rebuilding both the temple and the people, he sees these corporate resources as part of God's provision. As with other predecessors, the pagan king, Artaxerxes, marks the occasion of sending Ezra home to Jerusalem with an official gift and calls on the Jews to join the expedition by contributing as well (Ezra 7:20). Because the God of Israel exists for his people and is more than a name to be honored, the king understands that his royal donation should reflect the scale of his respect. Ezra consents to receive the royal donations as a tangible and courteous display that is consistent with the honor, power, and glory due to the God of Israel.

Rosa Ching Shao

---

1. Emily Mark, "Most Popular Gods & Goddesses of Ancient China," https://www.ancient.eu/article/894/most-popular-gods--goddesses-of-ancient-china/, accessed February 28, 2018.

EZRA 9:1–15

O LORD, YOU ARE RIGHTEOUS!

This chapter is about holiness, where the leaders urge the people of God to separate themselves from ungodly people who practice detestable acts. By keeping marriage holy, we can live a life that is pleasing to God.

The forbidden practice of mixed marriages within the Jewish community, including among priests and Levites, forces Ezra to tear his robe, pull the hair from his head and beard, and fall down on his knees to confess to God on behalf of the people (9:3–15) and then to respond to the issue with painstaking care (10:1–44). His commission from the pagan king is to teach the Torah to the community (7:14), and his conviction from God is to carry out the Torah in communal living. The Jewish leaders and officials inform Ezra about the situation in the hope that he will implement change.

As the chosen people of God who belong to a holy race (9:2), the Israelites are called to live a sanctified life. With the Torah as their guide, they are expected to live faithfully (9:3–4) by separating themselves from the detestable practices of the people of the land (9:1, 11, 14). Distressed and disappointed by the people's sin, Ezra acknowledges God as his Lord as he prays and pours out his confession to the righteous God of Israel (9:15).

9:1–5 ACCOUNT OF MIXED MARRIAGES

The Jewish leaders take the initiative to report the problem of mixed marriages among the people of Israel to Ezra. The report shows the maturity of the leaders in understanding God's desire, for they are reporting against their fellow Jews. This section consists of a public report (9:1–2) and a personal response (9:3–5), and its focus is on the Israelites as a holy race dedicated to the Lord alone. Being faithful to God means obeying the teaching of the Torah, which requires faithful marriages.

The opening phrase, "After these things," refers to the delivery of the precious articles to the house of God and their sacrifices of burnt and sin offerings before God (9:1; 8:33–35).[1] After such a great accomplishment in

---
1. Scholars such as J. Blenkinsopp (*Ezra-Nehemiah*, OTL, 174) and D. J. Clines (*Ezra, Nehemiah, Esther*, NCB, 118–119) conjecture that the events refer to Ezra's arrival in Jerusalem in the fifth

joining together to worship before God, the report from the leaders about mixed marriages within the community brings about necessary reforms. The teaching of the Torah requires total obedience, both inward and outward.

The report is given on the ninth month (compare 10: 9) by a small group of "leaders," who serve as both spiritual heads and political rulers within the community (compare Neh 3:9; 12:31). As leaders of the community, they blow the whistle, daring to speak out against the evil practices in their midst – even against other leaders and officials who have been unfaithful to the Lord (9:2).

The "detestable practices" can also be translated as "abominable practices." The practices refer to a custom of the Canaanites (Lev 18:30), which is a particular sexual perversion (Lev 18:13, 22, 26, 27, 29).[2] The worship of foreign gods is also an abominable action (Deut 17:4; Jer 44:22). In Malachi 2:11, as in this text, the detestable practices refer explicitly to mixed marriages. The people, along with the priests and the Levites, have not been careful in separating themselves from the neighboring peoples, but have assimilated with them. The rebuilding of the community's walk with God starts with the fidelity of the family unit.

The neighboring peoples (literally, "the peoples of the lands") are identified as "the Canaanites, Hittites, Perizzites, Jebusites, Ammonites, Moabites, Egyptians and Amorites" (9:1). Historically, the boundary principle – which is the strict prohibition to marry outside their own ethnic group – is for purity of the Israelite's faith. Although five of the banned ethnic groups – the Canaanites, Hittites, Perizzites, Jebusites, and Amorites – no longer exist in the post-exilic era, the Torah clearly instructs the people about the principle of separation (Exod 3:8, 17; 13:5; 23:23, 28; Deut 7:1; 20:17; Josh 3:10; 9:1; 12:8; Judg 3:5; 1 Kgs 9:20; Neh 9:8). The inclusion of the other three ethnic groups – the Ammonites, Moabites, and Egyptians – in 9:1 may reflect new concerns that have arisen since their return from exile (compare Neh 13:1). The Egyptians symbolize Israel's painful history of sojourning in the land of Egypt, and the Ammonites and Moabites are currently living among them. The list of "the peoples of the lands" in 9:1 differs from the earlier list in the

---

month (7:8). For them, Ezra's involvement in reading the law in the seventh month (Neh 8:1) should be placed before Ezra 9 to make better sense.

2. Brian Rainey, "'Their Peace or Prosperity': Biblical Concepts of Hereditary Punishment and the Exclusion of Foreigners in Ezra-Nehemiah," *Journal of Ancient Judaism* 6 (2015): 158–181, proposes a concept of "hereditary punishment" instead of fearing their idolatrous practices as the main reason that they do not mix with the people of the land. Because the people of the land committed offense against the Lord, their descendants should be punished based on Leviticus 18 and 20.

law of Moses, but the timeless Torah principle of holiness, which prohibits assimilation, remains the same.

The prohibition regarding intermarriage is meant to preserve "the holy race" (literally, "holy seed") so that they will worship the Lord God alone (compare Neh 9:2, literally, "the seed of Israel"). The "holy race" is a development of the old prophetic concept about the remnant of Israel (Isa 6:13). Because the leaders take the initiative in approaching Ezra, they demonstrate their desire for holiness within the community. The word "unfaithfulness" (literally, "disloyalty," "infidelity") is a strong theological word that suggests a treacherous action against God (9:2, 4; 10:2, 6, 10). In its normal usage, it refers to the marital infidelity of a wife against her husband (Num 5:12, 27), and God's punishment is very severe (Ezek 14:13; 15:8; 17:20). In the context of Ezra, intermarriage is a snare (Exod 34:11–16) and a sign of unfaithfulness that will lead to idolatrous and wicked ways (Deut 7:1–4).

Mixed marriages between Israelites and other peoples have some precedents: Joseph's wife was an Egyptian (Gen 41:45); Moses had mixed marriages (Exod 2:21; Num 12:1); Ruth, a Moabite, was integrated into the Israelite the community through her faith in God (Ruth 1:16). Yet the law forbade mixed marriages between Israelites and the inhabitants of Canaan (Exod 34:11–16; Deut 7:1–6; 20:10–18) because the patriarchs understood that Israelite men who married pagan women might adopt their religious practices (Gen 24:2–4; 27:46–28:9). Intermarriage brought apostasy (Judg 3:5–6), and royal marriages brought syncretistic practices into Israel (1 Kgs 11:1–8; 16:31–33). Hence the reason for the cautious separation is religious rather than racial (compare Mal 2:11) and is meant to preserve the purity of their faith so that future generations will continue to live as faithful people of God.

Ezra responds to the intermarriage problem with compassion, whereas Nehemiah is more assertive. Ezra tears his own tunic and cloak and pulls his own hair and beard (9:3), whereas Nehemiah rebukes the people, hits them, and pulls their hair (Neh 13:25). Moreover, Ezra responds to the intermarriage by fasting and making a private confession before the Lord (9:3, 5–15), whereas Nehemiah deals with the matter in the public square (Neh 13:25). Their different roles in the community shape their approach in responding to the situation. This can be seen before they even set out on their journey to Jerusalem, when Ezra prays to the Lord for protection (8:21–23), and Nehemiah asks the king for protection and explains it as a testament of God's grace (Neh 2:8, 18). Similarly, as a priest, Ezra prays to the Lord and expresses his emotional sorrow, whereas Nehemiah, as a governor, confronts the community and teaches them through aggressive actions. Though their different roles and personalities lead them to respond differently, God uses them both.

As the teacher of the Torah, Ezra knows that "the words of the God of Israel" are the proper guidance for the people (9:4). Knowing the truth about their unfaithfulness to the faithful God, the people gather before Ezra, and Ezra prays on their behalf at the temple area before God's house at the appointed time for the evening sacrifice (9:5). By kneeling and spreading his hands to the Lord in the public area, his prayer draws a crowd, who also weep (10:1). Ezra uses no coercion in facing the issue of intermarriage. His sorrowful quietness and his self-abasing sincerity to pray before God show his spiritual maturity in handling the case.

9:6–15 ASKING FOR FORGIVENESS

Ezra's prayer of confession can be compared with Daniel's personal prayer (Dan 9:4–19) and Nehemiah's corporate prayer (Neh 9:5b–37). Ezra's confession recognizes the people's communal shame, sin, and guilt. Although Ezra has not sinned by taking on a foreign wife, he identifies himself with the people's sins and confesses their collective guilt before God. Ezra's prayer can be divided as follows: (1) a sincere and penitential lament to God (9:6–7); (2) an affirmation of God's gracious provision (9:8–9); (3) a confession of the people's detestable sin of intermarriage (9:10–12); and (4) an acknowledgment of the people's guilt (9:13–15).

9:6–7 Sincere and Penitential Lament

The prayer begins in a spirit of humility as Ezra falls on his knees before God (9:5) and then utters a sincere and penitential lament to "my" God (9:6). As a prayer on behalf of the people, he appeals to "our God" (9:8–10, 13), who is the "Lord, God of Israel" (9:15). Because sin brings shame to the sinner, he can hardly lift up his face to God (compare Gen 3:8).

He identifies the people's guilt as grave and severe, for their sins reach higher than their heads and pile up to the heavens. Though the discovery of their sins is recent, Ezra understands that their unfaithfulness to the Lord is rooted in the past, just as it was in the days of their ancestors. Both the previous and current generations have to face the consequences of their sins, for they caused their ancestors, kings, priests, as well as the returned community to be subject to the sword, captivity, pillaging, and humiliation of foreign kings. The servitude of the people under the Assyrian and Babylonian kings continues to the present with the Persian king (compare Neh 9:32). As the teacher of the

Torah, Ezra understands all the more the gravity of sins and severity of the punishment. Though the returned community is now in Jerusalem, they are still under the reign of the Persian king. History seems to repeat itself with the sins of the returned community. These punishments are the result of their disobedience to the teaching of the Torah (Lev 26:14–33; Deut 28:15–68).

9:8–9 Affirmation of God's Gracious Provision

God's gracious provision includes the opportunity to survive with the remnant (9:8), to restore the temple, and to protect the community with a wall (9:9). No doubt, the numbers in the returned community are small, but by the grace of God, the "remnant" (literally, "survivor," "one who escapes") continues to exist in the post-exilic community (9:8, 13, 14). Ezra affirms that God's "brief moment" of graciousness has spared them from bondage as slaves (9:8). This bondage links their suffering with the historical troubles in Egypt. Though God's steadfast love may be for a short period, the remnant has learned to enjoy and be gratified by God's timely help.

Because of God's steadfast love upon the people, they are granted a new opportunity to rebuild the house of God, and they are given a protective wall in Judah and Jerusalem (9:9). This "wall of protection" (literally, "hedge") is the low fence used in a vineyard (Isa 5:5; Ps 80:12, MT 13), which symbolizes God's protection over his people. This protective hedge differs from Nehemiah's city wall (Neh 1:3). Judah is the major tribe that returns from the Babylonian exile, and Jerusalem is the focal city for their return. The combination of Judah and Jerusalem is a standard formula in the post-exilic period (10:7; 2 Chr 11:14; 20:17; 24:6, 9).[3]

9:10–12 Confession of the People's Sin

God's command not to intermarry summarizes Israel's history through the words of the prophets. Instead of the former phraseology, which is that the land is flowing with milk and honey, it is now a land that is polluted by the corruption of its peoples (9:10). The Lord handed this land to Abraham and his descendants because of the detestable practice of worshiping the gods of Canaan (Gen 15:16). Ezra links the worship of other gods with impurity in the land (9:11).

The possession of the land, though promised as a good and everlasting inheritance, comes with the simple condition that the people obey the commands

---

3. Compare the reverse order of "Jerusalem and Judah," which is taken to be of early date. See Isa 3:1, 8; 5:3; 22:21.

of the Lord. The concept of "everlasting" is connected with the covenant. Because of the corruption and pollution in the land, the Lord drove out the original inhabitants. Thus Ezra reiterates the Torah teaching of the Lord, which commands them to separate themselves from the people of the land. He offers a proper solution to their dilemma by giving them three imperatives: "do not give" your daughters; "do not take" their daughters; and "do not seek" treaties of friendship with the peoples of the lands (9:12). Holiness, therefore, is an active commitment to obey the teaching of the Lord.

9:13–15 Acknowledgment of the People's Guilt

In his confession, Ezra recognizes the seriousness of God's wrath as well as his authority to destroy the remnant. The remnant is both a reminder of the people's evil deeds and guilt as well as a testament of God's grace (9:13). Ezra raises a rhetorical question about breaking the covenant, but the question demands a negative answer. For if the post-exilic community refrains from intermarrying, God will have mercy on the remnant.

Finally, Ezra affirms God's righteousness and acknowledges that no one can stand before him (9:15). The Israelite people have been caught red-handed and found guilty of intermarriage and impurity against the righteous God.

SHAME AND GUILT

Ezra expresses his frustration about the recurring sinful acts of the leaders and people through his prayer of confession before God. The prayer is an outlet for his own personal sadness about the detestable living of God's people. The sense of guilt and shame overwhelms him as he prays on behalf of the people, confessing their sins even to the days of their forefathers. Ezra identifies himself as among those who are guilty of detestable practices, even though he is not guilty of intermarriage. As the teacher of God's law and the scribe who keeps records of God's law, Ezra humbly kneels down, confessing, "I am too ashamed and disgraced, my God, to lift up my face to you, because our sins are higher than our heads" (Ezra 9:6). This raises a question about how we can distinguish between guilt and shame.

In Scripture, guilt and shame are often expressed in the same passage. In Genesis 3, taking the forbidden fruit is a guilty act; hiding from God is the result of feeling shameful before God. Covering up our mistakes is our human way of seeking a solution (Gen 3:8). Hiding is a shameful response to the discovery of nakedness; God's garments remove our shame (Gen 3:10, 21).

Guilt and shame are also at play in the parable of the two lost sons (Luke 15:11–32). The prodigal son took off with his share of the inheritance before his father had even died. He brought shame to himself and removed honor from his father. Nonetheless, the father waited for the return of this son before any member of his clan could get near him. It would be fitting for the clan to kill this shameful son in order to bring back honor to the family name. On the cross, Jesus identified with our sinful deeds and bore shame for our sake (Heb 12:2).

In the prayer of confession, Ezra identifies with the guilt of Israel (Ezra 9:7). Earlier, he is ashamed to ask for protection on the dangerous journey to Jerusalem (Ezra 8:22). Because of the people's sin, he prays, "I am ashamed and disgraced to lift up my face to you" (Ezra 9:6). Guilt, then, can be understood as disobedience to God and his law, whereas shame is the loss of face or the feeling of humiliation before others. Muslims, for example, justify killing a family member who apostatizes to Christianity because of the shame that is brought on the whole family.

Both the Bible and psychology have much to say about the nature and origin of guilt. Narramore points out that the Bible tells us what legal guilt and theological guilt are, but it never tells Christians to feel psychological guilt.[1] Guilt is the objective state of being responsible for a wrongdoing or transgression. In the Bible, the words for guilt mean "to be liable to judgment or to be guilty of an offense." It never refers to the *feeling* of guilt. True guilt is not an emotion or feeling, but rather the status of being wrong. As Ezra confesses the people's guilt for the sin of intermarriage, he acknowledges the painful admission with sorrowful actions. Tearing his clothes, pulling his hair and beard, and sitting down in dismay are pictures of his inner conflict.

Carder distinguishes true guilt from false guilt, clarifying "true guilt as that voice we hear inside, which could either be the Holy Spirit prompting us or our conscience – letting us know that we have done something wrong."[2] 1 John 1:9 shows us the best way to deal with any offense we have committed. We only need to acknowledge and confess our sin to God, and then we are cleansed of all guilt by the blood of our Lord Jesus Christ, whose work on the cross is sufficient to pardon and redeem us.

Shame is pervasive in the social culture, even more predominantly among Asian countries, such as China and the Philippines. In the Asian way of doing things, people are driven by shame, such that a person who does wrong would carry his shame for life. No amount of restitution could remove the shame. In the West, the society is driven by guilt system. When someone does wrong, he will be punished for his guilty act accordingly. With the payment of his guilt done, he is now guiltless. Thus, in the Asian context, shame is seen as *who I am*; guilt is *what I do*.

The common Filipino psychological phenomenon of *hiya* (in Tagalog) has both positive and negative connotations. As a painful emotion, *hiya* is a sense of inadequacy and anxiety in a threatening situation; it resembles "shyness," timidity," "embarrassment," and "sensitivity." Because of *hiya*, no one dares to reveal good or bad secrets, and so many things are hidden in the closet. No one dares to report a wrongdoing to an authority if the culprit is related to someone known. With a big extended family, it can be difficult to correct evil practices due to a deep sense of *hiya*. However, Tagalog identifies the absence of *hiya* as *walang hiya*, a connotation that stigmatizes immoral or unconventional behavior when one violates certain social expectations. Thus *hiya* reflects an inner form of respect that is due to one's group or elders, and therefore society would "abhor anyone who is *walang hiya* because this person now tears apart the line of respect, its conventions and its rules."[3] The Chinese people also value *saving face* in relationships and tend to keep confrontations at arm's-length.

The Christian way to please God is to be tactful yet truthful – loving one's enemies yet hating the sins or guilt. The Holy Spirit, the Great Counselor, is given to guide us into all truth, to help us admit our sins and be restored to a right relationship with God. The truth from God's word can set us free from guilt and shame. When God forgives, God forgets: "For as high as the heavens are above the earth, so great is his love for those who fear him; as far as the east is from the west, so far has he removed our transgressions from us" (Ps 103:11–12).

Rosa Ching Shao

---

1. Bruce Narramore, *No Condemnation: Rethinking Guilt Motivation in Counseling, Preaching, and Parenting* (Eugene: Wipf & Stock, 1984).
2. Dave Carder, Earl Henslin, John Townsend, Henry Cloud, and Alice Brawand, *Secrets of Your Family Tree: Healing for Adult Children of Dysfunctional Families* (Chicago: Moody Press, 1991), 97.
3. Jaime C. Bulatao, *Phenomena and Their Interpretation* (Manila: Ateneo de Manila University Press, 1992), 219.

EZRA 10:1–44

REPENT OR BE PENALIZED!

Because of the shame embedded in Asian culture, taking disciplinary action can be very difficult. After a Bible school student committed adultery, the administration decided to face the issue prayerfully with guidance from the Bible. After the guilty parties were counseled and supported with much prayer, the student made a public confession and humbly faced the consequences, understanding it might mean dismissal from the school. Immediately after the public confession, the community of students and faculty surrounded the student and embraced him with forgiveness. After a period of guidance and counseling, the student was restored. The disciplinary action taken by the school reflects a proper balance between righteousness and love according to Scripture.

Ezra 10 is about the problem of mixed marriages and how Ezra responds to the people's sinfulness in order to restore their walk with God. Marrying pagan women from the "peoples of the land" is a grave religious impurity, for it is strictly forbidden in the law (Deut 7:3–4) and thereby demonstrates the Israelite people's unfaithfulness to God (10:2, 10, 11, 17, 18, 44). For when the Israelites begin to worship the idols of pagan wives, they lose their spiritual and physical identity as God's chosen people.

As a man of God, Ezra prays, teaches, and leads the community to return to the Lord. After Ezra's prayer of confession and his moving example of repentance, the people respond with repentant spirits as they weep and mourn at the house of God (10:1; 9:4). It is clear that Ezra's prayers and teaching take root in the community, because the leadership, family heads, and representatives from each family division initiate the reformation.

The chapter ends with a list of those who married foreign women, naming the priests (10:18–22), Levites (10:23), musicians, and gatekeepers (10:24), and then identifying the laity (10:25–43). Thus the list commences with the upper stratum of the society, moves to the lower classes, and ends with the common people. This arrangement emphasizes that the priests and Levites are to set an example of purity in order to preserve the people's faith.

This chapter can be divided into three sections: (1) the response: admission and proclamation (10:1–8); (2) the resolution: action and investigation (10:9–17); and (3) the revelation: authenticity and sincerity (10:18–44).

10:1–8 RESPONSE: ADMISSION AND PROCLAMATION

Ezra's dismay is directly proportional to his frustration about mixed marriages among the people of God. His indignation is described through four actions – praying, confessing, weeping, and throwing himself down before the house of God. His expressive display prompts a large crowd (10:1) to gather in a spirit of remorse. The first section of this chapter consists of Ezra's admission of the people's unfaithfulness (10:1–4), his response (10:5–6), and the proclamation to assemble (10:7–8).

In response to the problem of mixed marriages, a leader named Shekaniah suggests making a covenant, or a public declaration of faith, to send the foreign wives away in accordance with the teaching of God's law (10:2–3, 13). Shekaniah is a descendant of Elam and is listed among the first returnees. As a descendant of the faithful remnant that has returned from exile, he is aware of the problem of mixed marriages (2:7; Neh 7:12). His speech reflects the sentiments of the men, women, and children of Israel (10:1) and imparts hope for them (10:2). The counsel of spiritual leaders agrees to implement a covenant in order to rekindle the people's passion to return to the Lord. In the Old Testament, there are basically two types of covenant. The first is unilateral, made between God and humankind, with God initiating his actions. The second is usually bilateral, made between two parties of equal status. The covenant in Ezra 10 refers to a contract for the people by the people under the guiding principle and standard of God.

The phrase "counsel of God" denotes the overall revelation of God (10:3) through his commandments and laws (see 9:3). The "counsel of Ezra," on the other hand, refers to his spiritual guidance for the people. Those who fear the commands of God can share in giving counsel, and this is reflected in the large crowd that gathers around Ezra, hoping to make changes in their community. Thus the counsel that Ezra receives is not limited to one leader, but includes unanimity of ideas from those who fear God by obeying his commands.

A pastor of a mega-church in the Philippines says that even though his church has given him the authority to pastor, he has a group of elders to whom he is accountable. He values the opinions of members and listens to the counsel of these elders. Whenever the church needs to undergo change or make decisions, he consults his accountability group. If the elders do not agree in harmony, they continue to wait and pray. Looking back, the pastor recognizes that the counsel of the elders has always prevailed.

For instance, when an unmarried couple approached the pastor and told him about their premarital pregnancy, the pastor sought godly counsel from the elders before making a decision about how to respond. With the support of the elders, the pastor counseled the couple about their marriage, and then the man and woman confessed publicly during a Sunday service. Right after the confession, the pastor embraced and prayed for the couple. Together, they set a date for a church wedding. This response balanced righteousness and love.

In another church, when there was a premarital pregnancy, the pastor strictly followed the biblical principle and refused to solemnize the marriages inside the sanctuary without first seeking guidance from elders. Though he offered to marry the couple in a garden wedding instead, they just contacted another church pastor and asked him to officiate their wedding without telling him about their situation. This outcome led to alienation as well as criticism of the church and its members. Seeking to adhere to biblical principles while also receiving the counsel of church leaders, is a more balanced approach that can help leaders uphold the changeless teaching of the Scriptures amidst the changing values of the postmodern world.

Responding to the crisis, Ezra leads those who are gathered in taking an oath. Because the leading priests and Levites are the leaders, who are charged to teach the law of Moses to the people, they lead the group to repent before God (10:5). For this reason, they are identified first in the list before the other Israelites. After taking the oath, Ezra withdraws into a quiet place in the house of God, the room of the high priest, Jehohanan, who is the son of Eliashib (10:6). In this inner chamber, he fasts from both food and water as he mourns before the Lord (10:6), lamenting about the people's unfaithfulness toward their loving and faithful God.

A public proclamation is issued for all the exiles to assemble in Jerusalem in three days (10:7). The three-day period allows the information to be distributed throughout the Jewish community. Although Ezra is the spiritual leader of the returned community, the officials and elders of the community help to make and execute corporate decisions. While Ezra may have the right to issue a proclamation himself, since it is related to the people's unfaithfulness in following God's word (compare 7:26), he is open to suggestions from other leaders and waits for consensus before carrying out this proclamation (10:8). The people are warned about two consequences if they fail to appear in Jerusalem within three days: (1) they will have to forfeit their property; and (2) they will be expelled from the assembly. These are terrible punishments for any Jew. Forfeiting one's property means losing one's legal right to own land, which is to be disinherited. This consequence ensures that no pagan children will be able to claim Israel's land. Expulsion from the exiled community prohibits one from worshiping in the temple.

10:9–17 RESOLUTION: ACTION AND INVESTIGATION

This section can be divided as follows: (1) a gathering of the people and Ezra's speech (10:9–11); (2) the people's response and some opposition (10:12–15); and (3) an investigation of the people and the registration of names (10:16–17).

As Ezra prays before the house of God, a huge crowd gathers and sits in the open space at the temple (10:9). Those who gather are the men of Judah and Benjamin, the two southern tribes that have returned from exile. Ezra candidly states their unfaithfulness and asks them to confess to the Lord, the God of their fathers. Then he tells them to separate themselves from the neighboring peoples and their foreign wives (10:10–11).

The whole assembly responds to Ezra's message with a resounding affirmation, demonstrating their social support and willingness to work out the issue properly (10:12). The natural phenomenon of the rain in 10:13 is significant in the history of Israel, since the people interpret it as a reflection of God's fierce anger (10:14). This theology is informed by a similar historical event. When the Israelites asked Samuel for a king, he called upon the Lord to send thunder and rain in order to illustrate their disobedience (1 Sam 12:16–18).[1]

After making this resolution, the people develop a comprehensive plan for carrying out Ezra's instructions. They appoint leaders to oversee the matter and to work with the elders and judges and the religious and civil leaders in each town to deal with the issue directly (10:13–14). This principle applies what is written in the law of Moses (Deut 17:8–13).

Four people, whose names are listed, oppose the separation proposal (10:15), which suggests that different opinions can be freely given in the community. None of these four people have foreign wives. Meshullam may refer to one of Ezra's active leaders (10:15; 8:16); since he has returned with Ezra, he could not have taken a foreign wife. But Meshullam is a common

---

1. The demonstration of God's wrath through thunder and other natural manifestations is very much part of the prophetic message to the people of God. Samuel could have learned this basic principle from his mom, Hannah (1 Sam 2:10).

name, and so this voice of opposition should not be identified as one of the descendants of Bani who did take a foreign wife (10:29). Sabbethai the Levite also opposes the separation proposal. Both Meshullam and Sabbethai are Ezra's helpers and supporters in reading the word (Neh 8:4, 7).

In spite of this minor opposition, the leaders implement a careful investigation, distributing the responsibility for carrying out the separation to the family system by selecting one family head from each family division, designating each by name (10:16), and calling them to judge without prejudice or favoritism.

The reform is cautiously implemented over the course of three months. The people gather initially on the twentieth day of the ninth month (10:9); they begin the investigation on the first day of the tenth month (10:16); they finish the investigation on the first of the first month (10:17).

10:18–44 REVELATION: AUTHENTICITY AND SINCERITY

The list follows the post-exilic pattern for recording names, wherein the priests come before the Levites (10:18–24), who are followed by the musicians and the gatekeepers, and the list concludes with the people of Israel (10:25–43). The list does not include temple servants or the servants of Solomon, because they are not Israelites, and so they are not prohibited from marrying foreign women. The list of names suggests that the number of men who have foreign wives is not as large as it seems.

Compared with the first list of returnees (2:2–42), the names of the family heads are listed first, followed by the names of those who have married foreign women. There is no need to record a total number here, since all the names are recorded meticulously. The naming of the offenders indicates their sincere repentance and willingness to turn to the Lord.

The first returnees include four priestly family heads: Jedaiah (through the family of Jeshua), Immer, Pashhur, and Harim (2:36–37). The list of offenders also includes these four priestly family heads: "Joshua, Immer, Harim, Pashhur" (10:18–22; 2:36–39; Neh 7:39–42). The first two names follow the same order, but the last two are inverted. The resumptive summary in 10:19 states that the offenders have pledged to put away their wives and have presented a ram for their guilt offering. This description not only applies to Joshua and his descendants, but to every family named on the list (10:18–44).

Among the eleven Israelite family heads named on the list (10:25–44), most appear on the list of the first returnees as well (2:2–35). Parosh is named at the beginning of both lists (10:25; 2:2–3). The list includes the descendants of Elam, with the significant exception of Shekaniah (10:26; 2:7), who gives suggestions to Ezra about how to deal with the issue of mixed marriages (compare 10:2). This list includes Shekaniah's father, Jehiel (10:26, 2), which may mean that Shekaniah himself could be excommunicated from the assembly of the exiles.[2]

Harim and Nebo, which are listed as place names in the list of the first returnees (2:32, 29), are registered here as personal names (10:31, 43; compare 2:32, 29). The final verse summarizes the purpose of this list, which is to identify those who married foreign women and had children with their pagan wives (10:44).

Biblical scholars have two interpretations regarding the list of names. The first interprets the situation in a literal context, arguing that a separation (divorce) between husbands and foreign wives does take place. The fact that these names are formally recorded implies that the foreign women and children are forced to separate from their families. The second view interprets the situation figuratively, arguing that the separation (divorce) between husbands and foreign wives may not have actually happened; rather, the purpose of the list is to teach the people a lesson about holiness. Most of the narrative texts in the Old Testament include a summary statement to show that the described reformation is implemented in the society. Though the post-exilic community seems to be very serious about the issue of foreign wives, a corrupt variant of this concluding verse can be read as: "and they sent them away with their children" (10:44, NIV fn).[3] However, most textual critics accept the MT: "and some of them had children by these wives." This means that the accepted Hebrew text leaves it open.

If we accept the first interpretation, we could argue that the Old Testament accepts such separations, but the New Testament does not (1 Cor 7:10–11). But if we take the unity of the Old and New Testaments seriously, we cannot permit such discontinuities. Paul, a reader of the Old Testament texts, can guide us on this issue, for even if the separation is taken at face value, the nature of the text is descriptive rather than prescriptive.[4] The post-exilic community has to rectify the idolatrous situation brought about by the practice of mixed

---

2. Clines (NCB, 126) conjectures that Shecaniah (Shekaniah, NIV) almost advocates his own excommunication. His father, Jehiel, is a son of Elam. Likewise, Williamson (WBC, 150) surmises that Shecaniah may have been an adult already and become a member of the Jewish community in his own right as an observant follower of the Lord (6:21).
3. See 1 Esdr 9:36.
4. Williamson (WBC, 161) argues that Ezra 9–10 is descriptive rather than prescriptive for the Christian faith.

marriages, and registering the names of the offenders would demonstrate an uncompromising respect for God's law and each family's assigned role within the community. As a teaching vehicle, this would encourage the next generation to be careful with their marriages.

The prophet Malachi teaches the Israelites to maintain loyalty with their spouses and keep their marriage commitments holy in order to raise godly descendants (Mal 2:10–16). The union of godly parents ensures holy matrimony for a lifetime (Mal 2:15). Through Malachi, the Lord God of Israel declares: "I hate divorce" (Mal 2:16).

As we turn to Nehemiah, we will observe that even though Nehemiah aggressively expresses his anger about mixed marriages, there is no indication that a separation between the Jews and their foreign wives is actually implemented (Neh 13:23–24). Should this omission suggest further interpretation? Or, does the list of offenders' names indicate that a drastic measure is being implemented? Nehemiah uses the life of Solomon, who also married a pagan wife, to teach the people this painful lesson (Neh 13:26). Ezra uses this teachable moment among the community to sound out the message of true confession (10:10–11), which is not only to agree with God that they have sinned, but also to recommit themselves to do God's will by renouncing their disobedience.

COGNITIVE DISSONANCE AND COMPASSION

Ezra is appalled by the people's unfaithfulness to God through their mixed marriages, because the practice collides with God's ever-loving faithfulness. Though the Israelites claim that they are the chosen ones of God, they choose not to obey his will.

Social psychologists describe the state of psychological tension that is aroused when a person simultaneously holds two contradictory ideas or thoughts – cognitions – as cognitive dissonance.[1] Inconsistencies in our attitudes and behaviors cause unpleasantness, motivating us to attempt to reduce the dissonance as much as possible. Social psychologists point out that the greater the dissonance, the greater the pressure for changes in attitude. Hypocrisy is an experience of dissonance, wherein we recognize that we have not lived up to the attitudes we have publicly proclaimed.

The dissonance within the exiled community regarding holy living disturbs Ezra, who courageously and vulnerably shares his frustration with the community. Ezra's lament evokes a thorough response from the other leaders, who can no longer resist the need to instigate reforms in their families. The whole community recognizes their hypocrisy before God, and this confession sets them on the journey of adjusting their behavior to match their attitudes.

Biblical scholars have differing opinions about whether separation and divorce really took place in the post-exilic community. Some argue that separation and divorce would bring about more dissonance in the family system. I have tried to reduce my own cognitive dissonance with the episode about sending away the spouses and children in the article *Divorce: An Option or an Objection to God's Standards?*[2]

When a Christian marries a Muslim, Hindu, or Buddhist, the Christian usually either converts to the other's faith or becomes secular. In order to retain the faith, the Christian may have to separate or find a creative way to exercise his or her faith. Such marriages are to be discouraged. Yet in a pluralistic society in the postmodern world, many Christians are marrying non-believers. The church ought to extend compassion to them and find ways to create opportunities for them to feel loved in God's family.

In today's society, there are many single parents involved in caring for their children, but this causes much struggle and hardship. Some are single parents because of unforeseeable events, others because of separation or divorce. The dissonance felt by growing children in separated or divorced families can create imbalances in their psychological health. The church can be light and salt amidst this broken world by becoming a caring and healing community for these broken families. Those who do not have a responsible father figure or have been left with the scars of divorce could be adopted by a believing family to help restore faith, hope, and love within the lives of those who are suffering.

Rosa Ching Shao

---

1. Feldman, *Social Psychology* (Upper Saddle River, NJ: Prentice Hall, 2001), 344.
2. Rosa C. Shao, *Divorce: An Option or an Objection to God's Standards?* Philippine-Chinese Mission 2000 Newsletter of CCOWE Fellowship, Philippines (November 1997), 4.

THE BOOK OF NEHEMIAH

NEHEMIAH 1–6

REBUILDING THE WALL

The book of Nehemiah has two important sections. The first section, Nehemiah 1–6, deals with the rebuilding of the wall of Jerusalem. The second section, Nehemiah 7–13, highlights the rebuilding of the people.

In 445 BC, during the twentieth year of Artaxerxes I, Nehemiah's brothers inform him about the plight of Jerusalem with its broken city wall and burned gates. Nehemiah begins his personal account within the secured walls of the Persian palace. His memoirs, which are our most valuable and authentic source on the history of the post-exilic age, record his journey from Susa to Jerusalem and describe how he restores the city walls and gates of his ruined hometown in the land of Canaan.

Nehemiah belongs to a group of exiled Jews who rise to high office in the Persian administration. His first office was as a cupbearer to King Artaxerxes, where he became close to the Persian monarch and well-acquainted with Persian policies. In time, Nehemiah becomes a governor, but he retains a deep love for his country and a concern for the welfare of his fellow Jews.

After hearing about the state of Jerusalem from his own brother, Nehemiah mourns for several days while fasting and praying. Eventually, he is able to return to Jerusalem and Judah to commence the rebuilding of the city wall and gates. With the rebuilding project, he not only faces external oppositions from his enemies, but he also has to deal with internal issues. Despite personal threats to his life, he rallies the people to finish the project in fifty-two days.

NEHEMIAH 1:1–11

PRAYING TO GOD

A physical wall not only symbolizes the boundaries of a property, but it also protects the owner from intruders. The walls around our seminary were first built when it was founded in 1957. On numerous occasions, different parts of our wall have fallen down, sometimes due to flooding and other times due to earthquakes. The school personnel have to inspect the wall from time to time to figure out ways to resolve the problems.

This chapter is about the ruins in Jerusalem, especially the broken city wall and burned gates. Nehemiah's concern moves him to pray to God, asking for a smooth return to his homeland to lead the challenging task of repairing the walls of Jerusalem. His narrative begins with a visit from his brother, Hanani, who has just returned from Jerusalem. Nehemiah asks about his hometown, and when he hears of the gloomy state of his war-torn homeland, he mourns (1:4) and then he fasts and prays to God (1:5–11).

1:1–3 REPORT FROM JERUSALEM

Nehemiah records the time, place, and reason for his return to Jerusalem. His story is set during the month of Kislev in the twentieth year of King Artaxerxes (445 BC) at the citadel of Susa, the winter residence of the king.[1] Many years earlier (in 586 BC), Nebuchadnezzar, the king of Babylon at the time, destroyed the walls of Jerusalem (2 Kgs 25:8–10).

Nehemiah's story takes place more than a decade after Ezra leads the second group of returnees to Jerusalem (in 458 BC). The returnees do not attempt to rebuild the city and restore the walls (see Ezra 4:12–13, 16). Ezra might be in Jerusalem when King Artaxerxes issues the decree to stop the work of rebuilding (Ezra 4:17–23). Presumably, after this decree is issued, the wall is broken down and its gates are burned with fire. As the cupbearer to King Artaxerxes, Nehemiah knows that the king's decree will affect the people in Jerusalem, and he shows his concern by asking about the condition of the Jewish remnant.

---

1. The king's summer residence is Ectabana (Ezra 6:2).

Hanani is identified as Nehemiah's "brother," which is a common word in Hebrew that may refer either to a blood brother or to a countryman.[2] Here, it refers to a blood brother.

Traveling in those days was very common, so it is not surprising for Hanani to travel between Jerusalem and Susa. His report about great trouble and disgrace relates to the broken wall of Jerusalem and the burned gates.

"The Jewish remnant" refers to the exiles who returned to Jerusalem from the Babylonian captivity. The exile is a shameful event for the Jewish people, and so returning from exile is an escape from shame. The remnant is a small group of Jewish people who survive the exile and return to Jerusalem successfully, though sparingly, as prophesied by the prophets Jeremiah and Ezekiel (Jer 31:1–6; Ezek 36:24–32). The remnant is certainly a distinct entity who is segregated from the indigenous population as well as those remain in exile.[3]

1:4–11 NEHEMIAH'S RESPONSE

The penitential elements of Nehemiah's prayer follow the convention of post-exilic piety (see Ezra 9:3–15; Neh 9:6–37; Dan 9:4–19). His persistence in prayer over a period of four months[4] demonstrates his belief in prayer and his concern for his fellow Jews. Nehemiah's phenomenal religious devotion is evident throughout the book.

As a Jew, Nehemiah would know the wordings of the Torah and the prophetic writings by heart. He uses phraseology that is part of the prayer vocabulary of a believing Jew in his time. The closest parallels between the thought patterns and phraseology of this passage with antecedent books can be seen as follows:

---

2. The usage may mean: "full brother" by the same father (Gen 4:8; 44:20; Hos 12:4), "kinsman" with blood relationship (Gen 13:8; 14:16; 29:15), "tribesman" (Gen 31:32; Judg 9:18), or "countryman" (Exod 2:11; Lev 19:17).
3. In the stirrings of classical Jewish sectarianism, the Babylonian exile is the watershed in Israel's history, but there are factions in the society. The remnant, returning from exile, is the principal group. See Morton Smith, *Palestinian Parties and Politics that Shaped the Old Testament* (New York: Columbia University Press, 1971), 144–147, 173–174; Shemaryahu Talmon, "The Emergence of Jewish Sectarianism in the Early Second Temple Period," in *King, Cult and Calendar in Ancient Israel* (Jerusalem: Magnes, 1986), 165–201.
4. The month of Nisan (2:1) is four months after Chislev (1:1).

Nehemiah 1	Old Testament
v. 5	Deut 7:9, 21; 10:17; Dan 9:4
v. 6	1 Kgs 8:28–29; 2 Chr 6:40; 7:15; Ps 130:2; Isa 37:17
v. 7	Deut 6:1
v. 8	Deut 4:27; 28:64
v. 9	Deut 30:1–4; 12:5
v. 10	Deut 9:29; Exod 32:11

Nehemiah's prayer shows that he is familiar with Israel's liturgical tradition, yet he offers his prayer fervently and creatively, connecting national distress (1:10) with his personal need (1:11a). His prayer begins with lament and ends with a repentant spirit. Nehemiah's acknowledgment of the sins of the sons of Israel and his profound conviction about the need for reform are characteristic features of post-exilic faith. Nehemiah identifies himself with the post-exilic community as he confesses his people's sins before God.

Nehemiah's prayer consists of the following elements: agonizing before God (1:4); addressing God's name (1:5); acknowledging God's justice (1:6–7); affirming God's power (1:8–9); and anticipating God's action (1:10–11).

1:4 Agonizing before God

Nehemiah's initial reaction to the report from Jerusalem is to sit down and weep. Sitting down and weeping is a customary posture of mourning and fasting in expressing one's grief and sadness (compare Job 2:8, 13; Ezek 26:13; Ps 137:1). For some days, Nehemiah remains in profound sorrow, praying passionately for his homeland.

There are three ways to interpret the occasion of Nehemiah's prayer. First, the prayer might be a summary of Nehemiah's petition over four months in response to the news of his broken and stricken homeland, revealing his grief before God. Second, the prayer might be a record of his actual prayer when the opportunity to approach the king arose. Third, the prayer might reflect his very first prayer for God to open a way for him to help rebuild Jerusalem (1:11). The first two alternatives are possible. The third alternative, however, seems to be most logical, since it reflects Nehemiah's sense of urgency in asking God to open the door of opportunity for him. Nehemiah refers to God as "my God" throughout his memoir, making it clear that he is very close to God, and he sees God as a personal God to whom Nehemiah can draw near (2:8, 12, 18; 5:19; 6:14; 7:5; 13:14, 22, 29). As a devout Jew, Nehemiah is able to utter all the liturgical phraseology he uses in the prayer. Moreover, Nehemiah believes that his awesome God will create opportunity for him in the midst of his mournful sadness to help restore his beloved country's sorrowful condition.

1:5 Addressing God's Name

Nehemiah addresses God with two names and descriptions. The first, "Lord" (Yahweh), is the covenant name of God, given specially to the Israelites (Exod 3:14). This name is associated with God's imminent care for the Israelites. It is the name that God reveals to Moses when he asks God for his name (Exod 3:14; 6:1–3), and it speaks of God's nearness to his people. The second name, "God of heaven," is a shortened form for "God of heavens and earth." This title emphasizes God's cosmic and transcendent power over the whole universe (see Gen 24:3, 7; Jonah 1:9; Dan 2:18, 19, 37, 44).

Nehemiah's first description for God is that he is the great and awesome God (4:14, MT, 4:8; 9:32). The word "awesome" can be translated literally as "terrible," which means the God who should be "respected and feared." The Hebrew word "awesome" usually appears in the context of God's intervention on behalf of his people in the Exodus account (Exod 15:11; 34:11). Upon seeing God's intervention, the enemies of Israel fear and respect their God. Nehemiah and the rest of the exiles have experienced the pain of exile. Even though Nehemiah is in the Persian court, he does not have the same liberty as he might have in his own country. Along with his people, he has experienced the exile and captivity described by the prophets.[5] Though God judged the Israelites by bringing them into exile, he also caused miraculous things to happen, as he promised through his prophets, and so this awesome God should be "feared."

Nehemiah's second description of God is that he keeps his covenant of love. The phrase "love" (*hesed*) is correlated with God's covenant. God loves the Israelites because of his covenant. Though God's love seems to be conditional, it is strongly rooted in and sealed by God's covenant with "those who love him and obey his commandments." The Israelites not only enjoy the benefits of following God's will, but they also enjoy the blessings of his character. In the context of the Decalogue, God is the one who initiates his love to a thousand generations (Exod 20:6). There are two conditions to living

---

5. Both Jeremiah and Ezekiel emphasize the reality of exile because of the people's arrogance and sin against God. Jeremiah stands in front of the temple and preaches about the reality of exile (Jer 7–9). Ezekiel, likewise, uses extended allegories and historical lessons to depict the rebellious people of God and the humiliation of exile (Ezek 16, 20, 23).

under God's covenant: the first is to love God, and the second is to keep his law. Torah-obedience allows the people of Israel to respond to what God has done for them.

There is a big difference between Hanani's (along with his delegation's) perception of their country's woes and Nehemiah's discernment of the core problem. Whereas Hanani and his delegation report about Jerusalem and its wall (1:3), Nehemiah understands that the true nature of the problem is the faithlessness of the Israelites in keeping God's covenant (1:5). Nehemiah perceives that the miserable condition of Jerusalem is related to their rebelliousness toward God.

1:6–7 Acknowledging God's Justice

Nehemiah wants God to listen to his prayers, for he implores God using anthropomorphic terminologies: attentive ears and open eyes (2 Kgs 19:16; Ps 86:1; Isa 37:17; Dan 9:18). Attentive ears describe how God cares by listening. Open eyes describe God taking a careful look into their situation. The eyes of God watch over even the sparrow, and so they are also upon his people (Ps 84:3; Matt 10:29).

Nehemiah uses the phrase "your servant" to describe himself (1:6, 11) and Moses (1:8), and he describes the people as "your servants" (1:6, 10, 11). The concept of servant entails the idea of someone listening to a master, and it also depicts someone with a mission. Both Abraham and Moses are called the "servant of the LORD" (Deut 34:5; Josh 1:1) because of their work and task. This great title is only awarded to Joshua after he proves himself worthy and commendable (Josh 24:29). The servant is one who is obedient and quietly accomplishes an assigned task (Isa 42:1–4; 49:1–6; 50:4–11; 52:13–53:12). The expression "day and night" implies the thoroughness of Nehemiah's ongoing prayer.

Nehemiah's insight about the connection between the condition of Jerusalem and the people's rebelliousness moves him to confess the people's sin to God. As one of the great intercessors (compare Moses, Exod 34:9; Isaiah, Isa 6:5; Ezra, Ezra 9:6–15), Nehemiah doesn't blame others, but identifies himself with the people, acknowledging their sinful actions as well as his own. His identification with the sinful condition of the people differs from Ezra's confession (Ezra 9:6–15) in that Ezra correlates the people's sin as the sole reason for exile (Ezra 9:7), whereas Nehemiah sees the people's sin as against God himself (1:6). Though Ezra identifies with the people, he stands outside the circle of sinners and intercedes on their behalf; Nehemiah identifies himself as a sinner along with the people.

The three-fold designation of "commands, decrees, and laws" is a comprehensive description of God's law. The word "commands" appears in Deuteronomy forty-two times and in the Old Testament a total of 180 times. It refers to the words given by the Lord for the people to follow, such as the Ten Commandments (Exod 20:1–17; literally, "ten words," Exod 34:28; Deut 4:13). "Decrees and laws" refer to the totality of the law. The word "decrees" originally designated the divine announcements, such as the statutes of the Passover (Exod 12:14, 24; Num 9:14). The word "laws" (literally, "judgments") refers to the case law in a court (Judg 4:5).

The phrase ". . . you gave your servant Moses" reflects an important concept about God's revelation. The privilege of receiving God's laws firsthand through Moses upholds the nation Israel. Priests collect and compile God's laws and are expected to teach these laws to God's people (Hag 2:11–13; Mal 2:1–9). The prophets consistently expound his will through the laws given to Moses.

1:8–9 Affirming God's Power

This section of Nehemiah's prayer affirms God's power. The same God both scatters the exiles (1:8) and gathers the returnees (1:9). Disobedience brings disaster and adversity to the community, for it results in their being scattered (Lev 26:14–39; Deut 28:15–68). Nevertheless, God's punishments correct the people and bring them back to the Lord (Lev 26:14, 18, 21, 23, 27). Their obedience is a key to God's blessing (Lev 16:1–13; Deut 28:1–14), which is manifested when God gathers – or brings home – the diaspora Jews.

Nehemiah quotes Scripture from memory, summarizing the teaching from Deuteronomy about the relationship between disobeying God and the scattering of the people among the nations (1:8; see Deut 4:27; 28:64). Having experienced the curse statements of Deuteronomy, the exiles are called to return to the Lord, who can act to bring them back.

A whole complex of ideas has developed around the name "Zion" as the physical location for the dwelling place of God (1:9). The Lord chose Zion as his resting place forever (Ps 132:13, 14), and therefore the sanctuary is "consecrated forever" (2 Chr 30:8). The Lord chose Mount Zion (Ps 78:68–69) and let it be known by his name (Jer 7:11). In the prophecy of Zechariah, God is zealous for Zion (Zech 1:14; 2:12).

1:10–11 Anticipating God's Action

This section of Nehemiah's prayer anticipates God's action. Nehemiah appeals to the formulaic statement, "they are your servants . . . whom you redeemed by your great strength and your mighty hand" (10:10). The exodus account provides a concrete example of how God has redeemed them by his strong hand (Deut 3:24; 4:34; 5:15; 7:8; 9:26; 13:5). Nehemiah affirms his belief that they belong to God, and so God alone will redeem them with his mighty hand.

Praying on behalf of the people, Nehemiah affirms his conviction that the people will surely revere God's name (1:11). The redemptive aspect of God's name is a strong theme in Ezekiel for preventing disaster in the history of Israel (Ezek 20:9, 14, 22). The antecedent informing theology is the oft-repeated promise of God in the exodus event, which is that God is "the Lord their God" (see Ezek 20:5). By revering God's name, the people acknowledge that God is the Lord.

Nehemiah's urgent request to God is: "Give your servant success today" (1:11). Nehemiah implores God to act immediately upon his earnest plea to release Nehemiah from his work so that he can get involved immediately with the ministry in Jerusalem. The expression "this man" seems to be dishonoring the king of Persia, the self-proclaimed "king of kings," but Nehemiah is addressing his prayer to the Almighty God, and so the heart of the Persian king is in the Lord's hand and thus under divine control (Prov 21:1).

As a "cupbearer to the king," Nehemiah is in an important position, with access to the king. In antiquity, a cupbearer was obliged to select wine skillfully and had a duty to taste the wine against poison or any evil scheme of men who might desire to harm the king. Moreover, he is expected to be a friendly and tactful companion to the king. Since the previous monarch was assassinated, Nehemiah's role in the Persian court is even more significant.

ANXIETY AND PRAYER

When Nehemiah learns from his brother that Jerusalem is in ruins and its gates have been burned by fire, he mourns and prays to the Lord. He cannot remain calm and stay in his cup-bearing routine. At once, he feels connected to his homeland. As he keeps up with the news of his people, his thoughts and concerns run toward his hometown, and he feels as if he truly belongs there.

According to psychologists, any threatening situation often brings about an unpleasant emotion known as *anxiety*.[1] A person who is anxious or faces problems of great magnitude feels tense and vulnerable. How can we face our anxiety or problems? Some people immerse themselves in their own problems. Others try to find a scapegoat and blame their problems on other people. Still others run away from their problems. But some people face their problems directly and may ask for help from others. Few people are able to face their own problems while also offering to help others.

In the Bible, David has to live as a refugee while he is pursued constantly by the jealous King Saul in the wilderness. Even as he is fleeing for his own life, David accepts many indigent and destitute people who come to join him in his camp. Without knowing what may lie ahead, David warmly receives the four hundred people who are refugees and rejects like himself (1 Sam 22:2). Later, that number swells to six hundred people (1 Sam 23:13). David even has the courage to arrange for the well-being of his parents (1 Sam 22:3–4). Though David has real problems, he rises above them.

Nehemiah faces his problems and concerns about his country's welfare by committing them to the Lord. He waits on the Lord and asks for God's help while praying and watching. His commitment to God helps him to release his burdens to God, trusting that the God of heaven will carry them. Nehemiah's prayer on behalf of his country and people verbalizes his anxiety and gives him a concrete understanding about why his country is in ruins.

In the midst of sufferings and problems, we can pray to the Lord for his guidance and care. We can learn from David, who helped the problem-laden people around him. By helping others, we shift our focus from the problem to God, who creates people who both need and give love. Like Nehemiah, we can commit the solutions to the Lord, trusting that God, who is greater than us, will carry us through, taking away our stress, fear, and anxiety.

Rosa Ching Shao

---

1. Aileen Milne, *Teach Yourself Counseling* (London: Hodder Arnold, 2003).

Jerusalem at the Time of Nehemiah
(Nehemiah 2 and 3)

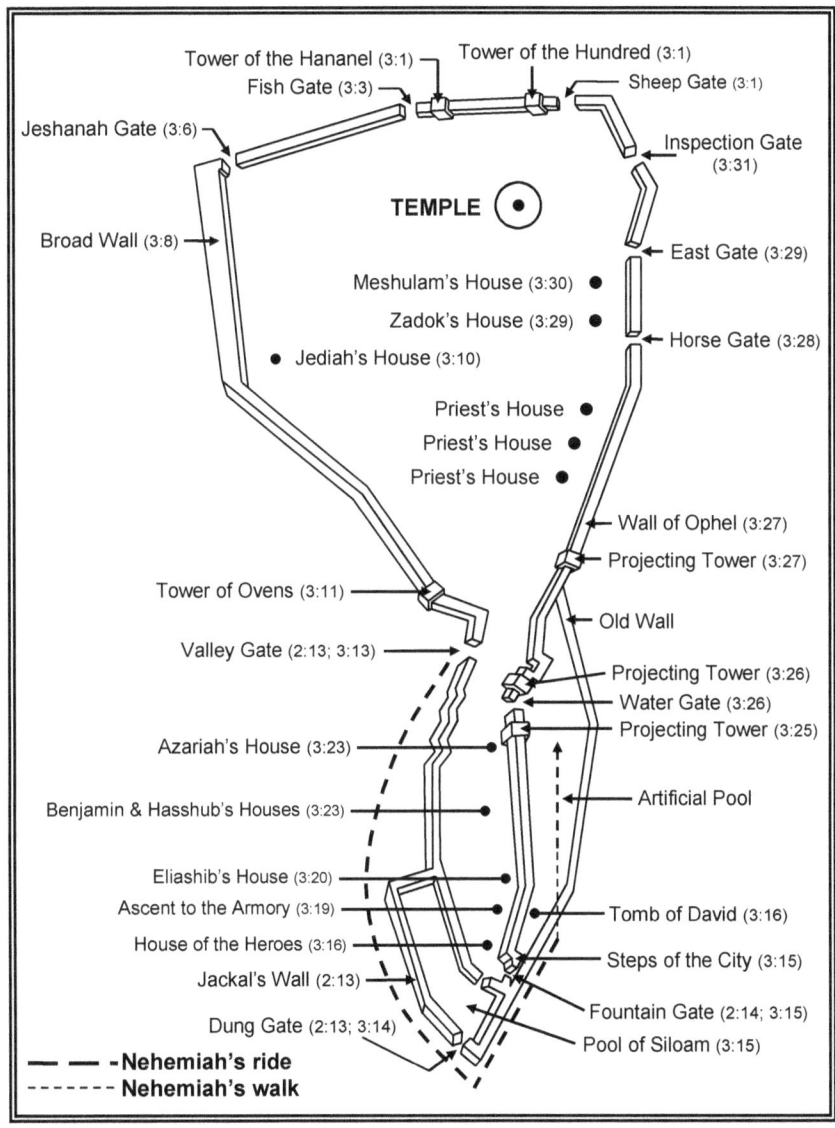

NEHEMIAH 2:1–20

JOURNEYING HOME

Journeying home is a desire of many travelers who work and reside in other countries. Today, many people groups are living in diaspora, and while it might be easy for some to return to their country of origin, it is not as easy for others. Usually, after waiting for proper timing and valid permission, the journey home can commence. Chapter 2 is about Nehemiah's return to Jerusalem after patiently waiting for the right opportunity (2:1–9). At the right moment, he rallies the leaders to start the work of rebuilding (2:10–20).

Because Nehemiah is devoted and patriotic, he wants God to bring him immediately to Jerusalem to do something for his country (1:11b). As soon as he perceives his mission from God, he is zealous to respond promptly to enact rapid changes in his environment. Yet God seems to have his own timetable in carrying out his work, for he does not answer Nehemiah's prayer instantaneously. This delay could be God's deliberate way of testing Nehemiah's patience and real motives, giving him a chance to form his character as he faithfully carries on his designated service as a cupbearer to the Persian king (1:11; 2:1). Nehemiah does not leave his job without God-given permission and human approval, but rather waits for his chance to present his burden to the king. Nonetheless, Nehemiah makes plans to take action as he waits for his mission to be in full swing, just like any well-balanced and prepared spiritual leader.

2:1–10 PERMISSION FOR NEHEMIAH TO RETURN

As a cupbearer of the king, Nehemiah is expected to be dependable. But after the terrible news about the pitiful state of his homeland reaches him, he realizes that the God of heaven wants him to return to Jerusalem. He knows what is expected of him in the Persian court, but he also knows he has a mission to rebuild the wall. As he wrestles with what to do, his grim facial expression reveals his inward struggle. Then an opportunity arises as he serves wine before the king (2:1).

2:1–3 The King's Concern
As a cupbearer to the king, Nehemiah holds the crucial task of overseeing the king's daily physical welfare, especially his food and drink. As a trusted

subordinate and competent steward, Nehemiah cannot leave his job without permission from the king. Nehemiah is waiting for the right time to present his request for a leave of absence, ideally during a felicitous occasion when the king might be in a generous mood (see Gen 40:20; Esth 5:6; Mark 6:21–25).

Then in the month of Nisan, during the twentieth year of King Artaxerxes, Nehemiah brings wine before the king. "Why does your face look so sad when you are not ill?" the king asks (2:2). The king's concern disturbs Nehemiah, because a cupbearer is expected to be jolly before the king. Nehemiah's sorrow might be interpreted as a disobedient or defiant act that could endanger his life. Since the cupbearer of the previous king stirred up trouble in an assassination attempt, this king is mindful about the condition and welfare of his cupbearer. Hence, Nehemiah expresses fear at this simple greeting from the king (2:3).

Nehemiah's sorrow may have come from his long devotion in praying and fasting on behalf of his forlorn country. Praying and fasting are post-exilic acts of spiritual piety. Indeed, there is an interval of four months between Kislev (1:1) and Nisan (2:1).[1] The Scripture, however, is not specific on this matter. Another interpretation sees Nehemiah's sorrow as a reflection of his inward struggle. On one hand, he urgently wants to return to Jerusalem to rebuild its ruined wall and burned gates. On the other hand, he has to proceed with his prescribed duties as a cupbearer for the king. This inner struggle burns inside him for four months and then becomes outwardly manifest in his countenance, a moment that unexpectedly becomes a timely occasion to present his desire before the king.

"May the king live forever!" Nehemiah responds to the king's question with the traditional blessing for longevity of life (2:3). Longevity is a wish of many people, especially a Persian king.[2] This greeting is expected of Nehemiah and was a common greeting among the Jews. For the Jews, life is the embodiment of God's blessing.[3] Living in the presence of God allows us to enjoy all the blessings from him.

Then Nehemiah tells the king that he is sad because the city where his ancestors are buried lies in ruins and its gates have been destroyed by fire. Rather than identifying Jerusalem by name, Nehemiah describes it as his ancestral city in order to avoid needless tension for the Persian king, who is the legitimate

---

1. See the Hebrew calendar.
2. In ancient Near Eastern royal hymns and prayers, longevity of life is the primary wish. See Joseph Too Shao, *A Study of Akkadian Royal Hymns and Prayers*, Jian Dao Dissertation Series 10, Bible and Literature 7 (Hong Kong: Alliance Bible Seminary, 2002), 20–37.
3. John 10:10.

ruler over Jerusalem. Nehemiah would certainly know about the letter that had arrived from the enemies of Israel (Ezra 4:1), which labeled Jerusalem as a "rebellious and wicked city" (Ezra 4:12) and identified the walls as symbols of the king's dishonor (Ezra 4:12–13, 16), as well as Artaxerxes's decree to stop the reconstruction in Jerusalem (Ezra 4:17–22). Any reference to Jerusalem would invoke harsh displeasure from Artaxerxes, and thus Nehemiah intentionally avoids the political bearing of his request.

By alluding to his ancestral city, Nehemiah makes a personal appeal for the king's mercy. Likewise, he mentions the scorched gates without specifying their locality. Nehemiah's reply portrays him as someone who is sensitive to the futile and forlorn state of the burial grounds of his forefathers. Nehemiah demonstrates sagacity by making a personal rather than political appeal for sympathy about his family's affairs. When the king asks about the reason for his sorrow, he answers transparently but prudently, for the king certainly knows about Nehemiah's ancestry without his mentioning it.

When my mother was about to die, I rushed home from my post-graduate studies in Cincinnati, Ohio, to be by her side and care for her needs, along with my father and siblings. During her last few days on the earth, she was sometimes fully conscious and other times she was in a coma. One day, my Dad and I had to leave the hospital to make arrangements for her impending death. That very day, she suddenly woke up and asked me where I was going with my father. I had to phrase my answer carefully, telling her the truth about going out with my Dad, but avoiding the fact that we were making plans for her funeral. She actually knew what we would be doing, but by not revealing our intentions explicitly, we avoided the unpleasantness of having her listen to the details about her impending burial.

2:4–10 The King's Consideration

Nehemiah prays to the Lord for the opportunity to present his case before the king, stating his wishes in minute detail. First, he prays for wisdom about how to answer the king (2:4). Second, at the king's request, he provides a time frame for his rebuilding project (2:5–6). Third, he presents his explicit needs (2:7–8) to the king, asking for letters to the neighboring governors that will allow him to travel smoothly in his journey to Judah (2:7) and also for a letter to the keeper of the royal forest so that he can access the materials needed to rebuild the city wall as well as his house (2:8a). Fourth, he praises God by acknowledging his grace (2:8a–9).

Before Nehemiah presents his plan to the king, he prays to the God of heaven (2:4), confidently committing his conversation with the king to God. Previously, Nehemiah prayed to be successful before the king. Now that an opportunity has arisen, he immediately commits the matter to God. Thus Nehemiah both prays for his plans and plans as he prays. Praying and planning are not mutually exclusive. One management principle states that if one fails to plan, one plans to fail. As a conscientious leader, he is both a man of prayer and also an effective planner.

In response to the king's second question (2:4), Nehemiah discloses his ancestral burial ground as "the city in Judah" (2:5; compare 2:3). Again, Nehemiah avoids using the name Jerusalem, but he does allude to it, since Jerusalem is, of course, the city of Judah. Nehemiah asks the king for the favor of being sent to Judah as a royal emissary so that he can rebuild it. During those days, Artaxerxes, as well as other Persian kings, regularly sent royal envoys to visit their satraps for military and political reasons.[4] To protect against the advances of Egypt and Greece, a strong ally such as Judah could be relied upon to guard the Persian border. Thus Nehemiah's desire to serve the king as a royal envoy is in line with Persian policies.

In response to the king's third question about Nehemiah's schedule, Nehemiah sets the timeframe for completing his mission, signifying his understanding of the king's benevolence. This question is practical, since Nehemiah will need to leave his post as cupbearer and later return to resume his royal task. As a cupbearer, Nehemiah shows conscientious time management skills, which can be confirmed by his record of building the wall in fifty-two days (6:15).

The presence of the queen during this dialogue between Nehemiah and the king could be interpreted in two ways (2:6). The first interpretation argues that only eunuchs are allowed in the presence of the queen, which proves that Nehemiah is a eunuch. However, in the book of Esther (another Persian environment), Haman, the chief minister, also has access to the queen (Esth 7:8), and he is most certainly not a eunuch (Esth 5:10; 9:13). Furthermore, even though LXX^{B,S} identifies Nehemiah as a "eunuch," LXX^A indicates that this is a scribal error for "cupbearer." Although some interpreters theorize that all cupbearers were eunuchs, not all cupbearers were eunuchs during this period.[5] Finally, if Nehemiah were a eunuch, he would not be respected as a Jewish

---

4. K. Hoglund, *Archaemenid Imperial Administration in Syria-Palestine and the Mission of Ezra and Nehemiah*, SBLDS 124 (Atlanta: Scholars Press, 1992); J. Berquist, *Judaism in Persia's Shadow: A Social and Historical Approach* (Minneapolis: Fortress Press, 1995), 105–120.
5. Edwin M. Yamauchi, "Was Nehemiah the Cupbearer a Eunuch?" *ZAW* 92 (1980): 132–142.

leader (in view of Deut 23:2), and his enemies would definitely discredit him, both inside and outside his community. Thus the idea that Nehemiah is a eunuch must be discarded.

The second interpretation is that the presence of the queen signifies the rapport Nehemiah has with the royal family. Because of his fidelity and loyalty, Nehemiah is permitted to appear while the queen is seated beside the king. Because of the presence of the queen, Nehemiah can present his case in a more intimate setting, apart from any royal officials who might be opposed to his proposal. This context depicts the king's confidence in Nehemiah and his closeness to the royal family.

After responding to the king's question about the timeframe for his journey, Nehemiah relates his need for introductory letters to neighboring governors for his safe passage (2:7) and to Asaph, the keeper of the king's forest, for the necessary materials to rebuild the city gates, wall and his own residence (2:8). As a cupbearer serving the king at the court, Nehemiah knows that traveling includes lots of hassles. With imperial letters endorsing his trip, he will receive royal treatment as the king's envoy, traveling before several Persian satraps with ease and protection. Nehemiah must have researched the Persian imperial systems of governance in order to know that Asaph is in charge of the king's forest. His request for materials shows his management skills in knowing what he will need to make the necessary repairs to the city gates and wall. The request for materials for his own residence may be for his immediate and practical need to have a place to stay in Jerusalem, or it may suggest that he is anticipating a longer stay in Jerusalem.

The king grants all of Nehemiah's requests because God's gracious hand is upon him (2:8). God's hand symbolizes power because it is the instrument of his saving acts of deliverance for his people (Exod 13:3, 14, 16; Deut 6:21; Josh 4:24). Just as the king's hand demonstrates royal liberality in giving bounty (1 Kgs 10:13; Esth 1:7; 2:18), God's "gracious hand" signifies his overflowing blessings (Ezra 7:6, 28; 8:31). The king even sends a military escort to accompany Nehemiah to Jerusalem (2:9). Any task imprinted with God's approval and prompting will never lack God's plenteous supplies.

Two enemies, Sanballat the Horonite and Tobiah the Ammonite, are displeased with Nehemiah's plans for the Israelites (2:10). Their unhappiness may be related to their own welfare, for Sanballat is the governor of Samaria, and Tobiah works closely with him. Without a wall surrounding Jerusalem, they can easily influence the Israelites, and they also may have many conniving friends inside Jerusalem (6:17–19; 13:8).

2:11–20 NEHEMIAH'S PLAN TO INSPECT THE WALL

The key to the historic rebuilding commences with observation. Without telling anyone else, Nehemiah, along with a few trusted men, personally inspects the ruins (2:11–12, 16) before challenging the people to join the rebuilding project (2:13–16).

2:11–16 The Nocturnal Visit

After a long journey to Jerusalem, Nehemiah rests for three days. Then he makes a secret, nocturnal visit to the ruined site to inspect the damage without raising suspicion or causing any disturbance (2:12, 16). By looking carefully at the ruined city wall and the scorched city gates, he will be in a better position to conceptualize a strategic rebuilding plan and then challenge others to get involved. His counter-clockwise inspection starts and ends at the Valley Gate (2:13, 15) as he moves around to discern which portions of the wall need the most urgent repair. The detailed account of his survey of the wall reflects his interest in Jerusalem's topography (2:13–15; see also 12:31–39). As the faithful men who accompany him (2:11) observe quietly, they become more convinced of the value of the project. This trustworthy team will work closely with him, and he needs their loyalty and support (see also 4:16, 23; 5:10, 14).

Nehemiah lists the people in Jerusalem who will eventually join him in the rebuilding mission: Jews, priests, nobles, officials, and other laborers (2:16). The "Jews" are the men of Judah who have returned from exile. Prior to the exilic period, they are living in Judah (2 Kgs 16:6; 25:25; Jer 32:12). In the book of Nehemiah, a "Judahite" refers to an individual person (4:10); "house of Judah" denotes ethnicity (4:16); "all Judah" signifies corporate entity (13:12); "the sons of Judah" indicates their blood lineage (13:16). During the post-exilic era, the Benjamites are integrated into the tribe of Judah (see 11:7–9). The "priests" are the ecclesiastical persons who lead the returnees in worship. The "nobles" are a special group within Jewish society who receive political and economic privileges (6:17; Eccl 10:17). The "officials" are the administrators and leaders of the Jews (4:14, 19; 5:7, 17; 7:5; Ezra 9:2).

2:17–20 The Challenge

Because Nehemiah can be trusted by his superior, King Artaxerxes, he gains the trust of his followers. After Nehemiah's nocturnal visit to the wall, he challenges the people to commit to the rebuilding project. By shifting his passion into persuasion, he creates interest and generates action. First, he acknowledges their troublesome situation (2:17a). Second, he accepts their shame (2:17b).

Third, he affirms the grace of God (2:18a). Fourth, he challenges them to start the rebuilding project (2:18b).

Nehemiah presents the dilemma to the people in a clear and truthful manner: "You see the trouble we are in: Jerusalem lies in ruins, and its gates have been burned with fire. Come, let us rebuild the wall of Jerusalem, and we will no longer be in disgrace" (2:17). At the same time, he inspires hope as he seeks to harness group support for the rebuilding project. Notice how carefully and sincerely he invites his audience to sense ownership of the project by using the pronouns "you," "we," and "us." This inviting tone encourages listeners to feel privileged to join in the work in order to remove the disgrace that will affect all of them if it is left unattended. Thus Nehemiah's concern becomes their concern, too. His underlying theme is: We can do it! We can work together successfully.

Nehemiah also shares with his audience the divine grace that he has experienced from God, which he describes as "the gracious hand of my God on me" (2:18). He also adds "what the king had said to me," attesting to God's confirmation of divine grace upon grace. The project is a sure success because it has all the affirmative signals from both heaven and earth.

Just as Nehemiah launches this call for followers, opposing parties appear to dishearten the people. These enemies are Sanballat the Horonite, Tobiah the Ammonite official, and Geshem the Arab (2:19), all neighboring inhabitants who live within the city. Their sharp accusations hinder the project before it even begins: "What is this you are doing? . . . Are you rebelling against the king?" (2:19).

Nevertheless, Nehemiah remains calm, and his strong conviction rebuts them: "The God of heaven will give us success. We his servants will start rebuilding" (2:20). Because Nehemiah and his followers are God's servants, their success is sure, but their enemies shall have no share or part in this historic work.

When the Biblical Seminary of the Philippines was about to rebuild its campus, there were a lot of financial, logistical, and personal problems that made this task seem impossible. The rebuilding process began when a portion of our campus walls broke down. The campus is situated lower than the street levels in the area, and so all the rain water naturally flows down to our campus, and the accumulated flood water caused the ground to loosen against the wall.

With very limited funding, our seminary could not afford to build a new wall. Nevertheless, we made a survey of the debris in faith, and as we quietly examined the extent of the ruins, we realized that the walls had fallen because our neighbors had blocked the passage of the drainage. Immediately, we rallied our Board members and friends to pray. Our neighbors tried every means to frustrate the rebuilding project, even trying to keep the repairmen from working on the site. They thought that we would have other motives for the rebuilding of the wall. After our thorough inspection of the ruined walls, however, we finally convinced our neighbors that danger was looming for them as well. God's gracious hand remained upon the seminary throughout the completion of this repair project. For friendship with our neighbors, we created another passage way for the rain water.

Then an even greater challenge awaited us when we started an enormous and expensive project to rebuild our campus. The first phase of the campus development was to set up a new 150-student dormitory, beginning the work at the height of the Asian economic crisis in 1997. This task was completed in March 1998. The second phase began in 2000, when we tackled the construction of the administrative building, along with a chapel and classrooms. This work was completed in 2001. The last phase was to complete another wing of the student dormitory. This work was completed in May 2006. Throughout each phase of rebuilding, God's gracious hand carried us through unforeseeable circumstances and faith-stretching experiences. Indeed, we experienced his faithfulness just in time for the fiftieth anniversary celebration of the founding of our university. The rebuilding of the campus is a testament to God's gracious hand!

TRUE SELF

As a cupbearer of King Artaxerxes, Nehemiah has inner strength. He is not afraid to state the reason for his sad countenance, and he confidently tells the king his heart's desire when the opportune time comes. Using a psychological term, his *true self* is intact, which means he is authentic inside and out, able to express his inner convictions through his outer conduct. Said another way, Nehemiah's beliefs and behavior closely correspond with his identity.[1] Because of the king's trust, he is able to return to Jerusalem.

Because of Nehemiah's training as a cupbearer, he can excel in his duty and win the trust of the king. His readiness to give a timeline suggests that he can envision his mission from beginning to completion. His ability to complete his mission is connected with his sense of well-being.

When Nehemiah reaches Jerusalem, he spends time alone, quietly inspecting the wall, without exposing his mission publicly (2:12, 16). Someone who is psychologically healthy does not need to appeal to the public before embracing the importance of the task ahead. As a leader of his team, he only has a few men working with him, but unity of vision is more significant than numbers. Nehemiah intentionally builds up this inner circle by modeling personal watchfulness.

Rosa Ching Shao

---

1. Robert S. Feldman, *Social Psychology* (Upper Saddle, NJ: Prentice Hall, 2001), 114.

Distribution of People at the Wall
(Nehemiah 3)

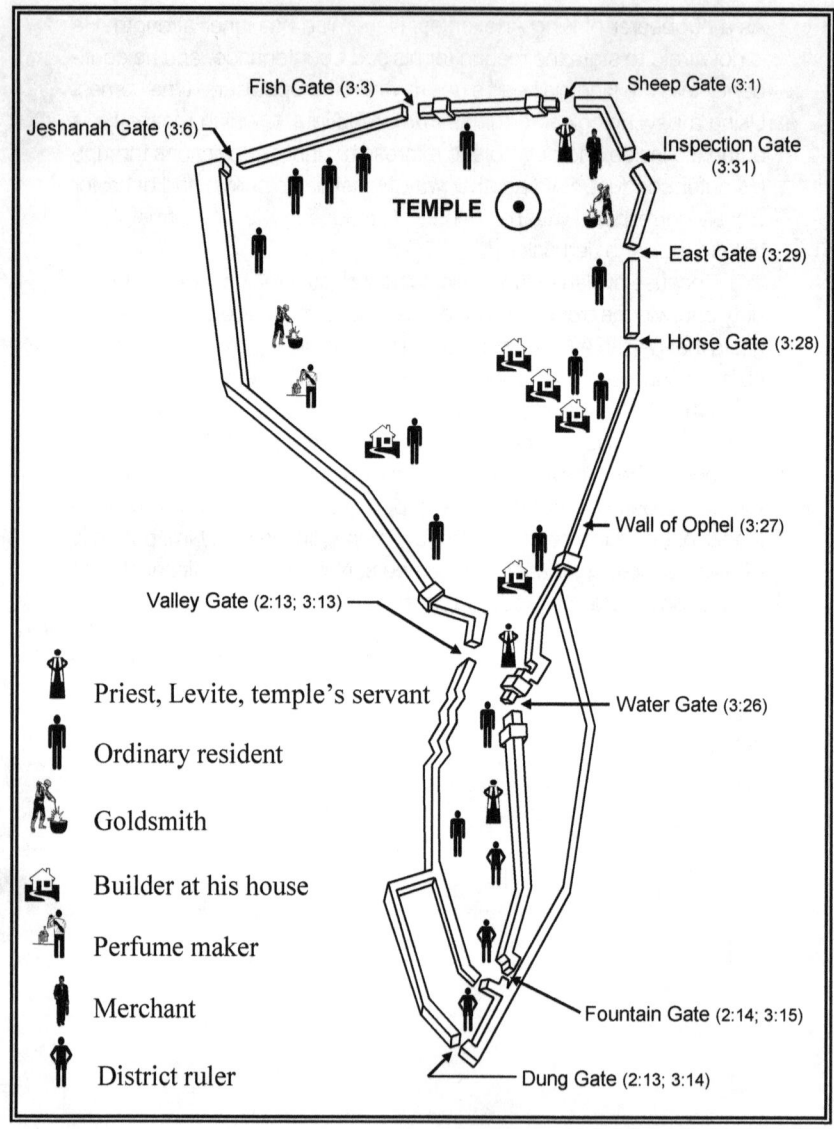

NEHEMIAH 3:1–32

WORKING TOGETHER

A church in Bandung, Indonesia, just celebrated its eightieth anniversary. The program for the celebration listed many momentous years of God's grace in the church's history. At one point in the service, the whole congregation paused quietly for five minutes to remember and thank God for those who had served the church in years prior. Though names were not publicly mentioned, it was a good opportunity to acknowledge many unsung heroes in the congregation. Nehemiah 3 is about the names of those who are involved in rebuilding the wall. The list includes the ancestors of some builders, showing the continuity of generations that are involved in serving the welfare of the returned community.

Having completed the strategic planning and preparation for the rebuilding (2:18–20), Nehemiah distributes the work among the people. This chapter summarizes the rebuilding process, including lists of names and the distribution of various tasks. Chapters 4 and 6 describe the details of the restoration process, and Nehemiah 7:1–3 records the final hanging of the doors. Nehemiah is behind the whole strategy. Because of his personal survey of the dismal state of the wall, he is able to divide the work into clear tasks and assign different groups of people to work alongside each other on various sections. Nehemiah's inner group of supporters is comprised of his brothers, servants, and guards (see 4:23). Though this small core group serves with him, he challenges many others to participate in the project so that they will own it. Except for a few nobles who do not want to get involved, everyone participates in the rebuilding of wall, from the priests to the leaders in the community (3:5).

Nehemiah assigns forty-two different sections of work to the people. His assignments move section by section around the wall in a counter-clockwise direction, beginning and ending at the Sheep Gate (3:1, 32), with each of the other gates serving as markers for the rebuilding project: the Fish Gate (3:3), the Jeshanah Gate (3:6), the Valley Gate (3:13), the Dung Gate (3:14), the Fountain Gate (3:15), the Water Gate (3:26), the Horse Gate (3:28), the East Gate (3:29), and the Inspection Gate (3:31).

This list bears the name of each builder for a particular section and reflects Nehemiah's organizational abilities as well as the multi-faceted character of the social and historical world of post-exilic Israel. Though not a genealogical record, the names include both the individual builders as well as the names of each builder's father and sometimes grandfather, reflecting the concept of family in ancient Israel. The social world of ancient Israel is reflected in the list of various professions, which includes cultic officials (3:1, 17, 22, 26, 28), political leaders (3:9, 12, 14–19), and various business fields, such as goldsmiths, perfume makers, and merchants (3:8, 32). Based on the usage of the word "ruler," the list identifies five administrative centers: Jerusalem (3:12), Beth-hakkerem (3:14), Mizpah (3:15), Beth-zur (3:16), and Keilah (3:17).

The work is divided according to various rebuilding tasks. Some are in charge of rebuilding the gate and setting the doors, bolts, and bars in place (3:1, 3, 6, 13, 14). Others roof the gate (3:15). The majority of builders are scattered along different sections of the wall, with some assigned to make repairs near their houses (3:10, 22, 28, 29).

This chapter is divided into two sections, with the first (vv. 1–15) joined by the repetition of the prepositional phrase *al-yad* (literally, "at [his] hand"), and the second (vv. 16–32) joined by the repetition of the preposition *aharav* ("after him"). Apart from their literary usage, both phrases reflect Nehemiah's good arrangement and planning.

3:1–6 NORTHERN WALL

The rebuilding commences with the most important area of Jerusalem: the vicinity of the northern wall, where the temple and palace are located. This area is the center of faith, culture, and business. In the Israelite history, the northern area is the main target for invaders. If enemies gain access through the northern wall, the destruction of Jerusalem is inevitable.

Thus the rebuilding starts and ends with the Sheep Gate (3:1, 32). Eliashib, the high priest, leads his fellow priests in this project. Eliashib is the grandson of Joshua (the high priest during the time of Zerubbabel) and the son of Joiakim (12:10). Eliashib and his fellow priests begin by dedicating the Sheep Gate before setting its doors in place. The dedication is significant, because it speaks of thanking and trusting God as the provider for and completer of the project. The dedication also reflects their declaration that the rebuilding is a sacred venture.

The "men of Jericho," along with the "men of Tekoa" and "men from Gibeon and Mizpah," are from the neighboring towns of Jerusalem (3:2, 5, 7). There are two probable reasons that commonplace rather than proper names are given in this list of participants. First, some men remain anonymous to the recorder. Second, commonplace names emphasize the participation of men from neighboring areas around Jerusalem. The rebuilding project is not only of interest to people in Jerusalem, but to all the Israelites.[1]

Meremoth, a descendant of Uriah and Hakkoz (3:3), is one of three builders to restore two portions of the wall (3:24). During the first return with Zerubbabel, Hakkoz was one of the three priests who could not locate his ancestry and therefore could not serve as priest (7:63). Later, during the time of the second returnees, Ezra weighs silver in the temple to Meremoth, "son of Uriah, the priest" (Ezra 8:33). Thus Uriah, the son of the undocumented Hakkoz, is given the title of "priest" and an important position in the temple. This significant detail suggests that the priestly family of Hakkoz is re-established during the time of Ezra and Nehemiah (perhaps along with other priestly families). In the post-exilic era, more priests are needed for right worship, and so certain priestly families can now legitimately join this remarkable work. The other two builders are Meshullum (3:4, 30) and Binnui (3:18, 24). Likewise, the men of Tekoa repair two portions (3:5, 27).

The nobles of Tekoa are the only group mentioned who do not want to participate in the rebuilding project (3:5). In contrast to their noblemen, the ordinary men of Tekoa appear to show enthusiasm for the project. They are given two sections of the wall and they work diligently (3:27).

Nehemiah's good planning links each worker to the next, as reflected in the use of "next to him/them" (3:4, 7, 10, etc.). The sense of unity in fulfilling a common task motivates each worker to finish the assigned task.

3:7–14 WESTERN WALL

This section records the repairs on the western wall. Team members are identified by ancestral line and occupation, including goldsmiths, perfume-makers (3:8), two rulers of half-districts of Jerusalem (3:9, 12), and other political officials (3:14–19). Shallum's daughters assist their father with repairing a section (3:12). They are the only women named in the record.

Most of the builders work on a designated portion next to each other. Jedaiah repairs a section opposite his house (3:10). Assigning some people sections near their own residences shows that the project is not only relevant to the community at large, but to the individual builders themselves. These

---

1. Whereas Chronicles prefers to refer to the participants as "all Israelites" as a sign of unity (1 Chr 11:3; 13:5), the name list of the first returnees in Ezra-Nehemiah registers place names to show that people from many different regions participate in the project.

assignments reflect Nehemiah's creativity in linking the significance of the work with the people so that they will work even harder and more effectively.

This section concludes with the only measurement used in the record to describe the extent of the work: "five hundred yards" (3:13). Since Nehemiah began his inspection of the ruined wall at the Valley Gate (2:13, 15), this record of five hundred yards reflects the broken portions that need special attention.

3:15–32 EASTERN WALL

Nehemiah recruits a lot of rulers to participate in the rebuilding project, but he does not assign identical tasks for all the rulers. While some are assigned to repair the wall (3:9, 12, 16–19), others are in charge of setting the doors with their bolts and bars in place (3:14–15). Doors are important because they guard the entrance to the city, and so this work needs to be assigned to dependable people. Yet the setting of doors is also assigned to priests and other people (3:1, 3, 6, 13), which suggests that the setting of the doors and the rebuilding of the wall are equally important. Shallum, the ruler from the district of Mizpah, participates by repairing the wall and then setting the door (3:15). Hashabiah, the ruler of the half-district of Keilah, repairs his district (3:17). Every task is vital. Everyone should follow the given orders and fulfill the assigned duties.

This section describes topographical details that correspond with the section that Nehemiah inspects during his nocturnal visit (2:14). Because of Nehemiah's familiarity with this portion of the wall, he records the assigned tasks for this area with meticulous descriptions. Starting with the Fountain Gate, the ruler Shullun is responsible for repairing the Fountain Gate by roofing it and setting its doors and bars as well as repairing the wall by the Pool of Siloam and the steps going down from the City of David (3:15). These topographical details reveal that Shullun has to do a lot of work. Nehemiah (not related to Nehemiah, the governor and son of Hacaliah) is responsible for repairing a point opposite the tombs of David as far as the artificial pool and the House of the Heroes (3:16).

The next section is near the residences of the Levites and priests, so it is logical for them to repair this portion of the wall. The Levites are responsible for rebuilding the wall near their quarters (3:17). Eliashib, the high priest, is responsible for repairing the portion in front of his house (3:21). Several other builders also work near their residences, motivating them to be involved (3:23, 30).

ASIAN FAMILY LEADERSHIP

Hanani, Nehemiah's brother, ignites Nehemiah's vision with his report about the state of the wall, motivating Nehemiah to spearhead the rebuilding project (Neh 1:2). From an Asian perspective, Hanani is reporting to the family leader, either the head of the family, an elder brother, or someone who is in a better position, to "fix" the problem. In a hierarchical culture, this is known as the "respect" principle, where the top person in the family or the clan is the prime mover. Examining the text from this Asian perspective, Hanani is not merely reporting a problem, but seeking Nehemiah's help.

Formation before Action

The four months that Nehemiah spends in prayer are normally treated as a spiritual period of waiting upon the Lord, but they can also be interpreted as a period for Nehemiah's character formation before he takes action (Neh 1:1; 2:1). The Chinese idiom *xiu xin yang xing* (修心養性) literally means "cultivate the heart and nurture the character." It speaks of cultivating one's moral and spiritual character. A famous Chinese idiomatic expression is "character formation comes first before leading a country and managing the world" (*xiu shen qi jia zhi guo ping tian xia*, 修身齊家治國平天下). Nehemiah does not just jump in, even though he has an urgent desire to ask God for success (Neh 1:11). Instead, he prays and waits for four months, a period of time that forms his character, prepares him spiritually, and focuses his passion and determination. This significant season of preparation ensures Nehemiah's success in leading the community in the formidable task of rebuilding the wall.

Community Involvement

In contrast to the Western style of leadership, which is to hire experts and rely on them to do the job, the Asian style of leadership prefers to involve everyone in the project. Total involvement means that everyone benefits from the results, which heightens the sense of ownership by all participants. Community development involves everyone (Neh 3:1–32). In the rebuilding project, three people seem to do more than any others: Meremoth (Neh 3:4, 21), Meshullam (3:4, 30), and Binnui (3:17, 24).

In the family style of business in Asia, members of the immediate and extended family all benefit from the business. Every member has to be involved even though some will always do more than others. Since all are involved in the family business, everyone in the family or clan is given the privilege of food and other related benefits, which is referred to as *da guo fan* (大鍋飯), or "communal feeding." This means that all members of the family can get assistance from the family business. A friend related that in the early 1950s in Manila, the Chinese understanding of the word "company" literally meant eating food together during noontime. For the company that his dad runs, it also includes the benefit of a monthly free haircut. Regular meals with extended family bring the family closer together.

Rosa Ching Shao

NEHEMIAH 4:1–23

FACING EXTERNAL OPPOSITION

Any significant work of God usually triggers opposition from the evil one. When a church in China wanted to build a sanctuary on a vacant lot they had bought, they faced opposition from top-level city officials. The pastor invited members of the church to gather around the vacant lot to pray. Though it took time, the hostile city official was replaced by someone who eventually granted the church a building permit. Today, a big sanctuary on the site attests to God's power in removing any hindrance to his work.

Nehemiah 4 is about the external opposition that Nehemiah faces when he returns with the people of God to seek the welfare of Jerusalem (2:10, 19). Every time God's people move forward in the rebuilding project, they face hostilities from their enemies. Upon learning about the commencement of the rebuilding project, Sanballat and his friends initiate opposition against Nehemiah and the builders. Once the wall reaches half its height, they threaten even more serious attacks to try to intimidate Nehemiah and the builders. Confident and secure in his mission, Nehemiah counteracts every hostile tactic with steadfast conviction in God and a suitable solution to motivate, encourage, and protect the builders.

Upon hearing what Nehemiah is doing for the wall, Sanballat and his associates hurl innuendos against the builders (4:1, 7, 15; compare 2:10, 19).[1] Serving as the governor of Samaria, Sanballat's reaction against Nehemiah comes naturally, since he and his cohort think they can control Jerusalem (2:10, 19). Nehemiah, on the other hand, asks God to hear his prayer promptly and gets his own people to hear his instructions clearly (4:4, 14, 19–20, 22). Nehemiah prays and implements his plans for the people as their enemies hurl opposing tactics at them. Nehemiah's confident prayers to God and his men's cautious surveillance enable them to continue with the rebuilding project (4:4–6, 9–10). God himself fights for them and with them to accomplish his purposes.

The enemies use all means to stop the rebuilding efforts of the people, beginning with the mockery of Sanballat and Tobiah (4:1–6), followed by

---

1. The English text that follows the LXX differs from the Hebrew text. In the MT, the English translation of Nehemiah 4:1–6 is 3:33–38.

the mobbing plot of Sanballat and company (4:7–9), and concluding with the murderous attack (4:10–12). Nehemiah, however, counters each of the intensifying clashes and leads the people by facing the challenges, trusting God through prayer (4:9), remembering God's greatness (4:14), and working hard (4:9, 13). Though the enemies eventually abort their attack (4:15), Nehemiah guides the people to be watchful and continue their hard work (4:16–23).

4:1–6 MOCKERY OF SANBALLAT AND TOBIAH

When Sanballat and Tobiah see that the work on the wall has started, they ridicule Nehemiah and his builders for their so-called insignificant project (4:1; compare 2:10) in an attempt to dampen their will. To instigate resistance to the rebuilding, Sanballat incites his accomplices and the military troops that support him as governor to make a collective effort to undermine the builders. Nehemiah counters their ridicule (4:1–3) with prayer (4:4–5) and by praising his builders (4:6).

4:1–3 Pressure through Ridicule

The first round of sarcastic intimidation consists of five questions that psychologically taunt the Jews. Sanballat's first question, "What are those feeble Jews doing?" attacks the character of the Jews. The word "feeble" is used here in the sense of "frail," "withered," "powerless," and "impotent" (1 Sam 2:5; Jer 15:9). His second question, "Will they restore their wall?" undermines the ability and competence of the builders. Normally, professional masons are hired to build lasting city walls with dressed stones. How could the Jews, as a group of amateurs, be able to build the wall? The third question, "Will they offer sacrifices?" scornfully challenges their religious motives. Sanballat knows that offering sacrifices will unite the Jews over the long haul and designate the rebuilding as a sacrosanct project that is even bigger than the rebuilding of the altar. His fourth question, "Will they finish in a day?" derides the energy of the builders and mocks their ability to finish the enormous project given their limited strength and power. His final question, "Will they bring the stones back to life?" questions their materials and methods. How could they build a strong wall with broken, chipped, and damaged stones from the rubbish heaps of Jerusalem? Although the stones are limestone, fire has damaged them and caused them to crack and disintegrate. Such materials are worthless and therefore lifeless. The natural answers to all five questions, of course, are damaging criticisms. The Jews cannot do it! The ridicule indicates that they have not counted the costs, and with their insufficient resources, they should think twice about their plan.

Incited by Sanballat's scornful mockery, Tobiah jeers that even a small animal, such as a fox, can break the wall, publicly announcing that the wall they are building is weak. Tobiah's ruthless insult engenders disdain for Nehemiah's project.

4:4–5 Plea for Divine Intervention

Upon hearing the taunting words of Sanballat and Tobiah, Nehemiah prays to God to intervene against his enemies. Though his prayer may seem reprehensibly violent to the modern reader, as do the "imprecatory Psalms" (e.g. Ps 79:12; 109:6–20; Jer 18:21–23), it is appropriate given the context. As a prayer of confidence, Nehemiah's prayer consists of two elements. First, there is a sense of urgency, asking God to intervene on behalf of his people. Second, there is a sense of trusting God to fight for his people. Hence, it is a prayer of trust as Nehemiah commits his people's troubles to the Lord.

Nehemiah, just like any New Testament saint, expresses his frustration and anger to God. He neither commits any crimes against his enemies, nor hides his passions from God. His praying about their insults, guilt, and sins proves that he is an orthodox believer in the doctrine of righteousness and justice, which is in accord with the biblical faith (Gen 18:19; Ps 106:3).

How could the concept of Christian forgiveness toward loving one's enemies be reconciled with Nehemiah's blunt words? As Nehemiah is vividly identified as an OT saint, the easiest way to solve this query might be to appeal to the discontinuity between the Old and New Testaments. Some people associate New Testament believers, with their emphasis on "love" principles, as having higher moral values than Old Testament believers. The "love" principle first quoted by Jesus in the New Testament, however, is embedded in the holiness codes of Leviticus. This antecedent theology of "love" is first employed in Leviticus 19:18 before it is quoted in the New Testament (Luke 10:25–37; Rom 13:9; Gal 5:13–14). In other words, though there might be some discontinuity between the Old and New Testaments, the theme of "love" originates in the Old Testament.

Is it fitting for Nehemiah to view Sanballat's hostility as enmity toward God? Through the prophets Isaiah, Jeremiah, and Ezekiel, God makes it plain that Israel should be restored to its land. Thus any opposition to the restoration of Jerusalem comes from God's enemies. The restoration project is both God-approved and God-initiated, and so when the enemies despise the Jews and hurl insults at the builders, they are doing these things to God. Therefore Nehemiah's prayer is not a humanistic request that serves the builders, but rather a theocentric prayer that appeals to God's holiness and justice and asks for God's earnest rebuke and intervention. God's holiness and justice entail respect for his work and demand high standards from his people.

Nehemiah's prayer to turn the insults of Sanballat and Tobiah "back on their own heads" is a plea for God's intervention. When God changed the prophet Balaam's intention to curse the Israelites into a "blessing" for God's people, his curses were essentially returned to the Moabites (Num 23:11, 25; 24:10–11). This boomerang effect is a striking concept in the Old Testament (Zech 5:5–11), and the similar idea of "return to sender" is a New Testament principle. When Jesus sends out his seventy to every town and place, their "peace" greetings will be returned to them if the householders do not deserve the "peace" (Luke 10:5–6). Likewise, curses will be returned to the senders if the targeted recipients do not deserve the curse. Thus Nehemiah's request for divine intervention is a biblical principle. Prayer is an act of faith, anticipating God's timely intervention on behalf of his servants.

The notions of "cover up their guilt" and "blot out their sins" are the ideas behind the Old Testament sacrificial system. The sacrificial system covers up and blots out both the guilt and the sins of the worshiper with animal blood, thereby restoring proper relationship between the worshiper and his Lord. The sins are thus shielded and cleansed. The sacrificial animal, through the God-given sacrificial system, temporarily wipes away the sins of the people, looking forward to the sacrificial Lamb of God. By asking God not to cover up the guilt and sins of his enemies, Nehemiah is appealing to the concept of justice, which sees, exposes, and punishes the offenders. Let justice be served!

4:6 Praising the People

In Nehemiah's memoirs, the progress of the wall building project is credited to the wholehearted efforts of the people. This verse reflects Nehemiah's practicality as a leader. As a spiritual leader, he prays to God, appealing for justice on the people's behalf and expressing their dependence on God. Nehemiah's prayer helps to sustain the people's efforts in proceeding with the project amidst destructive opposition. As a project manager, Nehemiah diligently executes his building plans. A diligent heart, as the wellspring of life, is needed to see the project through to completion (Prov 4:23), and so Nehemiah acknowledges the efforts exerted by the builders as they work with all their hearts. Because the builders know that they are building for God's glory, the wall soon reaches half its height.

4:7–9 PLOT OF SANBALLAT AND COMPANY

When ridicule does not halt the rebuilding project, the enemies resort to the threat of violence. They commence their plot when they hear about the progress on the wall, closing in upon the Jews from all sides of the surrounding geographical regions. Aside from Sanballat and Tobiah, the Ammonites from the east of Judah, the Ashdodites from the west of Judah, and the Arabs from the southeast region are added to the list of enemies. Previously, the attack comes from individual political leaders, now groups of people are engaged (4:7; compare 2:10, 19; 4:1, 3).

Nehemiah thwarts the violent scheme with earnest prayer to God (4:9). God is not only Nehemiah's personal God who blesses him ("my" God, 2:8, 18), but he is also the God of the builders ("our" God, 4:4, 9). Along with prayer, Nehemiah assigns a guard to watch vigilantly day and night to protect the builders from harm. Rather than worrying about the threat of violence from Sanballat, his associates, and his army, Nehemiah trusts that God is watching over the builders day and night, and then he posts a guard to do the same (Ps 121).

4:10–14 THWARTING THE DEATH THREAT

The third round of attack adds violent intensity to the first and second rounds of opposition. The mocking words of a troubling mob discourage, distress, and dishearten the builders (4:10–12). Nevertheless, Nehemiah confronts the problems and confesses faith in their great and awesome God (4:13–14).

4:10–13 Family Cohesiveness

The exhausted laborers express their dismay over the workload. The first statement about losing energy speaks of an inability to sustain the long duration of work (4:10). The people are about to quit. The task of rebuilding is overwhelming, and their energy level is dwindling. The second statement about there being so much rubble reflects the people's view that they are working with insignificant debris and so lack the motivation to finish the task (4:10). There seems to be no feasible end to their present task. This discouragement is a killer and spreads like fire. The more they become overwhelmed by their difficulties, the more convinced they become that they cannot finish the project.

Then a rumor about a looming assault spreads among the Jews, who do not bother to question the validity of the rumor (4:11–12). The goal of the enemies is to penetrate the Jews and put an end to the work. Those who live near the enemies express their fear of being attacked and ask for immediate assistance. "Ten times," as a round number, conveys the people's anxiety about the possible threat (4:12).

Just as with the first two rounds of attack, Nehemiah knows how to counteract this third violent blow. Previously, he posts a guard to deter the enemies, but now he stations the people in family groups "behind the lowest points of the wall at the exposed places" and arms them with weapons (4:13). This strategy has dual purposes. First, the enemies can observe that the people will fight for their lives. Second, they are organized by family groups, which publicly declares their unity.

As early as the era of Moses and Joshua, the family is the basic unit of the clan and tribe (see Exod 6:14; Josh 7:16–18). This grouping reminds each Israelite of the historical tradition of family cohesiveness. In the exodus event, they march according to their tribes, clans, and family units. Tribal confederacy and family interconnectedness are patterns of Israeli lifestyle based on their conviction that family members should support one another as a solid unit. Thus gathering in family units strengthens their commitment to the restoration project and heightens each family member's resolve to fight against their enemies with one accord, following the instructions of the family heads.

The purpose of distributing "swords, spears and bows" exemplifies the people's readiness to fight. This strategic display will not only convince the enemies about their seriousness, but also heighten the fighting spirit of the builders.

4:14 Confession of Faith

Nehemiah is a man of faith. He not only believes in the great and awesome God (1:5), but he also wants the people to be reminded of God's greatness. He speaks a short slogan, "remember the Lord, who is great and awesome," as a war cry to the nobles, officials, and the rest of the people (4:14). All are given responsibilities, but the nobles and officials are referenced before the people. The leaders are given the most challenging responsibilities foremost, and they are to serve as examples for the rest to emulate.

Nehemiah's war cry mirrors the "holy war" concept in the Bible. In the Red Sea event, the Israelites survive the pursuit of Pharaoh and the Egyptian armies because the Lord is their majestic and awesome warrior who works wonders (Exod 15:3, 11; Deut 7:21). Likewise, as they face the challenge of conquering Jericho and the Promised Land, the Lord fights on their behalf (Josh 6:1–27). This call to "remember" is not just a passive mental recital of historical facts, but a holistic and active reflection upon the great and awesome Almighty God who accomplishes his purposes throughout history and all time. Thus the joy of their war cry must be timed and carefully sounded with self-assured confidence (Josh 6:10, 16). Moreover, as Nehemiah shares his faith with the builders (4:14; compare 1:4), he invites them to affirm and attest to this great truth as well.

As a pragmatic leader, Nehemiah also exhorts the people to fight for their family members and their own homes.[2] This sagacious characterization draws the dispute close to their hearts, for they are even more willing to fight for their own brothers, sons, daughters, wives, and homes. Nehemiah's battle cry connects with the people's feelings of nationality, fidelity, loyalty, and chivalry for their country and God.

4:15–23 MOBILE WATCHFULNESS

When the various attacks fail to break down the rebuilding project, Nehemiah declares that the Lord has frustrated the plans of the enemies, and so all the people return to work. Again, Nehemiah gives glory to God and affirms the people for their faithful work.

As a pro-active leader, Nehemiah employs various strategies to complete the rebuilding project. First, he assigns clear job descriptions to his men and the builders (4:16–18). Second, he establishes a crucial line of communication by instructing a trumpeter to blow a warning blast when he wants to gather the people immediately (4:18). Third, he issues longer working hours in order to concentrate the building efforts and finish the project (4:21). Fourth, he cautions the people to stay in Jerusalem, serving as guards by night and workmen by day (4:21). This instruction also prevents the people from hearing the intimidation from their enemies. He further instructs his close associates and guards to dress properly and be ready for defense (4:22–23).

As the team leader, Nehemiah has developed an effective strategy for working with people. His operational team consists of associates and servants

---

2. For a discussion on the family system of God's people, see Christopher J. H. Wright, *Walking in the Ways of the Lord: The Ethical Authority of the Old Testament* (Leicester, UK: Apollos, 1995), 147–162.

who returned with him to Jerusalem (see 2:12), blood brothers (see 1:2), and Persian escorts who also returned with him to Jerusalem (2:9). These committed men all set good examples for the other builders. Nehemiah divides his men into two groups: the workers, who build the wall; and the guards, who are equipped with weapons of war to defend against any attack (4:16). Nehemiah also expects a sense of urgent readiness from his supporters, who never take off their work clothes and carry their weapons wherever they go (4:23).

Finally, Nehemiah presents a carefully planned war strategy (4:19–20) and devises clear signals for the nobles, officials, and people to follow. Upon hearing the sound of the trumpet, all the people will join him (4:19). He concludes his instructions to rally at the sound of the trumpet with a winning charge: "Our God will fight for us!" (4:20; compare Exod 14:14).

HANDLING HOSTILE SITUATIONS

As a task-oriented manager, Nehemiah is able to handle his situation with different strategies. What makes him so strong, sound, and steady? How can we train a group of new leaders to be able to lead the church in hostile environments? Sometimes speedy training courses are detrimental to the Lord's work because they do not develop character. When we push people into leadership positions too quickly, they often burn out and need healing or feel ill-prepared to handle complicated relational tasks.

How might we transfer Nehemiah's methodologies to our particular contexts? First, Nehemiah affirms those who do the work properly. The more he appreciates the people who are working with him, the more they are empowered to do the task. Learning to affirm others may sound easy, but it can be difficult. Yet we can start by giving affirmation and encouragement to members of our family and to our faith households at church and in the mission field.

Second, Nehemiah asks the people to form family groups, with each defending his own family members. How can we transfer the idea of being our "brother's keeper" into the modern family, which tends to have so many busy members going in so many different directions? In the midst of our busyness, family members who live in the same city can set a time each week or once a month for everyone to gather together for bonding time. Some families may prefer to use weekly prayer meetings to encourage one another in the Lord. When family members are really far apart geographically, which is the case with many families in Asia today, an annual family gathering could serve to bond people together. An active and conscientious member from each home might facilitate these homecoming events for the whole family. Family gatherings can help restore lonely members to loving arms and so hold them to our Lord. Food and laughter are great ways to heal miserable relationships. Let us use our families to glorify the great and awesome God, who will defend all of us!

Rosa Ching Shao

NEHEMIAH 5:1–19

CARING FOR THE POOR

A pastor wants to encourage his congregation to love one another, especially the poor in their midst, and so he shares this message regularly from the pulpit and Sunday school. Time passes, and he doesn't see any action in his church, so with his own money, he decides to start a ministry to feed the poor in the morning. By God's providence, a woman leader in the church catches the vision and mission. With the pastor's example of caring for the poor as a seed, a ministry of sharing Christian love with the poor eventually springs up in the city.

In contrast to the external attacks encountered in the rebuilding project, Nehemiah 5 focuses on the taxing internal troubles arising from within the Israelite community. The problem is that impoverished members in the community are facing food deficiencies, deteriorating mortgages, and a devastating harvest. Nehemiah leads the community to resolve the predicament by angrily challenging the leaders of the community (5:1–13). Then he sets a prudent example as the governor by sacrificially reducing his own privilege in order to share his portion with the poor (5:14–19). His generous model sets a precedent for his associates about how to concentrate on the wall while being guided by the principle of kindness toward their own people, especially the poor (5:15–16).

5:1–5 OUTCRY FROM THE POOR

The community is becoming discouraged by seemingly endless problems. The first problem relates to grain shortage. Under normal circumstances, children are regarded as an inheritance from God and a blessing to the family (Gen 1:28; Pss 127:3–5; 128:3), but with so many mouths to feed, the blessing of children has become a dilemma (5:2). Some people are even mortgaging their fields in exchange for food (5:3). The second problem is heavy taxes (5:4). When the people have to borrow money to pay taxes, they cannot earn basic living allowances for their survival. The third problem is slavery. Due to poverty and perhaps a failed harvest, the people are enslaving their sons and daughters. They feel as powerless as the laborers, farmers, and ordinary people who live in their midst.

There are several possibilities for this destitute situation in their midst. First, as they return from exile, the rebuilding of the wall triggers an age-old issue, which is that the skills that some have acquired have drawn people away from farming and grazing animals. Second, the famine aggravates the crisis (5:3). Those who can only survive by meeting their daily needs cannot cope with the sudden crisis due to the failed harvest. Third, the mortgaging of fields and the lending of money suggest that the skilled and rich in the community are taking advantage of the deprived and destitute.

The poor people cry out against their own Jewish brothers, appealing to the community principle about helping their own needy members. The antecedent theology of caring for one's brothers has its seed in the Genesis account, when the Lord asks Cain about his brother, Abel: "Where is your brother Abel?" (Gen 4:9). The brother's keeper concept is the key teaching here. Moreover, after the death of Jacob, Joseph expounds to his brothers about the concept of graceful brotherly love (Gen 50:20).

According to the Law, a Hebrew man can sell himself or his daughter into slavery (Exod 21:2, 7–11; Lev 25:39–41; Deut 15:12), but the Hebrew slaves have to be released on the seventh year. Moreover, any mortgaged homes, fields, and vineyards must be returned to the original owner on the Jubilee Year (Lev 25:10, 14–17, 25–27). Likewise, the eighth-century prophets urge the people to love God by loving the needy among them.[1] According to Amos, the needy, poor, and oppressed are the righteous, for they depend solely on the Lord to extend justice to them (Amos 2:6; 5:12).

The Covenant Code clearly codifies love for foreigners, widows, orphans, and the needy (Lev 22:21–27). Likewise, when the people come to the land to offer thanksgiving to the Lord, they have to share their blessings with the needy, such as the Levites, foreigners, orphans, and widows (Deut 26:13).[2] In caring for the poor and needy, the Israelite community should be gracious and generous (Deut 15:8, 11; compare 1 Tim 5:3–16). Such open-handed generosity brings freedom and joy to the givers as well as the receivers.

---

1. In addition to the "Commitment Model," "Ascetic Model," "Mystical Model," and "Contemplative Model" of prophetic spirituality, the "Community Model" lives out in the community. This type of spirituality is emphasized by the eighth-century prophets. Loving people in need is an expression of one's spirituality. See Joseph Too Shao, "Spirituality in the Prophetic Traditions: An Asian Perspective," in *Perjuangan Menatang Zaman* (*Kumpulan esai sebagai penghargaan kepada Pendeta Stephen Tong*, pada HUT ke-60, *Festschrift* for Stephen Tong), ed. Hendra G. Mulia (Jakarta: Reformed Institute Press, 2000), 137–139.

2. For a more detailed study, see R. Jewel Azyamah, "Theological and Ethical Reading of Deuteronomy 26: Loving God and Loving People," PhD Diss., (Asia Graduate School of Theology, 2017).

5:6–13 OUTRAGE AGAINST THE ABUSERS

When Nehemiah learns about the grievance, he angrily criticizes the nobles and officials. Then he calls a public assembly to explain the seriousness of the problem and to outline its solution (5:7, 13). If the people are called to redeem their brothers who have been sold to Gentiles, how can they buy and sell their own fellowmen and allow this vicious cycle of slavery to exist in their midst? The more the people sell their own brothers, the more Nehemiah and others will have to redeem them. Nehemiah wants the usury to stop, and so he encourages the people to fear God (5:9). Nehemiah's brothers and men lend the needy people money and grain without exacting heavy burdens or taking advantage of them. Nehemiah exhorts their benevolent examples in loving their brothers, living generously, and helping to solve the problem of poverty.

The antecedent theology for releasing debts for the sake of freedom is related to biblical sabbatical laws, which include a weekly Sabbath (one day of rest in seven), a Sabbatical year (one year of rest for the land), and the Jubilee Year (one year of rest for every fifty years). A central tenet of Israel's faith is that the land belongs to the Lord (Exod 15:13, 17). Divine ownership and divine gifts are associated with the tradition of the land. The people who are living in the allotted share of the Lord's land do not own it but are stewarding it as tenants (Lev 25:23).[3] All Israelites share the same status before the Lord. Therefore, during the Jubilee Year, the impoverished or indebted brothers in their midst should be cared for and restored to their original status of freedom from poverty, debt, and slavery.[4]

The group responds positively by taking an oath to give back what they have taken from their needy brothers without demanding anything in return (5:12). The biblical oath is a public promise before the Lord. By submitting themselves to the Lord, who cares for the impoverished, they show that they fear the Lord. This biblical fear of the Lord is not an abstract noun, but rather a concrete action verb.

In the Philippines, it is very common for the poor to borrow money from relatives and friends. When family loans are not available, the needy may borrow money from a lender in the community. The formula for such loans is termed "five-six," which means to borrow five portions, but pay six portions

---

3. Everyone is dependent on God. See Jonathan Burnside, *God, Justice, and Society: Aspects of Law and Legality in the Bible* (Oxford: Oxford University Press, 2011), 179–218.
4. See the discussion of Christopher J. H. Wright, "The Jubilee Year," in *Walking in the Ways of the Lord: The Ethical Authority of the Old Testament* (Leicester, UK: 1995), 197–212.

when returning the money. The borrower is usually at the mercy of the lender. For a short period of time, such as a week, a heavy 20 percent interest is charged to the borrower. Some Christian groups try to help the poor cope with this crisis by teaching them how to earn money. Instead of freely handing the poor some money, one organization divides the needy people into groups of five. Each group is challenged to write out a proposal about how their group intends to invest the available money. After the group consents to the written proposal, one member from their group can receive the money, and the other four members serve as accountability partners to help the responsible person implement the group's proposal. Unless the first member starts to earn money and repay the loan, the second member cannot receive any money. To make sure that capital investment will help others lighten their financial burdens, the Christian organization charges very low interest. This Christian organization has helped more than 400,000 members living in the impoverished area of Tondo, Manila, and has expanded throughout the country through the support of generous Christians who care for the poor.

Jackie and Elsie, a Christian couple, met the emergency needs of their employees by starting a cooperative company when they found out that there were some people waiting outside their store during payday. Many people on the street survived their daily and emergency needs by relying on friends and relatives. After praying, they started a cooperative company for their employees. By paying a minimum fee of 100 Philippine pesos (approximately 2 US dollars), any employee can be a member of the company. The cooperative company helps the members by lending money at a low interest rate. Both Jackie and Elsie invested funds to help start the lending cooperative company. At year end, as the company earns money, the dividends are distributed to the employees who "own" the co-op. Of course, this couple has also thought of some other creative ways to assist their employees. Every Christmas time, they not only give bonuses, but they provide other incentives for employees to earn extra cash. No wonder the Lord blesses their business and also gives them many faithful employees in return.

5:14–19 OUTDONE BY NEHEMIAH

The last section deals with issues of taxation and Nehemiah's fear of the Lord as well as the people's efforts in building the wall and not acquiring land for themselves (5:16–17). Nehemiah responds to the issue of poverty by living an exemplary sacrificial lifestyle during his twelve years of governorship.

Nehemiah's unselfish giving and benevolent lifestyle change the gloomy and depressing outcries of the poor into a hopeful and dazzling outpouring of communal sharing.

As a response to the heavy tax exerted upon the people, Nehemiah decides not to take the food earmarked for the governor (5:14). The allotment in an agricultural post-exilic society is normally given through food and wine. This privilege is definitely passed on to the taxes that are levied from the people. By giving up this privilege in food provision, Nehemiah lessens the load on the people. Moreover, his men are focusing on their work on the wall, thereby minimizing other unnecessary activities that may deepen the problems of the poor.

Nehemiah provides a daily meal of "one ox, six choice sheep and some poultry" during his twelve years of governorship. He feeds as many as 150 Jews and visitors who come to him from the surrounding nations (5:17–18). His generosity in serving wine every ten days is a joyous event for those who eat with him. These details reveal Nehemiah's generosity beyond the call of duty.

Nehemiah ends his exhortation to the people with a prayer to the Lord, detailing what he has done for God's sake and for God's people. Nehemiah leads the people by authentic and benevolent living. He speaks what he practices in actual life. His lip-service is in accord with his life example. Nehemiah displays his accountability to God for the rebuilding project and the welfare of the people in the land.

CARING FOR THE POOR

How can we help the poor among us? Nehemiah uses both direct confrontation and his personal example to help the poor in Israelite society. As we deal with the felt needs of our society, how can we implement an effective strategy in reaching the poor in our midst? In the Majority World, we see a big distinction between the rich and the poor. Many wealthy families live in well-guarded homes, while poor squatters live in dilapidated, makeshift huts just around the corner.

At the turn of the twenty-first century, mission societies began to employ a more holistic approach to reach out to the community, and many people have been reached by the love of God. How can we reclaim the opportunity given to us to care for these marginalized people in our societies? Many evangelicals have rediscovered the cultural mandate to be holistic as they reach out to people. As children of God, who are created in the image and likeness of God, the *haves* must help the *have-nots*! The *powerful* must help the *powerless* regain their dignity.

In the Old Testament law, there are at least five teachings about caring. First, there is a theme of "brotherhood and sisterhood" as an illustration of love. In the narrative of Abel and Cain, this principle is illustrated through the Lord's question, "Where is your brother Abel?" Cain is expected to be "the keeper" (guardian) of his brother (Gen 4:9). This theme is further developed in the Genesis narrative after the death of Jacob, when Joseph's forgiveness of his brothers clearly exemplifies brotherly love (Gen 50:20). This theme of harmonious relationships is a testimony of God's people (Ps 133; compare 1 John 3:11–15). Second, the people of God have a social responsibility to love the unfortunate. Loving the aliens, orphans, widows, and poor is a significant theme in the Covenant Code, which is rooted in the compassion of God (Exod 22:21–27). Third, love is really a "holiness" mark of God's people in the Holiness Code (Lev 19:13–18). Fourth, God's stewards should be channels of God's blessings. Gifts are not only for us to enjoy, but also for us to share with others, because people are God's tenants (Lev 25:23). Fifth, generous giving is encouraged. In the Deuteronomic Code, showing generosity with an open hand is a solemn reminder to God's people (Deut 15:7–15; compare Mark 14:7; 1 Tim 5:3–16).

The eighth-century prophets link the concept of spirituality with powerless and the poor.[1] For Amos, the righteous people are the poor (Amos 2:6–8; 5:12). Micah exhorts the people of God to exercise justice and compassion. To do justice means to help the powerless; to extend kindness means to show unconditional love to the less fortunate

(Mic 6:8). In discussing real faith, both Isaiah and Zechariah exhort the people to show mercy and compassion to the needy (Isa 58:6-7, 10; Zech 9:8-9).

In the Writings, Job presents his love for the less fortunate by showing them justice and generosity (Job 31:13-23). The psalmist emphasizes character formation for those who worship the Lord (Pss 15; 24:3-6). Those who fear the Lord will be led to administer justice and give generously to the needy (Ps 112).

In the book of Nehemiah, the concept of "brotherhood and sisterhood" is the guiding principle for extending love to the family.

As we deal with the issue of helping brothers and sisters in our midst, how can we apply the "brother-keeper" concept? Some churches have free clinics on Sundays for their own members. Others offer regular medical clinics for those in need within the broader community. Some churches teach illiterate people how to read and write. How can our churches become light and the salt in our communities? Paul exhorts Titus that the grace of God teaches us "to live self-controlled, upright and godly lives in this present age" (Titus 2:12).

How can we follow Nehemiah's footsteps in increasing the involvement of lay leaders in mission work? Because the Philippines and other nations have so many migrant workers working in foreign lands, we can try to encourage, counsel, and help them. Someone we encourage might turn out to be as gifted as Nehemiah. This person could be offered an administrative position to assist others and dispense God's grace in the community. In this way, the poor in our communities can experience God's love in action. If this love in action continues to spread through good modeling, spiritual leaders will be raised up who can multiply God's love and expand God's kingdom on earth.

Rosa Ching Shao

---

1. Shao, "Spirituality in the Prophetic Traditions: An Asian Perspective," in *Perjuangan Menatang Zaman* (*Kumpulan esai sebagai penghargaan kepada Pendeta* Stephen Tong, pada HUT ke-60, *Festschrift* for Stephen Tong), ed. Hendra G. Mulia (Jakarta: Reformed Institute Press, 2000), 125-150.

NEHEMIAH 6:1–19

DODGING THE PERSONAL PLOY

In Asian culture, the elderly and leaders are honored with position or status. When a leader retires and a new successor comes into an organization, the previous leader may be recognized with the highest honor during his retirement ceremony. However, a leader who has not received the confidence vote of the community may be criticized or attacked personally with detailed accusations even after years of faithful service.

This chapter is about how Sanballat and his associates personally attack Nehemiah.

At the final stage of the wall rebuilding, Sanballat and his group switch their opposition strategy by launching personal attacks against Nehemiah. These enemies accelerate their power to distract Nehemiah and deplete his morale by assassinating his character. By hurling allegations against Nehemiah, Sanballat and his group try to intimidate Nehemiah so that the rebuilding project will fail during its final stage. Nehemiah counters each personal blow with unyielding integrity, guarding the wellness of his own body, mind, and soul.[1] The personal attacks against Nehemiah are depicted in two episodes: the scheme to meet at Ono (6:1–9), where Sanballat and his team threaten Nehemiah directly, and the suggestion to meet at God's house (6:10–14), where Nehemiah is intimidated indirectly by his friend Shemaiah. The purpose of both episodes is to terrify Nehemiah (6:9, 14), but because of his careful discernment, he is not disheartened.

6:1–9 SCHEME TO MEET AT ONO

With the gaps on the wall closing and the rebuilding almost complete, there are only the doors to be set in the gates (6:1; compare 4:7). Upon learning that the wall is almost complete, Sanballat and Geshem make a last concerted effort to distract Nehemiah by cordially inviting him to meet in one of

---

1. For an alternative view that doubts Nehemiah's capability to discern, see David J. A. Clines, "The Nehemiah Memoir: The Perils of Autobiography," in *What Does Eve Do to Help? And Other Readerly Questions to the Old Testament,* JSOT Supplement Series 94 (Sheffield: Sheffield Academic Press, 1990), 144–152.

the villages on the plain of Ono, which is near Lod at the farthest northwest corner of the province (7:37; 11:35; Ezra 2:33). The Chinese idiom *diao hu li shan* (literally, "to move the tiger from the mountain") means "to get rid of an opponent by luring him from the task." This seems to be Sanballat and Geshem's simple strategy in trying to allure Nehemiah away from the wall. Without Nehemiah's leadership, the rebuilding may stop. Moreover, Ono is secluded and far from the wall.

Wisely, Nehemiah understands that the invitation might be a plot to harm him as he travels. Through messengers, Nehemiah tells Sanballat and Geshem that he is leading an enormous task and cannot be distracted from the rebuilding, for if he leaves, the work may stop. Although Sanballat and the rest of the enemies send four invitations to Nehemiah, he graciously and firmly declines each.

On the fifth attempt, Sanballat delivers an unsealed letter to Nehemiah (6:5). In the ancient Near East, letters are normally sealed with the imprimatur of the writer in order to ensure privacy for the recipient. This unsealed letter essentially becomes a public document that others are free to peruse and spread, far and near, without needing to authenticate its validity.

The open letter suggests that among the nations, it is public knowledge that the Jews are plotting to rebel against the Persian king and install Nehemiah, the cupbearer and appointed governor, as the king of Judah (6:6). Geshem, Sanballat's close associate, confirms these derogatory accusations. This two-pronged attack raises questions about Nehemiah's integrity and the Jews' motives in rebuilding the wall. Earlier, rumors about the rebelliousness of Jerusalem caused Artaxerxes to issue a decree that stopped the rebuilding project (see Ezra 4:21). The open letter also alludes to prophets who have been appointed to proclaim in Jerusalem, "A king is in Judah" (6:7). Apparently, Sanballat and his group understand that such a proclamation is part of the pre-exilic Israelite prophetic tradition (1 Kgs 1:34–39). The open letter closes with a duplicitous clause that warns Nehemiah that the allegations will be reported to the Persian king, thereby aiming to coerce Nehemiah to join Sanballat and his associates at the discussion table. The implication is that Sanballat and his cohorts can help suppress the rumor of Nehemiah's supposed uprising against the king.

Nehemiah confronts the rumors by immediately and vehemently denying them. He knows that the enemies are trying to frighten him and the rest of the Jews in order to denigrate the wall project, and so he strongly and swiftly unmasks their devious motives. After discerning the root purpose of the rumor and tackling it in a proper manner, Nehemiah prays to the Lord, asking God to strengthen his hands (6:9). Again, Nehemiah shows his effective leadership by executing what is needed (confrontation) while also seeking the Lord for strength (intercession).

6:10–14 SUGGESTION TO MEET AT GOD'S HOUSE

Nehemiah visits Shemaiah ("The Lord hears"), son of Delaiah, who is confined in his home. Delaiah's name is included in the earliest list of the returnees to Jerusalem, and so Shemaiah might be an influential person in the community (7:62; Ezra 2:60). Because Shemaiah is confined in his home, he might serve in both prophetic and priestly offices. Shemaiah must have been a friend of Nehemiah since Nehemiah is choosing to visit him, and their conversation suggests that their appointment might have been previously arranged (6:12).

Shemaiah suggests that Nehemiah meet him inside the temple of God and even proposes to shut the temple doors (6:10). He suggests that people are wanting to kill Nehemiah in order to intimidate him into panicked submission, since the tradition grants a hunted person safety at the altar inside the temple doors (Exod 21:14; 1 Kgs 2:28). Though Shemaiah seems to be concerned about Nehemiah's safety and well-being, it would arouse suspicion for a God-fearing man to secure his own safety.

Thus Nehemiah perceives Shemaiah's deception and discerns the meddling presence of his enemies behind the plot to oppose the rebuilding project. True discernment means not only distinguishing right from wrong, but also distinguishing the primary from the secondary. Aside from being a man of prayer, trusting the Lord in the midst of problems, and using his foresight and hindsight in assessment of facts, Nehemiah prudently recognizes the moral implications of his situation (6:9) and then follows a proper course of action (Ps 119:66).

If Nehemiah can be intimidated to flee from his task, his integrity and reputation as a leader will be effectively discredited. Moreover, all his previous accomplishments will be nullified if he foolishly abandons his God-given responsibility in order to save his life. With clarity, strength, and zeal, Nehemiah remains grounded in his rebuilding mission, focusing on finishing well rather than being distracted by petty hearsay (Phil 4:12–14).

Nehemiah commits his problem to the Lord by asking God to remember his enemies, Tobiah and Sanballat. In the Old Testament, pleading to the Lord for remembrance has both positive and negative connotations. In this prayer,

Nehemiah entreats the Lord not to cover up the sins of Tobiah and Sanballat, but to punish them instead (compare Ps 79:8). Tobiah's name is uttered before Sanballat, because Tobiah has exceeded Sanballat in his wickedness. Moreover, Nehemiah also names the prophetess Noadiah and other prophets who are hired to intimidate him.[2] He discerns their motives clearly and calls upon the Lord to remember their wicked deeds.

6:15–19 SUCCESS OF THE REBUILDING PROJECT

In spite of ceaseless opposition from the enemies, the work on the wall is completed within fifty-two days. At the start, the enemies carry on distracting tactics to frustrate the rebuilding project; later, they try to destroy Nehemiah's morale, personal integrity, and relational trust as a leader. Nevertheless, their divisive strategies fail to frighten or frustrate Nehemiah and his men. The enemies cannot deny that the Jews' rebuilding task is being accomplished with the help of their God, whom they cannot defeat, and so they begin to lose their self-confidence. This is a powerful witness to the builders as well as their enemies.

Still, many letters keep passing between the nobles of Judah and Tobiah, the ongoing adversaries to the rebuilding project. For no apparent reason, these letters praise the good deeds of Tobiah, the enemy of the exiled people. The nobles are in close alliance with Tobiah because they are under oath to him, having been pledged due to a friendly marital alliance. Specifically, Tobiah is the son-in-law of Shecaniah, the son of Arah. Moreover, Tobiah's son, Jehohanan, married the daughter of Meshullam, whose name is listed among those that made repairs on the wall opposite their living quarters. Thus Tobiah has marital connections with noble Jewish families and maintains ongoing ties with the local people.

Tobiah's wily friendship misleads these noblemen to circulate frequent reports about his good deeds. As the reports pour in, Tobiah hopes that Nehemiah will be threatened and intimidated. However, Nehemiah's untainted conscience, unselfish purpose, and unshakable faith ground him, and he sees through the Tobiah's guile and dismantles his plot before the public's eyes.

---

2. In the OT, there are many prophetesses: Miriam (Exod 15:20), Deborah (Judg 4:4), Huldah (2 Kgs 22:14; 2 Chr 34:22), and the wife of Isaiah (Isa 8:3), to list a few.

NEHEMIAH 7–13

REBUILDING THE PEOPLE

The second section of Nehemiah, chapters 7–13, deals with the rebuilding of the people. With the wall project finished after such a short period of time, Nehemiah could have immediately initiated a dedication ceremony. His first task, however, is to ensure the welfare and prosperity of Jerusalem by appointing leaders and managing the repopulation of the city (7:1–73). His second task is to work with Ezra on rebuilding the people through the law of Moses so that they can live faithfully as the people of God.

The community renewal project begins when the community gathers to listen to the law of Moses so that they can understand God's teaching (8:1–12). The next day, the family heads, priests, and Levites gather to gain deeper insight into the words of the law (8:13–18). After this time of learning, the community gathers to confess their sinfulness before God (9:1–37). Then they renew their commitment to the Lord by making a pledge to observe the commandments, ordinances, and statutes of God and to support the work of the priests, the Levites, and the house of God (9:38–10:39).

Using a ritual reading, Noli Mendoza understands Nehemiah 8–10 as a covenant renewal ritual that facilitates the transformation of the Israelite community. The community goes through a threefold stage of separation (8:1–12), transition (8:12–9:37), and reincorporation (9:38–10:39). They are no longer alienated from God, but are reconciled with God and in solidarity with one another.[1] As a renewed people wanting to live according to the covenant, the community is now ready to live in the city, and so Nehemiah sets about the work of repopulating Jerusalem and appointing provincial leaders (11:1–36). Once the people are established in Jerusalem, they are ready to dedicate the wall (12:27–30). Though the story could end here, Nehemiah continues to challenge the people and instruct them about the law of God (12:31–44; 13:1–30).

---

1. Noli P. Mendoza, "A Community in Becoming: Ritual and Social Transformation in Nehemiah 8–10. A Ritual Reading of the Covenant Renewal in Nehemiah." MTh Thesis, (Asia Graduate School of Theology, August 2016).

NEHEMIAH 7:1–73

FAITHFUL LEADERS AND MEMBERS

Honoring the older generation is a cultural value in Chinese communities throughout Asia. One way we do this is by retelling oral history or by keeping written records and old pictures that can help later generations understand previous events in the community. To honor the sixtieth anniversary of the Biblical Seminary of the Philippines, we made a showcase of old pictures, which we presented as a slideshow during our grand celebration. We also printed photos in a special anniversary calendar, which we distributed to people related to the seminary. Our purpose was to give glory to our Lord by honoring the faithful people who preceded us. Their stories remind us to be faithful as we move forward into unknown years of ministry with our Lord.

Chapter 7 can be divided into two sections. The first section explains how Nehemiah cares for the security of the city after it has been rebuilt by appointing faithful leaders (7:1–3). The second section chronicles the list of the first returnees to Jerusalem, since Nehemiah is about to repopulate the city (7:4–73; compare Neh 11). In Ezra, the list of names records the first returnees as the key characters in the second exodus event (Ezra 2). The list in Nehemiah 7:4–73 is more theological in nature, where the people who will repopulate Jerusalem are shown to be in continuity with the first returnees.[1]

With the completion of the wall, Nehemiah carefully assigns reliable workers and gives them specific guidelines for taking care of the wall and gates. As he oversees the registration of those who will be residing in Jerusalem, he finds the list of the first returnees. This list not only depicts the names of the returnees, but also their willingness to return to the ruined Jerusalem under the leadership of twelve key leaders. The records also indicate their offerings toward the work of God. These godly and generous leaders are excellent models for the new generation to emulate.

---

1. In the Old Testament, many important matters are listed twice with different purposes. For example, the two creation accounts each have their own purposes. The first account portrays the grand, cosmic design of the creator (Gen 1:1–2:3). The second account reveals the loving care of God in creating Adam and carefully providing him with a helpmate (Gen 2:4–25).

7:1–3 CHOICE OF LEADERS

With the wall rebuilt, Nehemiah proactively assigns leaders to guide and guard the city and provide for the future needs of the community. Good management of resources is necessary for the welfare and progress of the city. First, Nehemiah assigns "the gatekeepers, the musicians, and the Levites" (7:1). The gatekeepers guard the gates of Jerusalem; the musicians and the Levites assist in guarding the gates until they are needed at the temple.

Previously, Rephasiah and Shallum each took charge of a half-district of Jerusalem (3:9, 12). With the wall completed, Jerusalem needs an innovative leader to take up new challenges, and so Nehemiah appoints his brother, Hanani, as the overall leader. "Hanani" is an abbreviated form of Hananiah, which means "the Lord is gracious."[2] Having previously demonstrated his dependability as the commander of the citadel, a very important entrance to Jerusalem, Hanani is an excellent choice. He has proven himself to be both godly and trustworthy, and this dual modeling of integrity and godliness is the scriptural guideline for qualified leaders (Exod 18:21; Acts 6:3).

After selecting leaders, Nehemiah gives Hanani and the guards (the gatekeepers, musicians, and Levites, per 7:1–2) clear guidelines about guarding the gates of Jerusalem (7:3).[3] The gates mark the entrances into Jerusalem and are a key to its security and therefore a central theme in Nehemiah (1:3; 2:17; 6:1; 13:22). If they are not carefully guarded, enemies could enter Jerusalem in spite of the wall. Nehemiah gives the guards three instructions. First, they are not to open the door of the gate until the sun is hot, which corresponds to around noontime. Though this seems quite late, great care is needed for the protection of Jerusalem. Second, the on-duty gatekeepers are to close the doors and block them tightly. Third, Nehemiah appoints the residents of Jerusalem as additional guards, with some posted near their houses. Similar to the rebuilding, the dual management of posting someone near one's house is practical. Involving the residents of Jerusalem adds more responsible people to guard Jerusalem, who will pay careful attention to the welfare of Jerusalem when their own lives are at stake.

---

2. In this context, the Hebrew connective *waw*, normally translated as "and," should not function as an ordinary connective conjunction, but rather as an explicative *waw*, translated as "that is," explaining that Hananiah is the same person as Hanani. Hanani has proven worthy to be chosen for his faithfulness and other characteristics. Otherwise, Nehemiah could easily be accused of nepotism by asking his own brother to serve as the chief leader of Jerusalem.

3. For those who prefer to interpret Hanani and Hananiah as two different persons, Nehemiah's instruction to "them" is interpreted as given only to the leaders.

Nehemiah 7:1–73

7:4–73 CHRONICLES OF NAMES

With the wall completed, the next mission is to expand the number of residents residing in Jerusalem, since few people were living within the city because of the destruction of the wall (1:3). Nehemiah trusts God's hands to guide him in all his endeavors, and so he credits God for helping him assemble the nobles, officials, and common people to register by families (7:5). This system, which was used in Israel since the time of Moses and Joshua (Num 1–3; Josh 7:16–18), solidifies the bonds of the Israelite community and identifies the people within the greater context of their tribes and clans. Both the key leaders (nobles and officials) and the common people support Nehemiah's work (2:16; 4:14, 19; 5:7).

After Nehemiah starts the registration process, he finds the genealogical record of the first returnees. The Old Testament records names in Israel's early history (Genesis and Exodus) as well as in Israel's later history (Chronicles, Ezra, and Nehemiah). Genealogical records may appear as a list of names, as in Nehemiah 7:6–73 (compare Ezra 2:1–70), and may record names in descending order from parent to child (see 1 Chr 9:39–44) or in ascending order from child to parent (see 1 Chr 9:14–16).[4] Either way, the names themselves reflect the religious and social history of Israel. Simple and compound names may reflect people's religious walk with the Lord. The order of names and the categories in a list may provide sociological clues about people's relationships with one another and their different roles and responsibilities within the community.

The genealogical record of the first returnees reveals their setting and background (7:6–7), identifying ordinary people (7:8–38), priests (7:39–42), Levites (7:43), musicians (7:44), gatekeepers (7:45), temple servants (7:46–56), and the descendants of the servants of Solomon (7:57–60). The list also includes those who have questionable ancestry (7:61–65). The list concludes with a summary account (7:66–69) and a record of the people's contributions to the work of God (7:70–72). A final remark states that the priests, Levites, gatekeepers, musicians, and temple servants have settled in their own towns (7:73).

Compared with Ezra 2, twelve leaders (instead of eleven) are listed. Just as there are twelve leaders for the twelve tribes during the wilderness period (Num 13:3–16), there are twelve leaders who bring the first returnees back to

---

4. Robert R. Wilson, "Genealogy, Genealogies," in ABD 2:930. See also Marshall D. Johnson, *The Purpose of Biblical Genealogies*, 2nd ed. (Cambridge/New York: Cambridge University Press, 1988).

Jerusalem. Zerubbabel and Joshua are listed at the beginning of both lists (7:7; Ezra 2:2). Whereas Ezra 2:1 connects the first returnees with pre-exilic Israel, Nehemiah 7:4 connects the first returnees with the resettlement in Jerusalem (compare 11:1–36).

The list begins by naming "the men of Israel" (7:7), who are the fundamental components of the post-exilic community and sizable in number. The people are divided into seventeen clans (7:8–24) from many different localities (7:25–38). Among the seventeen clans identified on the first list of returnees, fourteen clans affix their seals when they bind the agreement (10:14–19), and eleven clans journey with Ezra during the second return (Ezra 8:2–14). Just as many faithful clans respond to the initial call to return to Jerusalem during the first return, the majority of these clans continue to show their loyalty and piety under the leadership of Ezra and Nehemiah.

There are two probable reasons for listing the men according to geographical places. First, the geographical places reflect the place names of the tribes of Judah and Benjamin around Jerusalem. Bethlehem and Netophah are located south of Jerusalem, and the rest of the place names are in the territories of the Benjamin tribes. This reflects the political reality of the post-exilic community, which is that only two tribes return to Jerusalem. Whereas Chronicles prefers to say that "all Israel" returns, only the tribes of Judah and Benjamin actually return. Second, the listing of geographical places suggests that some returnees are not from well-known clans, and so they are identified by their place of residence instead.

The priests, Levites, musicians, gatekeepers, temple servants, and descendants of the servants of Solomon are identified according to this order, which reflects the post-exilic method of compiling lists (7:39–56), with priests placed before Levites. The priests are composed of four clans (7:39–42). The clan of Jedaiah comes from the house of Jeshua, who was the great high priest during the time of the first return (12:1; Ezra 3:2). This implies that the line of the high priest continues in the post-exilic community.

The Levites are usually listed as a whole group, with the musicians and the gatekeepers listed separately. The Levites are generally responsible for all the duties at the temple and serve the descendants of Aaron (1 Chr 23:28). During the time of David and Solomon, some Levites are designated as musicians and are in charge of worship (1 Chr 6:31–47), and other Levites are identified as gatekeepers, whose main responsibility is to maintain security by guarding the gates (1 Chr 26:12–19).

The temple servants are the assistants of the Levites, who were established during the time of David (Ezra 8:20). The temple servants, along with the descendants of the servants of Solomon, are foreigners, and yet they become members of the society, enjoy tax-free status (Ezra 7:24), and can affix their signature to any binding agreement (10:29).

Those who cannot find their proper ancestry are listed by clan (7:61–65). Rather than being excluded from the sacred community, their identity can be re-established through a proper genealogy (7:61). Though the descendants of Habaiah, Hakkoz, and Barzillai are considered unclean and excluded from the priesthood, they can be restored once there is a priest ministering among them. This applies a process written in the Mosaic law. Originally, the death of a high priest marks a fixed point when a sinner who is seeking asylum in a city of refuge might receive amnesty (Num 35:25). In ancient Israel, the high priest is the religious and national leader who makes decisions on behalf of God. Thus if a priest rises up and ministers among the community, he shall represent God in making important decisions. In this way, "unclean" priests can be restored to their original service (7:64–65).

Among the three "unclean" priests, the descendants of Hakkoz are eventually restored to their positions as priests. Meremoth, "the son of Uriah the priest" (Ezra 8:33), who is "the son of Hakkoz" (3:21), serves faithfully in the rebuilding project by repairing the Old Gate (3:4) and repairing a large section of the wall (3:21). Earlier, Ezra hands Meremoth the silver and gold utensils in the house of God (Ezra 8:33). Hakkoz is listed among the first returnees, while Meremoth serves among the second returnees with Ezra.

The decision-making through "Urim and Thummim" is given to the high priest (7:65; Exod 28:16, 30; Lev 8:8; Num 27:21). When the priest enquires of the Lord, the Lord will guide the priest with either a divine "Yes" (1 Sam 23:9–12) or "No" (1 Sam 14:36–37). The "Urim and Thummim" method was employed during the early Israelite history of the Mosaic era (Exod 28:30; Num 27:21). Saul and David also asked God for guidance with this method (1 Sam 14:21; 23:6–12; 28:6; 30:7).

The summary account lists the total number of people in the community (7:66–67), along with the number of domestic animals, who are part of the property of the post-exilic community (7:68–69). This record implies that the post-exilic community follows proper historical accounting and classifying methods. The summary account also reflects the inclusive concerns of the community, as it includes both male and female slaves as part of the post-exilic community (7:67).

The contribution record (7:70–72) reveals that no record is complete without an offering to the Lord. The Israelites have always been a giving community, and this record confirms that this practice continues with the post-exilic community. The governor heads the list, followed by the heads of the families, and then the rest of the people. Their offerings include "work," along with gifts and garments for priests (7:70–72). Both the project and the people involved are important for God's ministry.

The concluding remark about the people settling in their own towns reveals the mercies of the Lord, who gives the post-exilic community a chance to return to their homeland in fulfillment of the prophetic message that they would return home after their exilic experience. The summary statement also portrays a peaceful environment, where all the people can now begin to rebuild their lives.

HONOR AND SHAME

Anthropological, missiological, and biblical studies confirm the values of honor and shame within Asian cultures, whereas Baltic cultures tend to emphasize guilt. Interpreted within the collective and communal culture of Asia, Ezra and Nehemiah have several unique features.

Honor and Recognition

When Cyrus returns the temple vessels to the house of God, it brings honor to Israel and the providence of God (Ezra 1:7–11). Contrariwise, when the Babylonians seize those articles from the temple, it brings about shame in the history of Israel (2 Kgs 25:13–17). As an honorable person, Cyrus makes a proclamation that enables the people of God to return to Jerusalem and the precious vessels to be reinstated in the temple.

Ezra and Nehemiah both cite the names of the first returnees (Ezra 2:1–70; Neh 7:6–73). Whereas Ezra identifies the names of family heads, priests, and Levites, Nehemiah honors the first returnees as those who will rebuild the community. Honoring the forefathers in both lists not only memorializes the people involved in this historic event, but also honors their descendants. Those who return with Nehemiah enjoy pride as the ancestors of those who dared to come back. The record of their giving also conveys admirable generosity during a time of uncertainty. As in Ezra 2:68–69 and Nehemiah 7:70–72, leaders are expected to be more generous than ordinary members.

Leadership and Honor

The key leaders are also given honorable positions in Ezra and Nehemiah. Zerubbabel, the honored leader of the first returnees, appears first among the family heads (Ezra 2:2; Neh 7:7). Along with Joshua, Zerubbabel rebuilds the altar and the house of God in Jerusalem (Ezra 3:2; 5:2).

Ezra, the admirable leader of the second returnees, is also a man of honor. He is a qualified leader by virtue of his character and also through his actions of "studying," "doing," and "teaching." He is a praiseworthy model as a leader (Ezra 7:6, 10).

In Nehemiah's memoirs, he identifies himself as a man of prayer first and a cupbearer second (Neh 1:4–11; 2:4). As the governor, he is revealed as a man of prudence and generosity when he does not take his allotted food allowance. He also gladly and abundantly feeds the people during his twelve years as governor.

Rosa Ching Shao

NEHEMIAH 8:1–18

THE DYNAMIC WORD OF GOD

Reading, studying, and seeking to understand God's word are instrumental practices in the spiritual growth of any church. In most cities in China today, church members gather on Chinese New Year to learn from God's word. With the recent migration of Wunzhou Christians to Europe, the diaspora Chinese continue to gather on Chinese New Year to listen to the teaching of God's word.

Nehemiah 8 is about the public reading and teaching of the Mosaic law to the community so that they will understand God's commandments. The Mosaic law was also read publicly to previous generations (Josh 8:30–35). During the post-exilic era, the Israelites followed two calendar systems, one civil and another religious. Tishri, the seventh month, marks the beginning of the year in the civil calendar system with a public holiday known as the Feast of Trumpets (Lev 23:23–25; Num 29:1). At an outdoor meeting in the public square, the people gather to begin the year with a celebration and reading of the law of Moses. The law (*Torah*) is the written record of God's commandments for Israel. Because it embodies the desires and will of God, it allows the people to learn and study the heartbeat of God.

With the city wall completed in fifty-two days (6:15), the people could easily jump into plans for a grand dedication ceremony (see 12:17–47), but this section of Nehemiah makes it clear that rebuilding the people's faith is far more important than the wall project itself. The celebration can wait until the community's faith is rekindled, for the people – not the wall – make a city![1]

Ezra is identified as both a scribe (8:1, 4, 9, 13) and the priest (8:2, 9), who is invited to read God's word to the public assembly as they gather in the square (8:1–3). After the reading, the Levites interpret and explain the law of God to the people (8:7–12). All who understand God's word are touched and respond accordingly (8:9, 12). A smaller group, consisting of the heads

---

1. The Greek historian Thucydides, who wrote in the same century as Nehemiah, offered this idea, which is cited in Raymond Brown, *The Message of Nehemiah: The Bible Speaks Today* (Leicester, UK: IVP, 1998), 127.

of the family, the priests, and the Levites, gather the next day to study God's word with Ezra (8:13–18).[2]

8:1–6 READING GOD'S WORD: GOD'S PEOPLE LISTEN CONSCIENTIOUSLY

Nehemiah 8 is known as one of the most important chapters in Ezra-Nehemiah, for it brings the word of God to the people, meeting them where they are and giving them what they need most. As the people gather before the Lord to hear his word read publicly, the community is renewed and revitalized. With the word of God at the center of the people's lives, they confess their sins (9:1–37). This chapter reveals the post-exilic community to be an intensely textual community,[3] where the word of God is the focus of their lives.

"The book of the law of Moses" records the commands of the Lord through Moses (8:1); it is also referred to as "the law" (8:2, 14), "the book of the law of God" (8:8, 18), and "the book" (8:5). God revealed his will and desires to Moses by giving him the Torah, which is God's commands and teachings. For this reason, the law of the Lord perfectly revives the soul (Ps 19:7).

Ezra is a teacher who is well-versed in the law of Moses (Ezra 7:6, 12) because he devoted himself to the study and observance of the law of the Lord (Ezra 7:10). On this special day, Ezra brings out the law of Moses to the men, women, children, and sojourners who have gathered "as one man" to listen to the word of God in the square (8:1). The people initiate the public reading because they are yearning for God's truth and longing for spiritual food. The reading of the law is done creatively (8:1–2), conscientiously (8:3), and confidently (8:4–6).

There is creativity in the way that Ezra reads the law to the people as they gather in the square before the Water Gate (8:1–2; compare 1 Tim 4:13), which is a neutral and public place. If the law of Moses were only read at the temple courts or the temple, the men alone would have priority to listen, while the women and children would be in the background. Moreover, sojourners and aliens would not be welcome to listen. But Ezra reads the law in the public square, where everyone has access – and so the audience that gathers to listen

---

2. The reading on the first day is at square before the Water Gate with Ezra and Nehemiah as the facilitators. With Ezra, the smaller group wants rigorous reading and understanding. The instruction of the law needs to be disseminated properly through the head of the families (Deut 6:6–9).
3. Walter Brueggemann, *Cadences of Home: Preaching among Exiles* (Louisville: Westminster John Knox Press, 1977), 105.

is more inclusive than exclusive. Because the Law is the word of God, which is for everyone to hear, there are no traditions restricting the audience.

When Ezra reads the law, the people listen conscientiously (8:3). He reads from daybreak till noon. Imagine those long hours standing or sitting under the hot sun at a public square! Though it would not be easy to pay attention in such circumstances, the people are passionate about hearing the word of God, for it penetrates their minds and stirs their hearts to accept God's will for their lives. In this scene, reading and listening are coordinates – as Ezra reads, the people listen attentively.

Ezra confidently brings out the law before the assembly and stands on a high wooden platform built especially for the occasion (8:4). Thirteen men stand with Ezra on the platform, six on his right and seven on his left, each identified by name (8:4). Their role is to support Ezra as he reads the law. This scene can inspire us to read and proclaim God's law boldly in today's world!

8:7–12 INTERPRETING GOD'S WORD: GOD'S PEOPLE RESPOND CHEERFULLY

The word of God should not only be read publicly, but it should also be interpreted accurately. Ezra cannot rekindle the people's love for the law of God by himself, for the Levites and Nehemiah are also instrumental in helping the people understand God's word. The Levites instruct the people cooperatively (8:7) and interpret the law carefully (8:8). Then the people respond cheerfully to Nehemiah's and Ezra's instructions (8:9–12).

Just as Ezra has thirteen leaders who stand with him on the platform, thirteen Levites are appointed to explain and teach the word of God to the people. Their names are listed and they may have been trained by Ezra (8:7). In pre-exilic Israel, the priests are responsible for teaching the laws and decrees given to the people through Moses (Lev 10:11; Hag 2:11–13). During the post-exilic era, the Levites share some of the responsibility for teaching and interpreting God's words with the priests (2 Chr 17:7–9; 35:3; Mal 2:1–9; compare Deut 33:10). The Levites are to read and interpret the law and instruct the people as a group, instilling in them a clear understanding of God's word (8:8). As the people stand in place in the public square (8:7b), the Levites bring the word to them, responding to their questions and concerns.

The phrase "making it clear" (*meporash*) has three possible interpretations (8:8). The first sense is "translating" (NJPS, JB). Scholars believe that sometime during the post-exilic era, the Jews began to lose their ability to speak and understand Hebrew. During the fifth century BC, most people could still understand Hebrew, but by the second century BC, rabbis had translated many Hebrew texts into Aramaic and collected them into the "Targum." In this sense, *meporash* may mean translating the law into the Targum for those who could not understand Hebrew. In 8:9, Nehemiah seems to realize that many of the people could not understand Hebrew, and so he instructs them about how to keep the festival holy, and then the people finally understand what has been read (8:12).

The second interpretation translates the phrase "making it clear" as "distinct, clear, or explicit." Using the practice of the Massoretes in dividing the text into "portions" (*parashat*), the phrase "making it clear" (*meporash*) means reading it distinctly, following the advice of the Massoretes. This sense implies that the Levites are reading the text with different intonations and feelings.

The third interpretation translates "making it clear" along with the next phrase, "giving the meaning," to denote "interpreting" (NRSV "with interpretation;" NAB "interpreting;" NASB "explained the Law").[4] The Christian practice of expounding on a text by making it clear belongs to this third interpretation. When Jesus reads the Isaiah texts and interprets them before the audience in the temple, he supports this third sense of the phrase (Luke 4:18–21). Paul's exhortation to Timothy in rightly handling the word of truth also supports this third sense (2 Tim 2:15).

Ezra reads the text while thirteen Levites make the text clear for the people of God. The people understand the word of God and accept it cheerfully. Due to the deep conviction of God's word, they begin to mourn and weep (8:9). Nevertheless, Nehemiah and Ezra instruct them to celebrate and enjoy the blessings of the word because the joy of the Lord is their strength (8:10). So the people celebrate with food and drink, because they understand the word of God that has been made known to them (8:12). Their communal joy is not simply because of the holiday celebration, but because they appreciate the reading and teaching from the Torah.[5] Their joy proves that they understand God's word.

---

4. Philip Y. Yoo, "On Nehemiah 8, 8a," *ZAW* 127 (2015): 502–507, presents the background on understanding the word as "interpretation" of the Torah.
5. L. Allen and T. Laniah, *Ezra, Nehemiah, Esther*, New International Biblical Commentary OT Series (Peabody/Carlisle: Hendrickson Publishers/Paternoster Press, 2003), 127.

8:13–18 STUDYING GOD'S WORD: GOD'S PEOPLE FOLLOW COMPREHENSIVELY

On the second day after the celebration, the heads of the families, along with the priests and Levites, gather around Ezra to study the word of God. Because Ezra has devoted himself to studying the law, he can lead the group towards understanding. This gathering is quite significant because it gives even more attention to reading and understanding the word. The more the people hear the word of God, the more they want to study it (8:13–15). The more the people study, the more they understand God's teachings. The more they understand God's teachings, the more they can follow God's laws.

As the people study the word of God, they read about the command regarding the Feast of Tabernacles, which celebrates the year-end gathering of crops (Exod 23:16; Lev 23:39) and the joyful time of gathering the produce of the threshing floor and winepress (Deut 16:13). From its beginning as a celebration of the ingathering of the harvest, it becomes a time of public worship and remembrance of God's provision by living in booths (simple structures or tents), where the people can enjoy the fruits of their labor. Hence, the celebration becomes the Feast of Tabernacles (Lev 23:42), which has two purposes. First, it is a reminder of God's protection and care during the people's historic journey out of Egypt and their sojourn through the wilderness to the land of Canaan (Lev 23:43). Second, it is a joyful feast celebrating God's provision in their present lives (Deut 16:15).

Having heard and understood this word, the people comprehensively apply the teaching by immediately proclaiming this feast, spreading news about it throughout their towns and Jerusalem, and calling everyone to participate (8:15–18). The community applies the teaching practically as they gather the tree branches that they have at that time (8:15; compare Lev 23:40) and build booths everywhere – on top of their own roofs, in public courtyards, and even in the courts of the house of God (8:16). Building a booth on the rooftop is a good reminder and teaching tool for the whole family. Building a booth in the courtyard allows the people to entertain guests as they eat and drink while sharing about God's grace and provision in their lives. Building booths in the courts of the house of God and in the square by the Water Gate invite all people to remember that the religious and secular life ought to be the same. There should be no distinction between the private and public life of thanksgiving. Hence the people apply the essence of the law in a spirit of joyful celebration (8:17) – not just for native-born Israelites, but also for those who live in the land (Deut 16:14; compare Lev 23:42).

LEADERS AND PARTNERS

It is not easy for two strong leaders to work closely together. The fact that Nehemiah can work so closely with Ezra reflects his humility. As a believing Jew, Nehemiah's knowledge of the Torah is solid, and so it might not be easy for him to accept a leader who is as gifted as Ezra. As the governor, Nehemiah is the highest civic leader in the community. As a scribe, Ezra would be considered an expert at reading and interpreting the Torah. Yet these two leaders complement one another as they work together.

In recent Chinese church history, God used the individual gifts of many spiritual "giants" to bless churches worldwide because they partnered with others to leave a lasting legacy for future generations. Since 1974, Lausanne has been instrumental in founding the Chinese Center of World Evangelization. Every five years, leaders from around the world gather to encourage one another in different regions for mission work. This movement has enabled Chinese evangelicals around the world to work with one another.

A good follower can become a good leader. Someone with an accommodating spirit who is willing to work with others will help God's work expand throughout the world. How can we develop a greater spirit of cooperation among gifted leaders? How can we encourage leaders to work with one another?

When we focus on the big harvests around us, we take a first step toward building a closer relationship with other gifted leaders. The more we are willing to work with one another, the more work we can do for the kingdom of God. In the Bible, we see the teamwork of Caleb and Joshua, Haggai and Zachariah, Peter and John, Paul and Barnabas, and many others. By focusing on the greater task of helping others understand the word, we can encourage leaders to join the real battle in the field rather than getting distracted by in-fighting. May we bring glory to our master through our concentrated and cooperative efforts.

Rosa Ching Shao

NEHEMIAH 9:1–37

CONFESSION OF SINS

The corporate confession of sin is a time for the leaders and members of churches to quiet themselves before the Lord. In Taiwan, many different denominations and independent churches gather annually to affirm their faith publicly and to confess their corporate sins before the Lord.

Though there is certainly a time for private prayers of confession in the Old Testament (see Ezra 9; Daniel 9), there is also a time for the people to gather corporately to express their grief and demonstrate their common faith in the God of all compassion and mercy. In Nehemiah 9, the people of God come together on the twenty-fourth day of the month to fast and pray corporately before the Lord. With the word of God in the center of their lives, the people celebrate the Feast of Tabernacles and then gather to confess their sins and the sins of their fathers (9:1–37).

The prayer in Nehemiah 9 is basically a prayer of confession to God as the creator, redeemer, lawgiver, protector, and judge. Looking at this prayer carefully, it is similar to the historical psalms, which retell Israel's history to illustrate how God continues to care for his people even though they repeatedly disobey God's commands.[1] Despite their recurring arrogance and rebellion before the Lord, God continues to deliver them and shower them with steadfast love.

Following the form of Psalms 105 and 106, the prayer presents the current situation in the course of Israel's history. It commences with praise for God as the creator (9:5b–6), which is followed by a retelling of the patriarchal period (9:7–8),[2] the exodus event (9:9–11), the wilderness period (9:12–21), and the settlement in the land (9:22–31). The prayer concludes with a confession of the people's current rebellion (9:32–37). Since the people are living in the land, the history in their prayer of confession focuses more on the land that God has given to them. These key themes can be diagrammed as follows:

---

1. Pss 78, 89, 105, 106, 114, 132, 135, and 136 are classified as historical psalms because they use history to convey thanksgiving or prayer to God.
2. Frank Charles Fensham, "Nehemiah 9 and Psalms 105, 106, 135 and 136. Post-Exilic Historical Traditions in Poetic Form," *JNSL* 9 (1981): 35–51.

	God's Love	Rebellion	God's Love
Patriarchal Period	9:7–8		
Exodus	9:9–11		
Wilderness Period	9:12–15	9:16–18	9:19–21
Land	9:22–25	9:26–27a	9:27b
	9:28a	9:28b	
	9:29a	9:29b	
	9:30a	9:30b	9:31

The prayer in Nehemiah 9 is rich in theological phraseology, reflecting the importance that the post-exilic audience places on the pietistic traditions in the life of Israel as a nation. The prayer displays the conscience of the people, expressing their faith to God and, at the same time, acknowledging their history of rebellious arrogance against their long-suffering and forgiving God.[3]

9:1–5a GOD'S PEOPLE IN CONTRITION

After the returning exiles hear God's word, they clearly understand God's desire for them to come back to him, and so they gather for corporate confession. First, they express their contrition by fasting, wearing sackcloth, and putting dust on their heads (9:1). In the Old Testament, these are the people of God's basic external expressions for expressing sincere lament for their transgressions. Second, they decide to separate themselves from all foreigners (9:2). In the post-exilic community, the separation from foreigners for the sake of holiness is a constant theme. By separating themselves from foreigners, the people show their awareness of their unique role as the people of God (Ezra 6:21; Neh 10:28; 13:3). These external expressions reveal the people's inward repentance as they prepare their hearts for prayer and confession. Repentance starts with a decision of the will.

As the people confess their sins, they spend time reading God's word (9:3), which leads naturally to a fruitful response by the prompting of God's spirit. Just as the Levites help Ezra interpret the law in chapter 8, a group of eight Levites leads the service by shouting to the Lord to show their sincerity in prayer. Then another group of eight Levites directs the people to offer praises

---

3. Compare how Ezekiel interprets the rebellious Israel. See Lyle Eslinger, "Ezekiel 20 and the Metaphor of Historical Teleology: Concepts of Biblical History," *JSOT* 81 (1998): 93–125.

to the Lord. The people can call out to God, who exists in eternity, to help them during their confession.[4]

9:5b–6 PRAISING GOD'S SPECTACULAR CREATION

The prayer uttered by the Levites begins with adoration and consists of four elements: (1) God's admirable name (9:5b); (2) God's absolute uniqueness (9:6a); (3) God's astounding creation (9:6b); and (4) God's amazing gift of life (9:6c). Adoring God affirms that he is their Lord, their true God.

First, the people praise God's glorious and honorable name. This distinguishing term is a standard phrase for beginning or ending a communication with God (compare Ps 72:19).

Second, the statement, "You alone are the Lord" (9:6a), affirms God's absolute uniqueness and supremacy over all things, which is similar in essence to the Shema (Deut 6:4). At Mount Sinai, it declares the teaching of Israel's monotheistic faith. Here at the Water Gate, it declares Israel's monotheistic faith in God. This is very significant, since the returning exiles have survived their immersion in a pluralistic and polytheistic environment. With the experience of hardship behind them, the people believe that God alone is the Lord.

Third, by praising God, the people acknowledge him as the creator of the heavens and the highest heavens, the earth and the seas, the cosmos, the starry hosts, all things and all creatures. Similarly, the psalmist extols God's greatness in creating the heavens, the earth, the seas, and all that they contain (Pss 24:1–2; 69:34; 96:11; 146:6; compare Acts 4:24). Everything comes through God and by God alone (compare Col 1:16).

Finally, as the creator, God is the great gift giver of life (9:6c; see also Gen 2:7).

9:7–8 PRAISING GOD'S STEADFAST PROMISE

These two verses acclaim God's faithfulness in the patriarchal period. As the Lord, God is the active mover in calling Abraham, the prominent patriarch, out of Ur. These verses sum up the salient patriarchal history in Abraham's life: (1) God's election of Abraham (9:7); (2) God's covenant with Abraham (9:8); and (3) God's gift of the land (9:8).

First, just as a monotheistic faith is declared through God's universal creation, the declaration, "You are the Lord God, who chose Abram," affirms

---

[4]. LXX accredits the prayer to Ezra, with the addition of the statement, "Ezra said."

God's election of Abraham (9:7). Both the theology of creation and the theology of election express God's universal dominion, power, and concern.

Second, as the righteous God, the Lord has kept his covenant with Abraham and found him to be faithful (Gen 15:6). The history of Israel as God's chosen people begins with Abraham's election. The book of Deuteronomy develops Israel's divine election into a theological concept (Deut 7:6; 14:2). Third, the oft-repeated ancestral promise is fulfilled in the settlement of the land under Joshua. The theme of God giving the land to his people is also the key patriarchal promise (Gen 12:1; 15:18–20).

9:9–11 PRAISING GOD'S SPLENDID DELIVERANCE

This section extols God's love toward his people in the exodus event through his compassionate understanding of their suffering (9:9) and his timely intervention on their behalf (9:10–11). By uttering this history of deliverance, the people not only remember, but they also express hope for God to deliver them from their current predicament.

In the exodus event, when God sees the Hebrew people's pain, he sends Moses to deliver them (Exod 3:7–10). His caring intervention is also demonstrated through the miraculous signs and wonders of the ten plagues against Pharaoh (Exod 7:3; Deut 4:34; 6:22; 7:19; 13:2; 26:8; Pss 78:43; 106:7; 135:9). When God hears the people cry for help at the Red Sea, he rescues them (Exod 12:31–42). This event consists of two equally important events: God's amazing deliverance and astounding power. First, God's people experience his goodness as they pass through the Red Sea on dry ground (Exod 14:21–22). Second, the people experience his power as God hurls their enemies into the depths of the sea (Exod 14:28). The fact that God listens to their prayers is a prominent and unforgettable experience of their salvation history (Exod 3:7; 7:3; 9:16; 14:10, 21–22).

Kidnappings have become rampant in the Philippines, and hardworking Chinese-Filipino families seem to be easy targets. In one such encounter, an elderly Christian man was kidnapped and driven to a remote village in Mindanao. His elder son and daughter, who are faithful believers in the Lord, immediately went to a church, knelt down, and cried out to the Lord for intervention. Meanwhile, as the kidnappers sped through the night, their van went off the road and crashed into a ridge. All the kidnappers were knocked unconscious, but the elderly father was not hurt. He quickly climbed the ridge and got back to the road, and then the Lord stirred some kind-hearted people to give him a ride home. Along the way, he saw a vehicle with his son and daughter as they were returning from church. He managed to flag them down, and they rejoiced together over God's timely and miraculous intervention.

9:12–21 PRAISING GOD'S STEADFAST CARE

This section traces God's steadfast love for the people of God despite their failure. It can be divided into the following three segments: (1) God's unwavering love (9:12–15); (2) man's unruly stubbornness (9:16–18); and (3) God's unceasing grace (9:19–21).

The first segment on God's unwavering love (9:12–15) has four elements: (1) God's guidance through pillars of cloud and fire (9:12); (2) God's gift of regulations and laws (9:13); (3) God's gift of Sabbath (9:14); (4) God's provision of food and water (9:15).

First, God leads the people by a pillar of cloud during day and a pillar of fire during the night (9:12, 19). God's caring guidance is part of their salvation history. When the Israelites start their journey through the desert, these two pillars guide them (Exod 13:21). Second, God speaks to the Israelites through Moses at Mount Sinai and lets them know his desires by giving them regulations, laws, decrees, and commands (9:13; Exod 19–24). Third, God's holy Sabbath is a special gift to his people.[5] In Genesis, there is no direct teaching on Sabbath except the narrative statement about God resting from his work on the seventh day (Gen 2:2–3). The Sabbath teaching comes right after the exodus event (Exod 16:23–30; 23:12; 34:21; 35:2–3) and is a sign of the covenant, showing how God made Israel his special people (Exod 31:12–17; Ezek 20:12, 20)[6] so long as they respond in faith by keeping the Sabbath holy. Throughout the Hebrew Bible, the Sabbath is described as holy (Exod 16:23; Lev 23:3; Isa 58:13), for when God blessed the Sabbath, it attained a holy status (Exod 20:11). The Sabbath is holy to the Lord (Exod 16:23; Lev 19:3; Deut 5:14) and also to Israel (Exod 16:28; Lev 16:31), and so its observance by the people links Israel's holiness with God's holiness.

In the Hebrew Bible, two theological traditions serve as the rationale for Sabbath observance. The book of Exodus in the Decalogue grounds the

---

5. For views comparing John Calvin with other reformers on the idea of Sabbath, see Richard Gaffin, *Calvin and the Sabbath: The Controversy of Applying the Fourth Commandment* (Rossshire, UK: Mentor, 1998).
6. With the last supper, Jesus made a new sign of covenant with his people. See Matt 26:28; Mark 14:24; Luke 22:20.

Sabbath in the creative act of God. God created the heavens and the earth in six days and rested on the seventh day. The seventh day, or the Sabbath, is a time for Israel to worship the Creator God because God set that day apart (Exod 20:11). God enjoys that day of rest, and so humanity ought to rest, too. On the other hand, the book of Deuteronomy in the Decalogue grounds the Sabbath in God's redemption of Israel from Egypt. All of God's people should participate in the Sabbath, but this can only be realized when both masters and slaves share in its observance. Recalling the redemption from Egypt is a good way for Israel to remember the meaning and the need for rest for everyone.

Fourth, God's care and unwavering love for the people of God are demonstrated through his provision of food and water (9:15). The people are given food and water right after they cross the Red Sea. The "bread from heaven" acknowledges God's gracious provision (Exod 16:14–15; Ps 105:40; 1 Cor 10:3) and is the food that God provides for the angels (Ps 78:25). God also provides water for the people during their sojourn in the wilderness (Exod 17:6; Num 20:10; Pss 78:15–17; 105:41; 1 Cor 10:4).

The second segment in this section on God's steadfast love focuses on the people's unruly stubbornness (9:16–18) and consists of two elements: (1) their seditious attitude of arrogance (9:16–17); and (2) their making of an image of a calf (9:18). This subsection accentuates God's compassionate character. As a compassionate and forgiving God, God does not desert his people even though they forsake God and turn to idolatry. The credal theme of God being gracious and merciful is first declared when they are unfaithful to God (9:17; Exod 34:6–7) and then repeated throughout history as they claim his grace (9:31; Num 14:18; Ps 86:15). For the prophets, this oft-repeated theme is a great reminder of God's character (Joel 2:13; Jonah 4:2; Nah 1:3).[7]

The third segment in this section on God's steadfast love focuses on God's unceasing grace (9:19–21) and consists of three elements: (1) God's guidance to lead them (9:19); 2) God's spirit to instruct them (9:20); and (3) God's provision to nourish them (9:20–21).

First, God's "guidance to lead them" repeats the image of God leading the people by a pillar of cloud during the day and a pillar of fire during the night (9:19; see also 9:12). God's guidance in the wilderness reveals his great compassion, for rather than forsaking his people, he showed them the way in

---

[7]. With the theme on repentance, Joel and Jonah stress the nature of God's compassionate love. Nahum, however, quotes God's character and expands the theme of his wrath. See Joseph Too Shao and Rosa Ching Shao, *Joel, Nahum, Malachi*, ABCS (Manila: Asia Theological Association, 2013), 23–24, 53–54.

which they were to go. Second, God's "Spirit to instruct them" is a significant post-exilic interpretation of the wilderness period about the role of God's Spirit in teaching the people of God (9:20; see also 9:30). Previously, God's instruction came through Moses, but in the wilderness period, God's Spirit equips his people for the work he assigns them (Exod 31:1–3; 35:30–31). God's Spirit also strengthens seventy elders to assist Moses in leadership (Num 11:17, 25). In 9:20, the instruction refers to the law of Moses that God gave to his people at Mount Sinai so that they could follow God's standard. Moses, as God's mouthpiece for instruction, teaches them in the Spirit of God. For Isaiah the prophet, the Spirit of the Lord's immanent presence is in their midst during the days of Moses (Isa 63:10–11, 14). Third, God's provision throughout the forty years in the wilderness is part of their redemptive history (9:21; Deut 2:7). God sustained them with food and water, provided them with sufficient clothes that did not wear out, and even saw that their feet were not swollen through all their years of wandering in the desert (9:22; Deut 8:4).

9:22–31 PROCLAIMING GOD'S SUPERB PATIENCE

This section consists of three important events as the people enter the land of promise: (1) God's work in the conquest of Canaan (9:22–25); (2) the people's waywardness in the period of the Judges (9:26–28); and (3) God's warning through the prophets (9:29–31).

First, the historic conquest is a success because God gives the land to his people (9:21). The Israelites know that God actively chased their enemies, Sihon and Og, out of the land, because both these kings were strong and powerful (Num 21:21–35; Deut 2:16–3:11; Deut 29:7; 31:4; Josh 2:10; 9:9–10). The Israelites are only able to enter the land because of God's great goodness (9:25).

Second, the period of Judges recounts a cyclical history of Israel's failures. The people disobey and rebel against the Lord, and so the Lord hands them over to their oppressors, who inflict tedious labor and slavery upon them.[8] When the people cry out to the Lord, he sends deliverers. The cyclical history

---

8. In this summary statement, the prayer uses the verb "give" with reference to their oppression under the enemies. Notice that God "gives" them privileges (9:22), but with disobedience, God "gives" them over to the enemies (9:27). In the book of Judges, the verb "sell" is used concurrently with the verb "give," and sometimes as an alternative of "give." Both verbs speak of God as the Lord and master of the Israelites (see Judg 2:13; 3:8; 10:7).

of failure is a good reminder of their recurrent weaknesses before their merciful God.

Third, the subsection on God's warning through the prophets contrasts God's patience, on the one hand, with the people's arrogance, on the other hand. By obeying God's ordinances, a man will walk with the Lord and live (9:29).[9] Though God's Spirit patiently and painstakingly admonishes the people through his prophets, they stubbornly refuse to listen. Aside from Zechariah, no other prophet expresses this doctrine of God's Spirit as the mediator of God's word to the prophets, who are themselves its mediators (Zech 7:12). The post-exilic community may have been aware of Zechariah's revolutionary interpretation and wanted to affirm that God teaches through his Spirit during the Mosaic period and admonishes by his Spirit through his prophets (9:20, 30). Because God's people do not listen to the warning of God's Spirit, God hands them over to the "neighboring peoples" (9:30, literally, "people of the lands"; Ezra 9:2), who subject God's people to slavery. But with God being gracious and merciful, he still cares for them (9:31; compare Deut 4:31).

9:32–37 PRONOUNCING THE CONFESSION OF GOD'S PEOPLE

The final section acknowledges the historical failures and shortcomings of the people of Israel as they come before the Lord for his judgment. It consists of two main segments: (1) an affirmation of God's steadfast love and an acknowledgment of the people's hardship from the past to present (9:32–35); and (2) an admission of their sins against God, resulting in their state of misery and slavery under foreign rulers (9:36–37).

The first segment wholeheartedly affirms God's steadfast love and plainly acknowledges the people's hardships. The communal prayer of confession names the suffering that has come upon all God's people, including their kings and leaders, priests and prophets, and fathers and grandfathers. The prayer acknowledges that the purpose of all these troubles is to bring the sinful people back to the Lord, who is faithful (9:33–34), and admits that the people did not serve God or turn from their evil ways (9:35).

The second segment of the communal confession presents the people's lowly status as slaves in the land and asks God to lift them out of their distress

---

9. This is a basic OT teaching on sanctification and not justification. See Walter C. Kaiser Jr., *Hard Sayings of the Old Testament* (Downers Grove: InterVarsity Press 1988), 86.

and desolation. Because of their sins, their abundant harvest goes to the foreign kings, who rule over their bodies and their cattle as they please.

In the midst of seemingly endless troubles in the Philippines – from human-made destruction, to terrorists, to natural disasters and sudden calamities – many people have uttered communal prayers for the healing and peace of the land. The leaders and members of Chinese-Filipino churches have often called God's people to join together for public rallies to pray for the country and to confess the nation's sins of idolatry and the people's self-centeredness before God. These corporate prayer meetings are announced through church bulletins and the media, including newspapers and radio broadcasts. During these all-night prayer rallies, people lift up God's name, admit humanity's sinfulness, and beseech God for mercy while also extolling his righteousness. At these times, God's people come together from many different denominations and pray with one heart and one burden for God to lift up the Philippines – the only professing Christian country in Asia – from its economic, political, and spiritual woes and desolations.

RETELLING AND MEMORY

Many prayers and teachings in the Bible include a long summary of Israel's history. In ancient Israel, most households did not hold copies of God's word. Instead, the teachings and legacies of the historic patriarchs were passed on orally. Thus, it was necessary to keep track of God's interventions from the past to the present in order to remind the people of their great heritage and of God's promises. The Israelites take it to heart to remember their founding history, repeating and reviewing it with their children and their children's children, so that it can be passed on to future generations (Ps 78:3–8). Recalling their history reveals their honesty in addressing their weakness and wickedness, their humility in seeking God's forgiveness, and their gratitude for his willingness to take them back into his loving embrace. Memories help bring the past into the present while also pointing to a hopeful future.

In the Bible, interpretative histories are not meant to recreate the historical events exactly as they happened, but to teach the people of God to love the Lord their God with all their heart, soul, mind, and strength. For example, Joshua gives a short history of Israel in his farewell speech (Josh 24:1–15). Likewise, Samuel summarizes the people's rebellious actions against God in his farewell speech (1 Sam 12:1–17).

Throughout the historical psalms, the psalmist retells the history of Israel to teach a lesson, focusing on the rebelliousness of God's people to reveal the graciousness of God. In Psalm 78, the psalmist retells the history from Abraham to the time of Samuel, pointing out why the tribe of Judah is selected over the tribe of Ephraim. In Psalm 89, the psalmist retells the story of the Davidic covenant and then appeals to God for his steadfast love to David's descendants. Psalm 105 recalls God's election of Abraham and the people's rebelliousness, which deserves God's punishment.[1] Psalm 114 narrates the exodus event and how God cares for his people. Psalm 132, a Song of Ascent, focuses on the resting place of the ark in Zion. Lastly, Psalms 135–136 praise God for his deliverance and the gift of land.

The study of human memory differentiates between short-term and long-term memory. Our short-term memory stores up a small quantity of information or images for relatively brief time periods. Our long-term memory contains a nearly limitless storage capacity and is used as a permanent storehouse for meaningful information that keeps updating itself. We hold our past in our long-term memory. Research suggests that our memories interface with one another, which leads to questions about accuracy in testimonies and recollections. Nevertheless, the elements found in these communal prayers, including their organized historical accounts and sequences, can serve to validate the reliability of earlier events. Many biblical writers recite, rehearse, and remind readers about how God was working in the past as well as in their period in history. This practice guards against indifference and forgetfulness.

What have we learned from the past? When we remember God's timely and gracious intervention and redemption in our lives, are we overwhelmed with a spirit of gratitude? How can we retell the story of Christ's saving grace in our lives and in the world truthfully and boldly?

Rosa Ching Shao

---

1. Shirley Ho and Feng Yi Lin, *Psalms 73–150*, ABCS (Manila: OMF, 2013), 120–128.

NEHEMIAH 9:38–10:39

SIGNING AND DECLARING ALLEGIANCE

A church in Manila challenges all its members to participate in God's work by pledging to support mission work. Every year, the pledges far exceed the church's goal, and actual contributions are often even larger than the pledges. Such generosity can be interpreted as a sign of the community's love for God, but from an Asian perspective, it is also honorable.

In Nehemiah 10, the community renews their pledge of faith before God in public. The renewal of the community begins as they read and study the law of Moses (ch. 8), which reveals Israel's unrelenting sins against God. This revelation leads to their honest and thorough communal confession before God (ch. 9). After this public confession, the leaders (priests, Levites, and chiefs) bind the people of God to a renewed covenant to return to God and live according to the law of Moses, putting their decision in writing as a sign of their sincerity (9:38–10:27). Then the people join in the covenant renewal ceremony by making a public oath (10:28–30).

This chapter can be subdivided into three sections: (1) admitting the pledge (9:38);[1] (2) approving the pledge (10:1–27); and (3) affirming the pledge (10:28–39).

9:38 ADMITTING THE PLEDGE

In the Philippines, the *balimbing*, which is a juicy, yellow-green, ten-sided fruit, is plentiful during the summer. If the fruit falls to the ground, it can stand alone on any one side, and yet it can easily change its position. When the fruit is cut crosswise, it looks like a star in the heavens, but its appearance can be deceiving, for it symbolizes the worst in human frailties. Philippine politicians who easily shift political parties for their own benefit are often compared to the *balimbing*. In election time, human *balimbings* are plentiful and full of excuses, and the virtue of loyalty seems rare. Though politicians may behave like Mexican jumping beans or flittering butterflies, the people are no fools.

The binding agreement introduced in Nehemiah 9:38 is a human-made arrangement that differs from the Abrahamic and Davidic covenants, which

---
1. In MT, this verse is Nehemiah 10:1.

were initiated by God. The leaders, Levites, and priests affix their seals as a public means of affirming the pledge, which encourages the people to be loyal and faithful. The covenant renewal ceremony shows the seriousness of the community's commitment.

10:1–27 APPROVING THE PLEDGE

The list of signatories who approve the pledge begins with Nehemiah, the governor (10:1), which is followed by the names of twenty-two priests (10:1–8), seventeen Levites (10:9–13), and forty-four leaders of the people (10:14–27). Listing the names of the leaders who affix their signatures gives weight to the pledge. Affixing a seal in public confirms the communal confession and acknowledges the people's need to return to the Lord. The list is arranged according to the importance of the signatories in the post-exilic community. Nehemiah, the governor, shows his unswerving support to the cause. As always, the priests (because of their sacred duties) are listed before the Levites. The leaders represent the laity in committing their steadfast support to help pay for the costs of the house of God.

In the list of signatories, some names are repeated, as some Levites also participate in the reading of the law (8:7) and some help lead the communal confession (9:4–5). Among the leaders, twelve participate in the rebuilding of the wall. This repetition implies that godly and active leaders are present in each generation. The first eighteen names of the leaders who affix their seals are the same as the first returnees with Zerubbabel (10:14–19; 7:8–25; Ezra 2:3–20). Although it might be hard to prove that they are from the same clan, it is possible that the same names are chosen to reflect the presence of the same clan in their midst. The younger generation may have purposefully used the names of members of their godly older generation to reflect the continuity with their ancestors. As in the practice of the Old Testament, the younger generation seeks to emulate the godly example of the older generation. From one generation to the next, people eagerly and continuously desire to serve the Lord!

In 2006, a Chinese-Filipino *taipan* (a billionaire in the community) expressed his desire to donate a large portion of his earnings to the community. His adult children, all schooled in prestigious schools and universities, followed his wishes and donated generously to a university in Metro Manila. Christian education through Christian day schools is a dynamic vehicle for nurturing the faith of believers. Though we want to spread the gospel to the ends of the earth, the younger generation of godly families also needs to come to the saving knowledge of our Lord. If the descendants of godly parents do not receive the gospel of Christ, they will become the "unreached" generation.[2] We need to be intentional in claiming both the younger and older groups of descendants for the Lord. It is a great blessing to see our clans serving the Lord from generation to generation.

10:28–39 AFFIRMING THE PLEDGE

The law of God is perfect and pure, and everyone who can understand it should seek to obey and observe it. Because of the people's recurring failure to obey God, which is vividly recounted to them as they hear the law of Moses, the people choose to return to God. The community and leaders show their willingness to separate themselves from the people around them, remembering their calling as God's holy people even in the wilderness days after the exodus from Egypt. Their decision to separate from foreigners reveals their commitment to God.

The principle of holiness, which requires the people to separate themselves from others who live in the land, is a central theme of the Mosaic law. The Israelite people must be holy to the Lord and make a statement to the world about their special distinction as the people of God. Having been exiled for many years as a punishment from God for their assimilation with the peoples around them, they have learned the lesson of obedience and are expressing their commitment to follow the law of God. Both young and old join the leaders in binding themselves to the written pledge. All who have had a chance to listen to God's word willingly declare the oath (8:2–3; 10:28). This sacred event is a comprehensive undertaking by the whole community, where everyone – without exception – swears obedience to God's law and all his commands, regulations, and decrees.

This agreement leads to a question about how we should interpret the specific pledges. Are they additive laws or explicative laws? Additive laws signify that the post-exilic community adds laws to the existing laws. Explicative laws signify that the existing laws and regulations are being applied to fit the new generation. The Jewish interpreter Fishbane argues that each generation has their new interpretation of Mosaic law. Every Scripture would have its traditional content (*traditum*), which would change in time (*traditio*) so that

---

2. Ironically, the "reached generation" in the book of Joshua is described as having raised up an "unreached generation" in the book of Judges (Josh 24:31; Judg 2:7–10).

it is fitting and proper for each new generation. Fishbane describes this process as "inner biblical exegesis."[3]

Similarly, Clines suggests that the pledges represent early Jewish biblical exegesis, revealing how God's laws have been interpreted and how they developed into the Mishnah and the Talmud. There are five stages in this development: (1) the creation of the facilitating law; (2) the revision of the facilitating law; (3) the creation of new prescriptions; (4) the re-definition of categories; and (5) the integration of separate legal prescriptions.[4] Thus the specific pledges in Numbers are explicative laws, which explain the salient issues facing the post-exilic community based on the written law. As in the celebration of the Feast of the Tabernacles, the community applies the essence of the law (8:16–17; Ezra 3:4).

The specific pledges are subdivided into four main areas of concern: (1) purity in marriage (10:30); (2) Sabbath rest (10:31); (3) offerings for God's house (10:32–34); and (4) support for the temple and temple personnel (10:35–39).

The first pledge regarding purity in marriage is intended to preserve the people's national unity and identity (10:30) by making a promise about their daughters. In the Hebrew world, parents hold the key to the successful married life of their children, as the parents make important decisions and give spiritual guidance on behalf of their descendants. Hence they promise not "to give" and not "to take" daughters from the peoples around them. This stipulation against intermarriage is based on the Mosaic law (Exod 34:11–16; Deut 7:1–4). Whereas the Mosaic law identifies the people groups by name, the all-inclusive terminology in the post-exilic period distinguishes the Israelites from the people who live among them as their neighbors (literally, "the peoples of the land," 10:28, 31). This instruction assures that the Israelite people will serve the one true God and not be tempted to follow after the gods of Canaan.

The second pledge focuses on Sabbath rest, which implies resting from buying material goods (10:31a), letting the land rest (10:31b), and resting from debts (10:31c). These Sabbath principles are explained together because the Mosaic law that they read and study during the Feast of Tabernacles includes the teaching about the sabbatical year (Deut 31:9–11). This teaching reminds the people that they are the covenant people of God, and they owe everything

---

3. Michael Fishbane, *Biblical Interpretation in Ancient Israel* (Oxford: Clarendon, 1985), 123–134, 165–166, 213–216.
4. David J. A. Clines, "Nehemiah 10 as an Example of Early Jewish Biblical Exegesis," *JSOT* 21 (1981): 111–117.

to God. The weekly Sabbath rest is a very important sign, as it mirrors the God of creation, who rests after his creation.

Sabbath marks the people of God and encourages them to rest from work (Exod 20:8–11; 23:12; 31:13–17; 34:21; 35:2–3; Lev 23:3; Deut 5:12–15). In the eighth century, the Israelites are forbidden from doing any trade on the Sabbath (Amos 8:5). Jeremiah reminds the people not to engage in any commercial activities or carry merchandise on the Sabbath (Jer 17:21–24). Likewise, Ezekiel encourages the people to keep the Sabbath holy (Ezek 20:20; 44:24). By pledging not to buy from the neighboring peoples on the Sabbath, the people are seeking to keep the Sabbath holy. To ensure that there will not be any trading between the Israelites and non-Israelites on the Sabbath, the pledge states the position of the Israelites unilaterally and comprehensively.

Similar Sabbath principles are assigned to the fallow year law as well as the remission year law. Both of these laws reflect the essence of Sabbath rest by ensuring that the land and the debtor can "cease" from their duties. This upholds the religious value of God-given rest. The fallow year law is agricultural and allows the land to rest every seventh year (10:31b). Giving the land a year of rest is just as important as the weekly Sabbath (Exod 23:10–11). The land, like the people, needs to rest, and the purpose of this law is to teach the people that God's provisions are for both humans and animals (Lev 25:1–7). The produce of the fallow year reminds them that the land does not belong to them, for God alone is the owner of the land and gives them permission to live by enjoying its produce (Exod 17:16; Lev 25:23; Deut 8:7–18). Of course, when the land is at rest, the people also rest. The people of God make this commitment upon their return from exile, since the reason for their exile was because the land did not rest (2 Chr 36:21; Lev 26:34–35).

The remission year law is economic and cancels all debts at the end of the sabbatical year. The idea behind this law is clearly explained in the debt (*semittah*) laws in Deuteronomy (Deut 15:1–15; compare Exod 21:2–6).[5] The purpose of cancelling debts at the end of the Jubilee Year is not so that debtors can run away from responsibility. Rather, debt relief is a loving and generous measure to free debtors from their obligations in order to promote social welfare for fellow Israelites who have become poor. Creditors who drop

---

5. The Hebrew word *semittah* means to "cancel" debts. The law is a way to free the debtors. The Mishnah further develops the stipulations related to debt (see Shevi'it 10:1–2). For further discussion, see David Baker, *Tight Fists or Open Hands? Wealth and Poverty in Old Testament Law* (Grand Rapids: Eerdmans, 2009), 278–285.

outstanding debts at the end of the sabbatical year point to the God who is the giver of all wealth.

Offerings for God's house can be subdivided into a temple tax (10:32–33) and the wood offering (10:34). Previously, a one-time tax was levied for the work of the tabernacle (Exod 30:11–16; 38:25–26) and the repair of the temple (2 Kg 12:4–15; 2 Chr 24:4–14). Here, the offering of "a third of a shekel each year" reflects the need to sustain the house of the Lord during the post-exilic era (10:32). This annual levy encourages Israelites to take care of God's house. The "service" of the house refers to daily and periodic offerings at the house of God (10:32–33). The "duties" of the house refer to the maintenance of the temple building (10:33).

The "wood offering" is a practical application of what is written in the law (10:34). In the existing law, the fire on the altar must be kept burning continuously (Lev 6:12–13), but there is nothing specific about who should bring wood to the altar. During the time of Joshua, the task for bringing the wood to the altar is assigned to the Gibeonites (Josh 9:27). After Saul eliminates the Gibeonites, no one is in charge of this service (2 Sam 21:1). Hence, the wood offering law ensures that the fire on the altar will be kept burning. This is an explicative law that applies what is written in the law.

Supporting the temple personnel is part of the work of the temple. In the Mosaic law, the people bring the first fruits of their crops and fruit trees each year as a reflection of giving their best to the Lord as an offering (Exod 23:19; 34:26; Deut 26:2, 20). These offerings benefit the priests (Num 18:12–13). Support for temple personnel can be subdivided into three areas of concern. The first area is the importance of having younger recruits. As written in the law, the firstborn of their sons belongs to the Lord (10:36; Exod 13:2; 22:29–30; 34:19; Deut 15:19). Just as Hannah gave Samuel to Eli, the giving of their firstborn sons will ensure that people will continue to minister at the temple (1 Sam 1–3). The second area of concern is the daily living needs of the priests, Levites, and other temple personnel, which will be met when the people bring crops and other offerings to support them. The third area of concern is a system for receiving offerings and tithes. To ensure that the people give tithes, the Levites collect the tithes in all the towns (10:37). The presence of priests with the Levites as they receive tithes (10:38) ensures accountability and proper checks and balances.

A newly elected deacon in a church in the Philippines was chosen as the treasurer because of his integrity and success in a business venture. During the weekly Sunday offering, the deacons assigned to collect the money would count it together immediately after the service so that it could be deposited the next day. During the new deacon's first week duty, he suggested that the other deacons simply count the money and let him know the total amount. Another seasoned and experienced deacon wisely resisted this idea, which could create doubts and questions regarding the integrity of the deacons. The new deacon joined the others in their weekly accounting task, and so the crisis was averted. Offerings and funds in any church or organization need to be managed by leaders with integrity. Moreover, there needs to be an effective system with checks and balances in place.

> ### **COMMITMENTS AND CHALLENGES**
>
> The key leaders of the Israelite people sign their names on a pledge to signify their commitment to obey God. How can we encourage key leaders in our churches to make such strong commitments? Both reading God's word and making a public confession brought about the spiritual revival of the community. Nehemiah reveals how instrumental these practices are in restoring people's relationship with God.
>
> In the postmodern era, with so many eclectic ideas around us, we need to focus on the fundamentals in our mission and outreach. What are some of the obstacles to our mission work? What key mission themes and strategies need to be addressed?
>
> Many churches have annual mission weeks to instill a burden for mission work into their members' hearts and enhance their love for God's work. To make action relevant, it starts with the pastoral team and core leaders who discuss and initiate changes, and all the members respond accordingly, just like the time of Nehemiah. Every annual mission week at Grace Gospel Church in the Philippines, members are challenged to get involved with the church's mission programs. As part of the member care program, the church provides free professional health services for their missionaries, including dental work and physical checkups, and also invites church leaders and members to host the missionaries by offering them lodging, meals, encouragement, and prayer support. Many of the missionaries look forward to these refreshing times of fellowship and prayer. The church also supports missionaries by hosting revivals and testimonial services and supplying them with books and other educational materials so that they can remain updated about the trends of the time. Through these efforts, both

church members and missionaries are strengthened in their common commitment to mission work.

The Asia Theological Association (ATA) helps participating member schools remain aware about key issues faced by theological schools and seminaries by hosting representatives from around Asia for annual assemblies. During these gatherings, participants discuss many relevant and challenging Asian issues and also develop significant guidelines about how Asian churches can connect with and learn from each other. The ATA also encourages both young and mature scholar-pastors and leaders to write articles and books for the church in Asia and beyond.

In the pluralistic world of our time, we may not be able to solve all our theological differences, but as we present and discuss the relevant issues of our time, our pastors and missionaries can become better-equipped to serve their constituents with clear biblical teaching, Christian values, and doctrinal truth. After the ninth annual Chinese Congress of World Evangelization, which was held in Taipei, Taiwan, in 2017, many delegates returned home with a refreshed spirit, an empowering vision for mission, and a renewed burden and passion to bring the holistic salvation of Christ to their respective communities.

Rosa Ching Shao

NEHEMIAH 11:1–36

RESETTLEMENT IN JERUSALEM

Resettling a people group is not easy. Sometimes resettlement happens because of calamities, such as famine or war. A missionary serving in southern China resettled a whole Christian community to Kota Kinabalu, Malaysia, for religious and economic reasons. Today, most of the churches in Kota Kinabalu continue to use Hakka as their language during worship. The community continues to thrive because of its first settlement.

Nehemiah 11 is about resettling the city of Jerusalem. Because of the sparse population in Jerusalem, the resettlement could have commenced right after finishing the wall (7:4–5). The community, however, needed to be taught and formed by God's word (8:1–10:39). Having pledged themselves to live according to God's word and will, the community is now ready to move into the next stage for stabilizing and safeguarding Jerusalem.

There are two essential groupings in the resettlement. First, the list records the names of those who are willing to live inside the holy city, along with their ancestry (11:1–24). Second, the list records locations of those who prefer to remain in their ancestral homes (11:25–36). Both settlements show the theme of faithfulness. The first list indicates the faithfulness of the people, who comprise a reliable and rising community. The second list confirms God's faithfulness to the returned community by bringing the people back to their ancestral homes, as prophesied by Isaiah, Jeremiah, and Ezekiel.

11:1–24 LIVING IN HOLY JERUSALEM

This section can be subdivided into four segments: (1) commending the leaders and volunteers (11: 1–2); (2) listing the lay families in Jerusalem (11:3–9); (3) listing the priests in Jerusalem (11:10–14); and (4) listing the Levites and the gatekeepers in Jerusalem (11:15–24).

The people who live in Jerusalem are leaders and volunteers (11: 1–2). The leaders of the people set a good example by settling in Jerusalem, the holy city, where they can be closer to the temple (11:1). The holy city is also known as the holy mountain (Joel 3:17; Isa 65:25). According to the law of Moses, the people have to worship God in Jerusalem three times a year (Exod 23:14–19; Deut 16:16). Hence, Jerusalem is the center of worship, and this motivates the leaders to live nearby so they can worship at the temple and set a good example for others to follow (11:18; Isa 48:2; 52:1).

The rest of the people cast lots to decide which one out of every ten should live in Jerusalem. This method is used throughout the Old Testament to make decisions (compare 10:34; Num 26:55–56; Josh 7:14–18; 14:2; 18:6–8; 1 Sam 10:20–21; 14:41–42; Prov 16:33). Ten percent of the people are eager to live in Jerusalem, but others prefer to live outside Jerusalem in their own ancestral homes in the towns of Judah (11:3, 20).

The list of names in this chapter is similar to the list of those who returned to Jerusalem (1 Chr 9:2–17), but the emphasis here is to recognize those who reside in Jerusalem (11:4). This list begins with the descendants of Judah (11:4–6), followed by the descendants of Benjamin (11:7–9), and then the priests (11:10–14), Levites (11:15–18), and gatekeepers (11:19).

The list identifies the heads of the families of Judah – Athaiah (11:4) and Maaseiah (11:5), as well as Benjamin – Sallu (11:7) and his followers, Gabbai and Sallai (11:8). The list also gives the total number of men: 486 from Judah and 928 from Benjamin (11:6, 8). The descendants of Judah trace their roots to Perez (Gen 38:29; 46:12) and Shelah (Gen 38:5; 46:12). Perez, the ancestor of David (Ruth 4:18–22), is the prominent ancestor of Judah. In the New Testament, the ancestral line of Jesus is traced through Perez (Matt 1:13; Luke 3:33). Compare with 1 Chronicles 9:7–9 where there are four clans, the descendants of Benjamin listed here come from one clan (11:7–9). The paucity of data during the post-exilic period could be a reason why only one clan is listed here. Moreover, the sad historical incident where the tribe of Benjamin was almost wiped out because of their perverted behavior during a chaotic period of the judges (Judg 19–21) may add to this issue. As part of the southern kingdom, the tribe of Benjamin returned with the tribe of Judah.

The list of priests reflects three faithful priestly families who are willing to live in Jerusalem:[1] 822 men from Jedaiah (11:10), 242 men from Adaiah (11:12), and 128 men from Amashsai (11:12–14). The associates of Jedaiah, who head the list of the priestly families, are responsible for general and significant involvement at the temple (11:12; compare 1 Chr 28:13). The associates of Adaiah are only heads of the families (11:13), whereas the associates of Amashsai are in charge of defense (11:14) One of the ancestors of Jedaiah, Zadok, is one of two priests during the time of David (11:11; 2 Sam 8:17),

---

[1]. For an alternative view, see Joseph Blenkinsopp, *Ezra-Nehemiah: A Commentary*, OTL (Philadelphia: Westminster, 1988), 321–325, who argues for the listing of six priestly families: Jedaiah, Joiarib, Jakin, Seraiah, Pashhur, and Immer.

and he eventually ascends to the sole possession of the Jerusalem priesthood in the time of Solomon (1 Kgs 1–2). The descendants of Zadok continue to serve until their exile (586 BC) and even after being exiled. Pashhur, one of the ancestors of Adaiah, and Immer, one of the ancestors of Amashsai, are two of the four priestly heads during the first return (11:12, 13; 7:40–41; Ezra 2:37–38).

The list of Levites reflects six important families: Shemaiah, Shabbethai, Jozabad, Mattaniah, Bakbukiah, and Abda (11:15–18). Mattaniah, Bakbukiah, and Abda are Levite musicians. Shemaiah is a descendant of Hashabiah, who returned to Jerusalem with Ezra (Ezra 8:24) and was one of the three leaders of the Levites (12:24) that belonged to the Merari clan (1 Chr 9:14). Whereas the priests work at the temple, the two Levites – Shabbehai and Jozabad – work outside the house of God, doing miscellaneous tasks, such as collecting tithes and supplying materials. Mattaniah is a descendant of Asaph, one of the three choir leaders during the time of David (1 Chr 25:1–2).

The gatekeepers consist of two important leaders: Akkub and Talmon (11:19). Together with four other gatekeepers, they are in charge of guarding the storerooms of the temple (12:25). There is a total of 172 gatekeepers. Ziha and Gishpa are the leaders of temple servants (11:21).

Regarding the musicians living in Jerusalem, the record includes some supplementary notes (11:22–24), identifying Uzzi as one of the descendants of Asaph, and outlining specific job descriptions for the work of the musicians in the house of God. King David is credited for giving the royal order that regulates the activities of the musicians (11:23; 12:24; 1 Chr 16:4).

11:25–36 LIVING IN ANCESTRAL TOWNS

The rest of the Israelites from the tribes of Judah and Benjamin choose to live in their ancestral towns (11:20). The descendants of Judah live in the ancestral towns of Judah (11:25–30), and the descendants of Benjamin live in the ancestral towns of Benjamin (11:31–35). There is a special note about some Levites who settle in Benjamin (11:36).

All the towns listed as the ancestral towns of Judah, except for Dibon (11:25), Jeshua (11:26), and Meconah (11:28), existed in the time of Joshua and were allotted to the tribe of Judah (Josh 15:20–62). The list starts with Kiriath Arba, an archaic name for Hebron (Judg 1:10; Josh 15:13–14). The phrase "from Beersheba to the Valley of Hinnom" is geographical terminology that describes the traditional inheritance of Judah (11:30; Josh 15:8). The ancestral towns are further divided into categories of villages, fields, and settlements. Whereas cities may have walls, the villages are normally without walls (compare Lev 25:31). The fields may refer to tilled soil with domesticated animals (Gen 29:2; 30:16; Exod 9:3) or untilled soil with wild animals (Jer 14:5). The settlements (or "villages," NASB) are the smallest category of divisions.

The descendants of Benjamin also settle in their own ancestral towns. The towns of Geba, Bethel, and Ramah were allotted to the tribe of Benjamin in the time of Joshua (Josh 18:22–25).

GATHERING IN AND REACHING OUT

It would not be easy to assign people to live in the holy city of Jerusalem during the days of Nehemiah's resettlement, but a number of groups are willing to relocate. Of course, many families prefer to live in their own towns as a fulfillment of the promises of the prophets. Some missional principles about our involvement in the expansion of God's kingdom on earth can be drawn from the resettlement in Jerusalem.

One church plants churches by assigning a group of mature believers and a faithful pastor or elder to be stationed in an outreach point. This group of forerunners agrees to attend the regular Sunday worship at their outreach point faithfully and to invite newcomers and seekers to join them. This particular group of core believers thus forms a "daughter" church.

Sometimes, only a handful of believers are willing to move to an outreach point because they have become so used to the worship services in the mother church. However, after much prayer and waiting, as in the Book of Acts, a group of committed believers is gathered and sent out to attend and promote the ministries in the new location. These believers sacrifice longtime friendships with mother church members and often struggle to make new friends at the new location. Most people like to stay in their familiar comfort zone, and so only those with a missional heart and a burden for lost souls will strive to see a budding group of new believers grow in the new place of worship.

We need to raise up new generations of believers from the existing Christian families in our churches by nurturing new and younger generations of faithful believers. Though many pious parents rear pious children, and in every church there are family clans of generational followers of Christ, we need to be intentional about outreach in order to beget more kingdom followers of Christ. We need to take a serious look at how generational believers are born and reared. Many times, we cannot see the benefits of bringing the whole family into a newly established outreach point, where a shortage of ministerial staff might turn off or even disappoint zealous members.

Three families of a metropolitan church made the decision to heed God's calling for missional outreach in a remote area. These committed families saw their children take up vacant ministries by serving as song leaders, teaching children, and even doing visitation work. Thus the spiritual gifts of their families were put to good use in the Body of Christ.

In the missiological context, how can we channel special interest groups to do what they feel called to do for the glory of God? Some can shine for Christ in the public marketplace, while others can tend one-on-one ministries in their personal spaces.

Gathering people together in a concentrated place and scattering them into the world are both necessary aspects of mission. A missional church should use both approaches to reach out and touch those who need God's love. The "unreached" groups need God's workers to share the gospel with them. At the same time, the "reached" groups need pastors to help them deepen their faith so that they mature as Christians and become disciple-makers for Jesus.

Rosa Ching Shao

The Processional Routes
(Nehemiah 12)

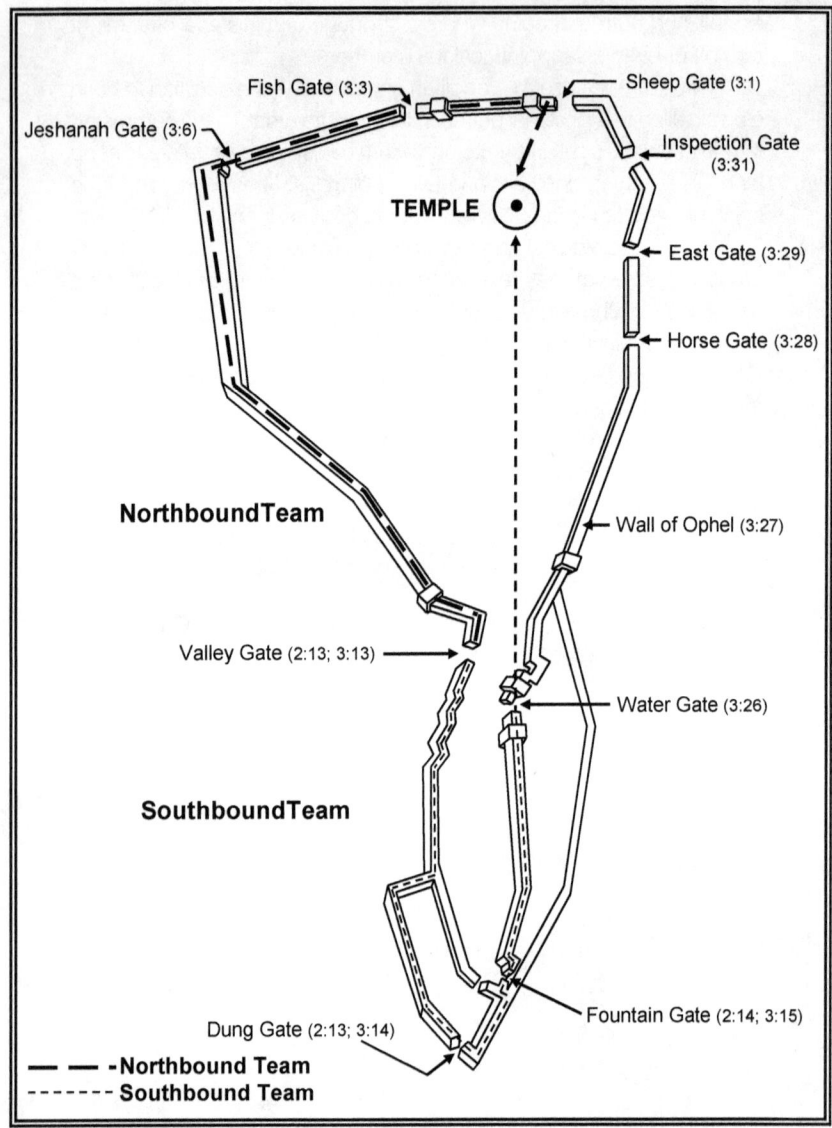

NEHEMIAH 12:1–47

CLANS AND CELEBRATION

The traditional Chinese custom of extending oral or written invitations to festive celebrations shows respect and honor to one's relatives and friends. During Chinese New Year, birthdays, and weddings, people extend special invitations to extended family or clan members as well as others in the community. As relatives and friends gather for these celebrations, conversations often include both what is happening now in people's lives as well what happened in the past. The characters and deeds of those in previous generations may be remembered or honored during the gathering.

Nehemiah 12 is about the dedication of the wall in Jerusalem. Prior to the dedication ceremony, Nehemiah records the names of the priests and Levites from both the past and present (12:1–26). The celebration is a festive occasion for everyone, and so invitations are extended to all Levites, both active and non-active (12:27–43). Under the leadership of the priests and Levites, the people celebrate and dedicate the city wall, reflecting David's system of assigning temple worshipers and gatekeepers many decades earlier. Finally, Nehemiah instills a system to care for those who serve in God's temple (12:44–47).

12:1–26 REGISTERING THE PRIESTS AND LEVITES

Throughout the book of Nehemiah, recording names is an important way to acknowledge those who are involved in the rebuilding of Jerusalem during the post-exilic period (3:1–32; 7:6–73). Identifying the names of the priests and Levites who serve at the temple is particularly important, since names depict their root lineage and thus bestow credibility on those who perform the holy tasks at the temple worship. Chapter 12 records two clans of priests and Levites, one from the time of Joshua and the other from the time of Joiakim (12:1, 12). Joshua represents the generation immediately after the return from exile, whereas Joiakim signifies the second generation after the return. The content of this section can be divided into five lists: (1) priests in the days of Joshua (12:1–7); (2) Levites in the days of Joshua (12:8–9); (3) a chronological list of high priests (12:10–11); (4) priests in the days of Joiakim (12:12–21); and (5) chief Levites in the days of Eliashib to the time of Nehemiah and Ezra (12:22–26).

Twenty-two priests served with Joshua during the first return (12:1–7). These priests are then listed as the family heads of the next generation (12:12–21). Joshua is the son of Jehozadak, the high priest before the exile, and so he is the first high priest after the exile (Hag 1:1; 2:2, 4; 1 Chr 6:15). Hence, Joshua serves as the reference name for the first returnees (12:7, 10; Ezra 3:2l). Following the method commonly employed in Chronicles, Joshua's priestly genealogy is listed down to Jaddua in descending order (12:10–11; compare 1 Chr 6:3–15). In the summary list, Joiakim and Eliashib serve as the high priests during the time of Nehemiah and Ezra (12:10, 26; 3:1).

The list of high priests is as follows:

Joshua	(ca. 570 BC)
Joiakim	(ca. 545 BC)
Eliashib I	(ca. 545 BC)
Johanan I	(ca. 520 BC)
Eliashib II	(ca. 495 BC)
Joiada I	(ca. 470 BC)
Johanan II	(ca. 445 BC)
Jaddua II	(ca. 420 BC)
Johanan III	(ca. 395 BC)
Jaddua III	(ca. 370 BC)
Onias I	(ca. 345 BC)
Simon I	(ca. 320 BC)

Only four priestly families were listed among the first returnees (7:39–42; Ezra 2:36–39), but twenty-two priests are eligible and willing to serve during the time of Joiakim (12:12–21). Compared with the list in Chronicles, it seems that the names here are placed in the order that they served, and over time the list grew to twenty-four families (1 Chr 24:7–19).

The list of Levitical family heads includes six names in addition to the seventy-four listed among the first returnees, including Binnui, Sherebiah, Judah, and Mattaniah (12:8–9; compare 7:43; Ezra 2:40). The two antiphonal choirs, which face each other, are part of the common practice in worship after the return from exile (12:8–9, 24).

Nehemiah looks into the book of annals (12:23) for accurate data, which was a regular practice during this time. The book of annals refers to the temple archival materials, which differ from 1 and 2 Chronicles. The family heads of the Levites and the names of the high priests are historical signposts (12:12–22) that refer to the authentic names of actual servant-leaders. Earlier, the lifetime of a high priest marked the successive eras of the monarchy, but now, without a ruling king in their midst, the heads of the Levitical families delineate their times.

The title "man of God" (12:24) is used in earlier biblical literature as an honorific title for prophets who are used by the Lord God, such as Shemaiah (1 Kgs 12:22; 13:4, 6), Samuel (1 Sam 9:6–7), Elijah (1 Kgs 17:18, 24), and Elisha (2 Kgs 4:7; 13:19). King David is also identified as a "man of God" throughout the biblical narrative (Deut 33:1; Josh 14:5; Ps 90:1; Ezra 3:2; 1 Chr 23:14; 2 Chr 30:16). During the post-exilic period, David continued to impart an enduring mark in the religious life of Israel, for he instigated meaningful innovation to the worship system during his reign[1] by developing the order of worship (12:24; Ezra 3:10; 2 Chr 8:14) and the musical instruments used in worship (12:36; 2 Chr 7:6). Because David understood God's heart, he was given this title.

12:27–47 REJOICING OVER THE WALL DEDICATION

Having finished the rebuilding of the wall (6:15), renewed the people's covenant with God (8:1–10:39), and established the resettlement of the people in and around Jerusalem (11:1–36), it is finally time for Nehemiah to plan a joyous wall dedication celebration. Before the dedication, an invitation is sent to the Levites, who are living in many different places, so that they can join in the celebration through song and music (compare Ezra 3:10; 2 Sam 6:5; 2 Chr 13:8; 15:16, 19, 28). This section can be divided as follows: (1) preparing the guest list for the celebration (12:27–30); (2) staging the celebration (12:31–43); and (3) plotting out the financial system that will support God's workers (12:44–47).

As Nehemiah and the post-exilic community carefully plan the wall dedication, they intentionally seek out the Levites and the musicians, both those who are residing in Jerusalem (11:15–18) and those who are living around Jerusalem (11:36; 12:28–29), so that all can join in the celebration (12:27–28). Under normal circumstances, the Levites and musicians living outside Jerusalem would be left alone to tend their plots of land, but the

---

1. S. de Vries, "Moses and David as Cult Founders in Chronicles," *JBL* 107 (1988): 619–639.

community's inclusive approach gives the "fallen" Levites a chance to return to Jerusalem to participate in the Lord's work (compare 13:10).

Before the dedication of the wall, both the leaders and participants have to be ceremonially purified to show their respect for God and to demonstrate their uniqueness as a people who worship the holy God.[2] Purification is not only a symbolic act, but also an outward expression of their internal commitment. The theology of holiness both emphasizes the greatness and uniqueness of God and also reminds the people to be holy before the holy God. This theology begins on Mount Sinai when God teaches them about the concept of purity (Exod 19:5–6, 10–15). The priests and Levites must purify themselves and then purify the rest of the crowd as well as the gates and wall (12:30). The purification process for the priests and Levites may involve cleansing the body and clothes with water, abstaining from sexual relationship, and offering sin-sacrifices (Exod 19:10, 14–15; Lev 14:49–53; Num 8:5–8, 21; 19:18). The purification process for the people, the gates, and the city wall may involve a sprinkling of water (Lev 14:7–9; Ezek 36:35).

As Nehemiah executes the wall dedication, the spirit of joy is clearly visible in both the southbound choir (12:31–37) and the northbound choir (12:38–42). Then all who are gathered celebrate with joy (12:43). The twin choir processions lead the corporate singing with thanksgiving and confession, and Ezra is the leader of the whole procession (12:36). The design for each choir is as follows:

Southbound Choir	Northbound Choir
First choir (v. 31)	Second choir (v. 38)
Seven priests (vv. 33–35a)	Seven priests (v. 41)
Zechariah as precentor (v. 35b)	Izrehiah as precentor (v. 42)
Eight musicians (v. 36)	Eight musicians (v. 42)
Hoshaiah as leader (v. 32)	Nehemiah as leader (v. 38)
Half of the officials (v. 32)	Half of the officials (v. 40)

---

2. The post-exilic community is especially sensitive to the concept of holiness. Prior to the passover celebration, the priests and Levites purify themselves first before taking charge of the feast (Ezra 6:20). Before returning the sacred vessels to the room that Tobiah occupied in the house of God, the room is purified (13:9). The Levites have to purify themselves before guarding the gates (13:22). In concluding his work, Nehemiah purifies the priests and Levites of everything foreign (13:30).

The celebratory route is reminiscent of Nehemiah's nocturnal surveillance of the damaged wall (2:12–15). As the people process, the Fountain Gate and the Water Gate serve as markers along the way (12:37, 39). Many key leaders are also duly recognized as they walk around the wall towards the house of God (12:40). The celebration climaxes as the people offer great sacrifices and rejoice because God has given them great joy (12:43).

One significant aspect of the dedication is that Ezra, who is identified in the text as the scribe, leads the whole procession on top of the wall (12:36), and so he is also symbolically identified as the religious leader of the two choirs. Just as Ezra led the reading of God's word at the Water Gate, Ezra also leads this celebration. As the priest, Ezra knows the proper way to worship with the musical instruments prescribed by David, and respecting this tradition is important for the post-exilic community.

Nehemiah, on the other hand, is merely the section leader of the southbound choir, and Hoshaiah is the section leader of the northbound choir (12:32, 38). This decision shows Nehemiah's humility and greatness. As the key leader behind the rebuilding of the wall, Nehemiah could have asserted his leadership and led the whole celebration, but he lets Ezra have the honor of leading the celebration instead.

All the people, including women and children, gather for this grand celebration of God's goodness and grace. Though food is not mentioned, it would be a normal tradition for them to include food in the fellowship offering (see 1 Kgs 8:62–66). Just as the Lord made the rebuilding work on the wall possible, the people's joy in this celebration also comes from God. When the foundation of the temple was laid by the first returnees, their cry of celebratory joy was heard from afar (Ezra 3:11–13). Similarly, in this celebration of the wall, the people rejoice with joy that can be heard from afar (12:43).

In the post-exilic community, some Levites are staying in their own towns around Jerusalem, working with their own hands for their survival rather than relying on the support of the community. After the celebration, Nehemiah plots out a financial system to support the priests and the Levites. The purpose of this financial system is to ensure that continuous worship through the priests and Levites can be sustained. Most significantly, Nehemiah assigns men to take charge of the storerooms to gather the contributions, first fruits, and tithes (12:44a). With proper support, the priests and the Levites can minister to the people in the community, following the teachings of David and Solomon (12:44b–45; 2 Chr 8:13–14). The commitment of the post-exilic community in supporting God's ministry follows what they pledged during the covenant renewal ceremony (10:35–39).

The ability to be generous to the ministering priests and Levites is in direct proportion to the people's gifts. The phrase "in the days of David and Asaph" (12:46) states the proper procedure for orderly worship through the directors of the musicians in conducting songs of praise and thanksgiving. The concluding phrase, "in the days of Zerubbabel and of Nehemiah" (12:47), describes their obedience to God by setting aside "portions" to God, so that the proper daily "portions" or other designated "portions" can be given generously even to the musicians and the gatekeepers. The "portion" is sustained by their obedience to God (12:44, 47), and the people willingly bring in daily "portions" as contributions to God's work. With this good system of management in place, along with strong leadership and the people's understanding of and obedience to the law, the priests and the Levites can be supported. Moreover, the musicians and gatekeepers can serve joyfully. The Levites, having received their portions, can continue to practice giving their tithes as contributions to the descendants of Aaron. It is always a great privilege to give back to God what already belongs to him!

PORTIONS FOR PASTORS

Today's pastors and Christian workers are not the priests and Levites of the Old Testament. However, the books of Ezra and Nehemiah can guide us about how we can respect and care for our pastors and provide for their needs.

The priests and Levites do not have an allotment of land or inheritance in the land of Israel (Num 18:23; Deut 18:1–3), and so the Old Testament makes other provisions for them. The priests receive the unconsumed portions of the offerings along with the Levitical tithes (Num 18:8–20, 26–29); the Levites receive Israel's tithes (Num 18:21–24). Before entering the promised land, forty-eight cities are designated to meet the needs of the Levites (Num 35:1–8; Josh 21:1–42). Within the Levitical cities, six are designated as cities of refuge,[1] with three on each side of Jordan (Num 35:13–15). Both the priests and Levites also share a portion of the spoils of battle (Num 31:25–30). Although the Torah teaching is very clear, actual provision of care for the Levites by the people of God is lacking. The Levites are typically classified in the biblical narrative along with the poor, aliens, and widows who need God to allot a special portion for them (Deut 14:28–29; 26:12).

For the restoration of worship in the post-exilic era, both the priests and Levites are needed. When the people renew their covenant with God, Nehemiah makes sure to restore the system of offerings and tithes to provide for the needs of the priests and Levites (Neh 10:36–39). Similarly, after the celebration of the wall, the storerooms are arranged so that portions can be given to the priests and Levites (Neh 12:44–47). Unfortunately, however, due to communal neglect, the Levites eventually have to return to their own fields (Neh 13:10–11).

In the New Testament, Paul gives thanks for the way that the church at Philippi generously supports him with gifts (Phil 4:14–18). Though Paul is a tentmaker, he wants God's servants to receive double honor, especially those who are involved in preaching and teaching (1 Tim 5:17–18). Moreover, he teaches that they should be respected with love (1 Thess 5:12–13; Heb 13:7, 17).

Rosa Ching Shao

---

1. The Levitical city of refuge is to grant asylum to accidental manslaughter. The aim is to control the blood avenger from doing justice on his own against the culprit. Although the city of refuge may give safety to the "fugitive," his stay there is also a punitive detention.

NEHEMIAH 13:1–31

RETURNING TO THE PROPER TASKS

Nehemiah 13 is about the reforms that Nehemiah institutes in the post-exilic community when he returns to Jerusalem after a short absence. For twelve years (445–433 BC), Nehemiah serves as governor to the returnees in Jerusalem (5:14). Sometime after the wall dedication, he goes to Persia to visit King Artaxerxes. When he returns to Jerusalem, he is appalled to discover that the people have gone back to their unfaithful ways toward God (13:6–7). Thus many of his previous reforms have to be dealt with again. After a brief opening note that describes the context for this chapter, Nehemiah returns to the first person.

Every major segment of Nehemiah's reformation ends with a simple remembrance prayer (13:14, 22, 31) that consists of three simple elements: a call for active remembrance, a request for mercy, and a summary of what Nehemiah has accomplished for God and his people.

13:1–3 COMPREHENDING GOD'S WORD TO BAN FOREIGNERS

After reading from the book of Moses, the people learn that no Ammonite or Moabite should be admitted into God's assembly (13:1; compare Deut 23:3–6). As noted previously, the book of Moses is also referred to as the law of Moses (2 Chr 25:4; 35:12). The post-exilic community interprets the "tenth generation" of the law as a "forever" or lasting prohibition. The term "assembly of God" is synonymous with the post-exilic Jewish community (see 5:13; 8:2; Ezra 10:12, 14) and is also used to refer to the national origin of the assembly of Israel during the wilderness period (Num 16:3; 20:4).

Upon hearing God's word, the people realize that they must exclude all who are of foreign descent, since the Ammonites and Moabites did not extend love to the Israelites by meeting them with provisions, but rather maliciously hired Balaam to call down a curse upon them (Num 22–24). The Israelites' exclusion of foreigners is directly related to their profession of faith.[1]

---

[1]. Unlike LXX, the book of Ruth is part of the "Writings" in the Hebrew canon along with Ezra-Nehemiah. The book of Ruth, therefore, gives a clear answer that the believing foreign

13:4–14 CHALLENGING GOD'S PEOPLE TO GIVE GIFTS

When Nehemiah returns to Jerusalem after visiting King Artaxerxes, he discovers that the people have been making compromises in godly living.[2] As a governor, he manages and participates in a public vow to live righteously before God, and so he must initiate reforms in the community once again. First, he reinstates the proper use of a large room as a storehouse inside the house of God (13:6–9). Second, he restores the proper roles of the Levites and musicians (13:10–11). Third, he rebuilds the system of tithes and offerings (13:12–13).

Nehemiah discovers that the people are no longer giving gifts to support God's work because Eliashib, the priest who is in charge of the storerooms of the house of God, is closely related to Tobiah, an Ammonite and enemy of the Jewish community (6:17–19), and has impudently given him a large room in the house of God as a residence. This room is supposed to be used to store provisions for the Levites, musicians, and gatekeepers, along with contributions for the priests. Whereas the grain offerings, incense, and temple articles are connected to the liturgical ceremonies of the temple, the tithes and contributions are meant to provide for the primary needs of the temple personnel. By giving the large room designated for the sacred storage to Tobiah, the tithes for the Levites, musicians, and gatekeepers, along with the contributions for the priests, cannot be stored appropriately. As a man of action, Nehemiah deals with this issue at once by throwing all Tobiah's household goods out of the room (13:8). Then he orders the servants to purify the rooms and restore them to their proper use in the house of God (13:9).

Next, Nehemiah discovers that the Levites are not being given their designated portions or tithes (13:10; Num 18:21–24). Earlier, the post-exilic community publicly reiterates their commitment to support the Levites and priests through tithes and offerings (10:37–39). The portions for the priests and the Levites are stored in the temple storerooms right after the dedication of the wall (12:44), but then the people begin to neglect the Levites and musicians, and so they have to return to their own fields. Without support, the Levites and musicians cannot properly serve the house of God, and so

---

descendants, such as the Moabite Ruth, can be included in the believing community because of their faith in God. This is an alternative view on the exclusion of foreign descendants in the Old Testament.

2. In trying to solve the issues pertaining to the chronology of Ezra-Nehemiah, Greg Goswell, "The Handling of Time in the Book of Ezra-Nehemiah," *Trinity Journal* 31 (2010): 200–203, argues that the chronology makes more sense if Nehemiah 13:4–31 follows immediately after the community oath of Nehemiah 10.

Nehemiah courageously rebukes the officials for neglecting the house of God. By looking after the essential needs of the Levites and musicians, Nehemiah restores them to their proper roles in the house of God.

A senior pastor in Bandung, Indonesia, welcomed a new pastor to start serving at his church. Though the church could meet some of the financial needs of the young pastor and his family, the senior pastor knew that the new pastor might need some assistance. So the senior pastor brought monetary gifts to the new pastor to help with the educational expenses of his children. When senior pastors take good care of younger pastors, it encourages them to remain faithful in God's service. Senior pastors can also offer valuable social and emotional support by looking out for the welfare of younger staff. When senior leaders volunteer to care for and mentor younger servants of the Lord, God's work will continue to grow, and God's ripened fields will have more harvesters.

Nehemiah's third reform is to rebuild the system of distribution in order to restore the people's confidence in giving tithes and offerings. As Judah brings gifts into the purified storerooms, Nehemiah appoints trustworthy and dependable leaders to oversee the storehouses (compare 7:2). He appoints Shelemiah as priest, Zadok as scribe, and Pedaiah and Hanan of the Levites to assist them (13:13). With equal representation from the priests and the Levites, Nehemiah ensures that the supplies will be distributed equitably to their brothers. By appointing a scribe, Nehemiah ensures that there will be careful accounting of the supplies, which will restore the people's confidence in the system. By selecting assistants, Nehemiah ensures that the work will be done in a timely and efficient manner.

At the conclusion of this section, Nehemiah utters a short prayer of celebration, asking God to remember his faithful work for the house of God and its "services" (13:14), or temple personnel. By taking care of the needs of the temple personnel, Nehemiah restores the Levites and musicians to their proper service in the house of God. Nehemiah addresses his prayer solely to God, for the Lord is his personal God, and as God's servant, he is accountable to God alone.

The essential needs of school faculty in a developing country such as the Philippines are often marginalized. The Philippine Commission on Higher Education (CHED) encourages all colleges and graduate schools in the Philippines to safeguard the essential needs of faculty members by including a clause in the school's policy that prescribes proper compensation. Yet some Christian pastors argue that religious schools operate by faith in God, and so their faculty need to trust God to supply their needs. Though Bible schools need to trust in God, the family members of the faculty also need to be assured that their essential needs will be met as they serve both God and people. Thus we need to have balanced thinking about trusting in God and faithfully providing for God's people.

13:15–22 CHARGING GOD'S PEOPLE TO OBSERVE THE SABBATH

Nehemiah is a faithful believer who adheres to God's commands. When he sees the men in Judah doing all sorts of work and carrying out business on the Sabbath, he is immediately up in arms (13:15–18). Because Sabbath observance plays an important role in the Jewish community, he wants to restore it as a holy day to the Lord. For those who have become complacent about keeping the Sabbath holy (compare 2 Kgs 23:21; 2 Chr 30:2), Nehemiah uses the following strategy: (1) he cautions workers and merchants about desecrating the Sabbath (13:15–16); (2) he criticizes leaders for not consecrating the Sabbath (13:17–18); and (3) he commands his men to shut the gates of Jerusalem before the Sabbath (13:19–22).

First, Nehemiah zealously corrects those who are pressing grapes, carrying loads on donkeys, and bringing fish into Jerusalem to sell on the Sabbath. Although the people of Tyre and Judah may be foreigners, their profiteering profanes the sanctity of the Sabbath.

Second, Nehemiah teaches the leaders about the importance of the Sabbath by reminding them of the historical connection between the desecration of the Sabbath and God's wrath and punishment. The prophets Jeremiah and Ezekiel inform the theology that interprets calamity as a consequence of profaning the Sabbath (Jer 17:27; Ezek 20:23–24, see also 12–13, 16, 20–21). Nehemiah also teaches the leaders that they should take the initiative for consecrating the Sabbath as a holy day to the Lord.

Third, Nehemiah issues a command to close the gates of Jerusalem so that no load can be brought in on the Sabbath day (13:19). Whereas Jeremiah stands at the gate to call the people to keep Sabbath holy (Jer 17:19–27), Nehemiah stations his men by the gates of Jerusalem to make sure that they will remain closed. Then he warns the traders not to spend the night by the wall outside Jerusalem (13:20–21). Finally, he commands the Levites to purify themselves and guard the gates.

Nehemiah believes that the Sabbath is a blessing to all who live in Jerusalem (Isa 56:1–7), and so he enforces Sabbath observance for everyone:

Jews and foreigners, merchants and sellers, the nobles of Judah, his own men, and the Levites. As the leader of the community, he takes every precaution to ensure that the Sabbath will be a consecrated day to the Lord. During the eighth century, keeping Sabbath was a self-imposed restriction that prohibited the Jews from selling goods on the Sabbath (Amos 8:5). The public vow in 10:31 is seen as a commitment from the Jews not to buy merchandise on the Sabbath. Here, Nehemiah enforces the "no buying, no selling" policy for everyone who lives in the community in order to ensure that the Sabbath will be a day of rest and worship.

We need to rethink how we can keep the Sabbath holy so that we will enjoy the benefits of its teaching. Because the Sabbath is a day of rest that is connected to the creation of God (Exod 20:8–11), it is for all members of the family and community, including servants and animals (Deut 5:12–15). Of course, Jesus reminds us that he is the Lord of the Sabbath (Matt 12:8; Luke 6:5). In the market-driven economy, many have to work on Sunday and cannot find time to worship and rest.[3] But in the midst of our busy lives, the Sabbath teaching is an important corrective.

Chantry distinguishes the Mosaic and Christian observance of the Sabbath. According to Chantry, the same standard of morality is found in the Mosaic covenant and in the new covenant. He believes, however, that the moral law is wielded differently in the hands of Moses and Jesus.[4] On the one hand, Moses teaches about Sabbath rest by giving very exact external details for living. He insists that when narrowly defined lines are crossed, stiff and unsparing punishment will be applied to the offender. For instance, "whoever does any work on it (the Sabbath) is to be put to death" (Exod 35:2). Jesus, on the other hand, emphasizes the internal heart motives. Though he fully upholds the moral law and reminds us of God's judgment, he does not give any civil reprisals for breaking the Sabbath rest. This can be seen in the way Jesus tolerates how his disciples pick grain on the Sabbath.

This raises a question about how the fourth commandment should be understood and applied in our present days. Two opposing outlooks about Sabbath observance challenge its relevance to our present postmodern world, where anything goes, and everyone seems to be clamoring for individual expression. Because of our age's collapse of morals, some people would like to reinstate Mosaic strictness as a way of trying to restore order in religious life.

---

3. Walter Brueggemann, *Sabbath as Resistance: Saying No to the Culture of Now* (Louisville: Westminster John Knox Press, 2017).
4. Walter Chantry, *Call the Sabbath a Delight* (Carlisle, PA: Banner of Truth Trust, 1991), 62–66.

Others who fear Mosaic legalism and wish to modify its strictness, prefer to emphasize the inward benefits of reflection and a worshipful spirit. The latter group might suggest setting aside a few hours to go to Sunday worship rather than living the whole day restfully before God.

The concern about legalism has led many Christians to neglect the spiritual disciplines that Roman Catholics have adhered to through the centuries. Going back to the creation story, Lundy reminds us that the main purpose for honoring the Sabbath is to rest fully on one day in seven, and this purpose needs to be set aside from taking time to worship with a community of believers.[5] There is also a celebratory reason for observing the Sabbath, as it is a time for believers to join together to give praise and thanks for God's grace throughout the week's long and toilsome labor. Lundy suggests connecting the observance of Sabbath rest with other holidays, specifying that how one spends the day of rest will be unique for each person. Nonetheless, Nehemiah's zeal for keeping the Sabbath is translated into public righteousness in adherence to God's law. He fights for the Lord of the Sabbath, threatening the people with personal confrontation if they do not keep it holy. At the end of this section, Nehemiah offers another short prayer of celebration, asking God to remember him and to show mercy to him with his great love (13:22). Nehemiah's deepest longing is to connect with God, to bring his personal struggles to God, and to implore God to grant him mercy. In all that Nehemiah does, God is never out of his sight.

13:23–29 COMMANDING GOD'S PEOPLE TO CONSECRATE MARRIAGE

During this same time, Nehemiah observes that some men have married foreign women from Ashdod, Ammon, and Moab (13:23). Ashdod is located on the Mediterranean coast, a region controlled by the Philistines. Ammon and Moab are across Jordan to the east. All these nations are despicable to the Israelites. The children from these mixed marriages do not know how to speak the language of Judah (13:24), and so Nehemiah curses and strikes the violators (13:25) and makes them take an oath that they will not to give into

---

5. J. David Lundy, *Servant Leadership for Slow Learners* (Carlisle, UK: Authentic Lifestyle, 2002), 146–154.

interracial marriages (13:25). Moreover, he drives away a priestly descendant who has taken a foreign wife (13:28).

In tackling this issue, Nehemiah shows his anger by beating some of the men and pulling their hair. His actions are very different from Ezra, who tears his own clothes and pulls his own hair when he faces this issue (Ezra 9:3). Nehemiah forces the people to make a public oath about this matter (13:25) and then gives them a historical lesson about Solomon's sinful interracial marriages and their ongoing unfaithfulness to God (13:26–27). The issue is so important to Nehemiah that when he meets a descendant of Eliashib, the high priest, who is a son-in-law of Sanballat, the Horonite (13:28), Nehemiah boldly drives the priestly descendant from his presence.

Again, at the conclusion of this scene, Nehemiah utters another short prayer of celebration, asking God to remember what he has just accomplished by reinstating the sanctity of marriage in the Israelite community. Because the priestly descendant of Eliashib did not marry properly, he defiled the priestly office. The covenant of the priesthood ensures that those who serve the most holy God will themselves be holy and consecrated unto the Lord.

13:30–31 CONCLUDING REMARKS

In his final remarks, Nehemiah summarizes his accomplishments for God, which consist of two key items: (1) the consecration of the personnel at the temple (13:30); and (2) the systemization of contributions for the temple (13:31).

First, Nehemiah purifies the priests and the Levites of everything foreign and detestable before God. By ensuring their marital purity, Nehemiah restores the sanctity of the priests and the Levites. Just like David, he assigns designated duties and tasks to them.

Second, Nehemiah systematizes the contributions of wood and first fruits so that the temple can function properly. The contribution of wood at designated times ensures that worship can continue to function without any interruptions. The contribution of first fruits supports the work at the temple.

Nehemiah concludes his prayer of remembrance by asking for God's personal favor. Under Nehemiah's management, the wall is rebuilt in fifty-two days, but Nehemiah knows that only God can keep all his accomplishments from crumbling. Thus Nehemiah's primary concern is to be accountable to God and be faithful as he does the Lord's work.

MENTORING

How do we raise up good leaders like Nehemiah, who are bold enough to confront and sincere enough to right every wrong? As a cupbearer for King Artaxerxes, Nehemiah receives the best training in administration. His inner world is solid and healthy as he ventures out to help others. He is strong enough to speak for truth even when he is in the minority. He is neither selfish nor timid about tackling issues that others have left unresolved. Rather, as he zealously carries out the necessary reforms in the community, he demonstrates his skill in resolving conflict. Confident of his calling and connected to God, he constantly seeks divine favor and mercy.

While some appear to be born with leadership abilities, others can be trained for leadership. The Ministry Apprenticeship Program (MAP) is a mentorship program that aims to prepare young men and women for full-time service to God by providing them with ministry exposure under the guidance of specified mentors. This discipleship training program prepares those who have a heart for full-time service to God with two years of guided internship in a church setting. The founder of this program is Philip Jensen, who first envisioned this training model for Australia, where it is known as Ministry Training Strategy (MTS).[1] Mentors train participating youth and guide them as they gain hands-on experience in serving the church. This period of learning and working with a team of pastoral staff can help young recruits discern if they have the vigor and calling for full-time service to God.

Rosa Ching Shao

---

1. See http://www.mts.com.au.

SELECTED BIBLIOGRAPHY

Allen, L., and T. Laniah. *Ezra, Nehemiah, Esther*. New International Biblical Commentary OT Series. Peabody/Carlisle: Hendrickson/Paternoster Press, 2003.

Baker, David. *Tight Fists or Open Hands? Wealth and Poverty in Old Testament Law*. Grand Rapids: Eerdmans, 2009.

Berquist, J. *Judaism in Persia's Shadow: A Social and Historical Approach*. Minneapolis: Fortress Press, 1995.

Blenkinsopp, Joseph. *Ezra-Nehemiah: A Commentary*. Old Testament Library. Philadelphia: Westminster, 1988.

———. *Opening the Sealed Book: Interpretations of the Book of Isaiah in Late Antiquity*. Grand Rapids: Eerdmans, 2006.

Brehony, Kathleen A. *Living a Connected Life*. New York: Henry Holt & Co., 2003.

Brown, Raymond. *The Message of Nehemiah*. The Bible Speaks Today. Leicester, UK: Inter-Varsity Press, 1998.

Brueggemann, Walter. *Cadences of Home: Preaching among Exiles*. Louisville: Westminster John Knox Press, 1977.

———. *Sabbath as Resistance: Saying No to the Culture of Now*. New Edition. Louisville: Westminster John Knox Press, 2017.

Bulatao, Jaime C. *Phenomena and Their Interpretation*. Manila: Ateneo de Manila University Press, 1992.

Burnside, Jonathan. *God, Justice, and Society: Aspects of Law and Legality in the Bible*. Oxford: Oxford University Press, 2011.

Chantry, Walter. *Call the Sabbath a Delight*. Carlisle, PA: Banner of Truth Trust, 1991.

Chrostowski, Waldemar. "An Examination of Conscience by God's People as Exemplified in Nehemiah 9:6–37." *BZ* 34 (1990): 253–261.

Clines, David J. A. *Ezra-Nehemiah and Esther*. New Century Bible Commentary. Grand Rapids, MI: Eerdmans, 1984.

———. "The Nehemiah Memoir: The Perils of Autobiography." In *What Does Eve Do to Help? And Other Readerly Questions to the Old Testament*. JSOT Supplement Series 94, 124–164. Sheffield: Sheffield Academic Press, 1990.

———. "Nehemiah 10 as an Example of Early Jewish Biblical Exegesis." *JSOT* 21 (1981): 111–117.

Coggins, Richard J. *The Book of Ezra and Nehemiah*. The Cambridge Bible Commentary. Cambridge: Cambridge University Press, 1976.

Davies, Gordon F. *Ezra and Nehemiah*. BERIT OLAM Studies in Hebrew Narrative & Poetry. Collegeville. Edited by David W. Cotter. Collegeville, MN: Liturgical Press, 1999.

Duggan, Michael W. *The Covenant Renewal in Ezra-Nehemiah (Neh 7:72b-10:40): An Exegetical, Literary, and Theological Study*. Atlanta: Society of Biblical Literary, 2001.

Eskenazi, Tamara C. "Ezra-Nehemiah: From Text to Actuality." In *Signs and Wonders: Biblical Texts in Literary Focus*. Edited by J. C. Exum, 165–197. Atlanta: Scholars Press, 1989.

———. *In an Age of Prose: A Literary Approach to Ezra-Nehemiah*. Atlanta: Scholars, 1988.

———. "The Structure of Ezra-Nehemiah and the Integrity of the Book." *JBL* 107 (1988): 641–656.

Eslinger, Lyle. "Ezekiel 20 and the Metaphor of Historical Teleology: Concepts of Biblical History." *JSOT* 81 (1998): 93–125.

Fensham, Frank Charles. "Nehemiah 9 and Psalms 105, 106, 135 and 136. Post-Exilic Historical Traditions in Poetic Form." *JNSL* 9 (1981): 35–51.

Gaffin, Richard. *Calvin and the Sabbath: The Controversy of Applying the Fourth Commandment*. Ross-shire, UK: Mentor, 1998.

Georges, Jayson. "Get Face! Give Face! A Missional Paradigm for Honor-Shame Contexts." *Evangelical Missions Quarterly* 53, no. 3 (July 2017): 1–6.

Goswell, Greg. "The Absence of Davidic Hope in Ezra-Nehemiah." *Trinity Journal* 33 (2012): 19–31.

———. "The Attitude to the Persians in Ezra-Nehemiah." *Trinity Journal* 32 (2011): 191–203.

———. *Ezra-Nehemiah*. EP Study Commentary. Darlington, UK: Evangelical Press, 2013.

———. "The Handling of Time in the Book of Ezra-Nehemiah." *Trinity Journal* 31 (2010): 187–203.

Gunneweg, Antonius H. J. *Esra*. KAT 19/1. Gütersloh: Gerd Mohn, 1985.

———. *Nehemia*. KAT 19/2. Gütersloh: Gerd Mohn, 1987.

Ho, Shirley, and Feng Yi Lin. *Psalms 73–150*. ABCS. Manila: OMF, 2013.

Hess, Richard S. *The Old Testament: A Historical, Theological and Critical Introduction*. Grand Rapids: Baker, 2016.

Hoglund, K. *Archemid Imperial Administration in Syria-Palestine and the Mission of Ezra and Nehemiah*. SBLDS 124. Atlanta: Scholars Press, 1992.

House, Wayne H. *Divorce and Remarriage: Four Christian Views*. Downers Grove: InterVarsity Press, 1990.

Hwang, Jerry. "How Long Will My Glory Be Reproach?: Honour and Shame in Old Testament Lament Traditions." Old Testament Essays 30, no. 3 (2017): 684–706.

Japhet, Sara. *I & II Chronicles*. OTL. Louisville, KY: Westminster John Knox Press, 1993.

Selected Bibliography

———. "Composition and Chronology in the Book of Ezra-Nehemiah." In *Second Temple Studies 2. Temple and Community in the Persian Period*, 189–216. JSOT Supplement 175 (1994).

———. "The Supposed Common Authorship of Chronicles and Ezra-Nehemiah Investigated Anew." *VT* 18 (1968): 330–371.

Johnson, Marshall D. *The Purpose of Biblical Genealogies*, 2nd ed. Cambridge: Cambridge University Press, 1988.

Johnston, Graham. *Preaching to a Postmodern World: A Guide to Reaching Twenty-first-Century Listeners*. Grand Rapids, MI: Baker, 2001.

Kaiser, Walter C. Jr. *Hard Sayings of the Old Testament*. Downers Grove: InterVarsity Press, 1988.

Kalimi, Isaac, ed. *New Perspectives on Ezra-Nehemiah: History and Historiography, Text, Literature, and Interpretation*. Winona Lake, IN: Eisenbrauns, 2012.

Kang, Bin. "The Rhetoric of Honor and Shame as a Significant Role in Understanding the Judgement Oracle against Tyre in Ezekiel 28:1–19." MTh Thesis, Asia Graduate School of Theology, 2019.

Kidner, Derek. *Ezra and Nehemiah*. Tyndale Old Testament Commentaries. Downers Grove: InterVarsity Press, 1979.

Kim, Raeyong. "The Characteristics and the Roles of the Aramaic Epistles in Ezra 1–6." Theological Thought 148 (2010): 7–40.

———. "Historiographic Characteristics of Ezra-Nehemiah." *Korean Journal of Christian Studies* 75 (2011): 105–123.

———. "A Study on the Connecting Links in the Book of Ezra-Nehemiah." *Korean Journal Christian Studies* 84 (2012): 5–19.

Kissling, Paul J. "The So-Called 'Post-Exilic Return': Already-But-Not-Yet in Ezra-Nehemiah." *Stone-Campbell Journal* 17 (2014): 207–220.

Kring, Ann M., Gerald C. Davison, John M. Neale, and Sheri L Johnson. *Abnormal Psychology*. Hoboken, NJ: John Wiley & Sons, 2007.

Lai, Hung-Chuan. "Processes of Judean Identity Formation in Ezra-Nehemiah: A Social-Anthropological Analysis." *Taiwan Journal of Theology* 39 (2014): 1–44.

Levering, Matthew. *Ezra & Nehemiah*. Theological Commentary on the Bible. Grand Rapids: Brazos Press, 2007.

Lundy, J. David. *Servant Leadership for Slow Learners*. Carlisle, UK: Authentic, 2002.

McConville, J. G. *Ezra, Nehemiah and Esther*. Daily Study Bible. Philadelphia: Westminster Press, 1985.

Mendoza, Noli P. "A Community in Becoming: Ritual and Social Transformation in Nehemiah 8–10. A Ritual Reading of the Covenant Renewal in Nehemiah." MTh Thesis, Asia Graduate School of Theology, 2016.

Milne, Aileen. *Teach Yourself Counseling*. London, UK: Hodder Arnold, 2003.

Myers, Jacob M. *Ezra, Nehemiah*. Anchor Bible. Garden City: Doubleday, 1965.

Narramore, Bruce. *No Condemnation: Rethinking Guilt Motivation in Counseling, Preaching, and Parenting*. Eugene, OR: Wipf & Stock, 1984.

Nicholls, Bruce. *A Living Theology for Asian Churches: Contextualization-Syncretism Debate*. Asian Perspective Series 21. Taipei, Taiwan: Asia Theological Association.

Packer, J. I. *A Passion for Faithfulness: Wisdom from the Book of Nehemiah*. Wheaton, IL: Crossway, 1995.

Rainey, Brian. "'Their Peace or Prosperity': Biblical Concepts of Hereditary Punishment and the Exclusion of Foreigners in Ezra-Nehemiah." *Journal of Ancient Judaism* 6 (2015): 158–181.

Reid, Frank M. III. *The Nehemiah Plan: Preparing the Church to Rebuild Broken Lives*. Shippensburg, PA: Treasure House, 1993.

Roberts, Mark D. *Ezra, Nehemiah, Esther*. Mastering the Old Testament. The Communicator's Commentary. Dallas, TX: Word, 1986.

Shao, Joseph Too. "An Asian Reading of the Theological Themes of Nehemiah." In *Light for Our Path: The Authority, Inspiration, Meaning and Mission of Scripture*. Edited by Bruce Nicholls, Julie Belding, and Joseph Shao, 119–129. Manila: Asia Theological Association, 2013.

———. *A Study of Akkadian Royal Hymns and Prayers*. Jian Dao Dissertation Series 10/Bible and Literature 7. Hong Kong: Alliance Bible Seminary, 2002.

———. "The Changing Mission of the Church in Changing Asia." In *The Church in a Changing World: An Asian Response. Challenges from the Malang Consultation on Globalization*. Edited by Bruce Nicholls, Theresa Roco Lua, and Julie Belding, 17–25. Manila: Asia Theological Association, 2010.

———. "Spirituality in the Prophetic Traditions: An Asian Perspective." In *Perjuangan Menatang Zaman (KumpulanesaisebagaipenghargaankepadaPendeta Stephen Tong, pada HUT ke-60, Festschrift for Stephen Tong)*. Edited by Hendra G. Mulia, 125–150. Jakarta: Reformed Institute Press, 2000.

Shao, Joseph Too, and Rosa Ching Shao. *Joel, Nahum, Malachi*. ABCS. Manila: Asia Theological Association, 2013.

Shao, Rosa Ching. *Divorce: An Option or an Objection to God's Standards?* Philippine-Chinese Mission, 2000 Newsletter of CCOWE Fellowship, Philippines (Nov 1997): 4.

Smith, Gary V. *Ezra-Nehemiah Esther*. Cornerstone Biblical Commentary. Carol Stream, IL: Tyndale House, 2010.

Sugirtharajah, Rasiah S. *Asian Biblical Hermeneutics and Postcolonialism: Contesting the Interpretation*. Maryknoll: Orbis, 1998.

———, ed. *Voices from the Margin: Interpreting the Bible in the Third World*. Maryknoll: Orbis, 2006.

Selected Bibliography

Talmon, Shemaryahu. "Ezra and Nehemiah." In *The Literary Guide to the Bible*. Edited by Robert Alter and Frank Kermode, 357–364. Cambridge, MA: Harvard University Press, 1987.

Thomas, Derek W. L. *Ezra & Nehemiah*. Reformed Expository Commentary. Phillipsburg, NJ: P & R Publishing, 2016.

Thronveit, Mark A. *Ezra-Nehemiah*. Interpretation. Louisville: John Knox Press, 1992.

———. "Linguistic Analysis and the Question of Authorship in Chronicles, Ezra, and Nehemiah." *VT* 32 (1982): 201–216.

Turaki, Yusufu. "The Role of the Ancestors." In *Africa Bible Commentary*. Nairobi, Kenya: WordAlive Publishers, 2006,

Uayan, Jean Uy. *A Study of the Emergence and Early Development of Selected Protestant Chinese Churches in the Philippines*. Carlisle, UK: Langham Monographs, 2017.

Ulrich, Dean. "David in Ezra-Nehemiah." *Westminster Theological Journal* 78 (2016): 49–64.

de Vries, Simon. "Moses and David as Cult Founders in Chronicles." *JBL* 107 (1988): 619–639.

Ward, Colleen A., Stephen Brochner, and Adrian Furnham. *The Psychology of Culture Shock*. New York: Methuen, 1986.

Weiten, Wayne. *Psychology Themes and Variations*. Pacific Grove, CA: Brooks/Cole, 1995.

Whitehead, Brady. Jr. *Ezra, Nehemiah, and Esther*. Cokesbury Basic Bible Commentary. N.p: Graded Press, 1988.

Williamson, H. G. M. "The Composition of Ezra i-vi." *JTS* 34 n.s. (1983): 1–30.

———. "Did the Author of Chronicles Also Write the Books of Ezra and Nehemiah." *BR* 3 (1987): 56–59.

———. *Ezra, Nehemiah*. Word Biblical Commentary. Waco, TX: Word, 1985.

———. "Post-Exilic Historiography." In *The Future of Biblical Studies: The Hebrew Scriptures*. Edited by Richard Elliot Friedman and Hugh G. M. Williamson. *SBL Semeia Studies* 16 (1987): 189–207.

———. "Structure and Historiography in Nehemiah 9." In *Panel Sessions, Proceedings of the Ninth World Congress of Jewish Studies: Biblical Studies and the Ancient Near East*. Edited by Moshe Goshen-Gottstein, 117–132. Jerusalem: Magnes Press, 1988.

Wilson, Robert R. "Genealogy, Genealogies." In *Anchor Bible Dictionary* 2. Edited by David Freedman, 930. New York: Doubleday, 1992.

Wright, Christopher J. H. "The Jubilee Year." In *Walking in the Ways of the Lord: The Ethical Authority of the Old Testament*. Leicester, UK: Inter-Varsity Press, 1995.

———. *Walking in the Ways of the Lord: The Ethical Authority of the Old Testament.* Leicester, UK: Apollos, 1995.

Wu, Daniel. *Honor, Shame, and Guilt: Social-Scientific Approaches to the Book of Ezekiel.* Winona Lake, IN: Eisenbrauns, 2016.

Yamauchi, Edwin M. *Persia and the Bible.* Grand Rapids: Baker, 1990.

———. "Ezra, Nehemiah." In *Expositors' Bible Commentary Vol 4: 1 Chronicles-Job.* Grand Rapids, MI: Zondervan, 2010.

———. "Was Nehemiah the Cupbearer a Eunuch?" *ZAW* 92 (1980): 132–142.

Yoo, Philip Y. "On Nehemiah 8, 8a." *ZAW* 127 (2015): 502–507.

Asia Theological Association
54 Scout Madriñan St. Quezon City 1103, Philippines
Email: ataasia@gmail.com Telefax: (632) 410 0312

OUR MISSION

The Asia Theological Association (ATA) is a body of theological institutions, committed to evangelical faith and scholarship, networking together to serve the Church in equipping the people of God for the mission of the Lord Jesus Christ.

OUR COMMITMENT

The ATA is committed to serving its members in the development of evangelical, biblical theology by strengthening interaction, enhancing scholarship, promoting academic excellence, fostering spiritual and ministerial formation and mobilizing resources to fulfill God's global mission within diverse Asian cultures.

OUR TASK

Affirming our mission and commitment, ATA seeks to:

- **Strengthen** interaction through inter-institutional fellowship and programs, regional and continental activities, faculty and student exchange programs.
- **Enhance** scholarship through consultations, workshops, seminars, publications, and research fellowships.
- **Promote** academic excellence through accreditation standards, faculty and curriculum development.
- **Foster** spiritual and ministerial formation by providing mentor models, encouraging the development of ministerial skills and a Christian ethos.
- **Mobilize** resources through library development, information technology and infra-structural development.

To learn more about ATA, visit www.ataasia.com or facebook.com/AsiaTheologicalAssociation

Langham Literature, along with its publishing work, is a ministry of Langham Partnership.

Langham Partnership is a global fellowship working in pursuit of the vision God entrusted to its founder John Stott –

> *to facilitate the growth of the church in maturity and Christ-likeness through raising the standards of biblical preaching and teaching.*

Our vision is to see churches in the majority world equipped for mission and growing to maturity in Christ through the ministry of pastors and leaders who believe, teach and live by the Word of God.

Our mission is to strengthen the ministry of the Word of God through:
- nurturing national movements for biblical preaching
- fostering the creation and distribution of evangelical literature
- enhancing evangelical theological education

especially in countries where churches are under-resourced.

Our ministry

Langham Preaching partners with national leaders to nurture indigenous biblical preaching movements for pastors and lay preachers all around the world. With the support of a team of trainers from many countries, a multi-level programme of seminars provides practical training, and is followed by a programme for training local facilitators. Local preachers' groups and national and regional networks ensure continuity and ongoing development, seeking to build vigorous movements committed to Bible exposition.

Langham Literature provides majority world preachers, scholars and seminary libraries with evangelical books and electronic resources through publishing and distribution, grants and discounts. The programme also fosters the creation of indigenous evangelical books in many languages, through writer's grants, strengthening local evangelical publishing houses, and investment in major regional literature projects, such as one volume Bible commentaries like the *Africa Bible Commentary* and the *South Asia Bible Commentary*.

Langham Scholars provides financial support for evangelical doctoral students from the majority world so that, when they return home, they may train pastors and other Christian leaders with sound, biblical and theological teaching. This programme equips those who equip others. Langham Scholars also works in partnership with majority world seminaries in strengthening evangelical theological education. A growing number of Langham Scholars study in high quality doctoral programmes in the majority world itself. As well as teaching the next generation of pastors, graduated Langham Scholars exercise significant influence through their writing and leadership.

To learn more about Langham Partnership and the work we do visit **langham.org**

Who are better equipped than the Shaos, both long-standing faculty of Biblical Seminary of the Philippines (BSOP) since the early eighties, to offer an Asian perspective when expounding the living messages of Ezra-Nehemiah relevant to the Christian churches in the Majority World? Integrating critical scholarship and practical wisdom, this outstanding commentary is a must for consulting alongside Hugh Williamson's award-winning volume in the Word Biblical Commentary series.

Stephen Lee, PhD
President and Lam Ko Kit Tak Professor of Biblical Studies,
China Graduate School of Theology, Hong Kong

For decades, the ministries of Joseph and Rosa Shao have been much like the work of the protagonists of these biblical books, Ezra and Nehemiah. Like those great leaders of the past, the authors' devotion to God and their service to God's people in strengthening the faith of others have been exemplary. This edition of their commentary on these important texts will perpetuate their ministry and it is a welcome contribution to our understanding of Ezra and Nehemiah.

Bill T. Arnold, PhD
Paul S. Amos Professor of Old Testament Interpretation,
Asbury Theological Seminary, Wilmore, Kentucky, USA